WOMAN AND LAW

WOMAN AND LAW

B. Ramaswamy

ISHA

Woman and Law

ISBN : 81-8205-531-8

Published in 2013 in India by
Isha Books
B-69, New Gupta Colony
New DDA Market
Delhi - 110009

Laser Type Setting : Rajender Vashist, Delhi
Printed at : Chawla Offset Printers, Delhi

Contents

Preface

This publication titled "Woman and Law" is an integral part of women studies curriculum being followed in India and abroad. This book provides readers with an introductory overview of women's right in legal terms. A historical perspective has been given so as to have a complete knowledge of the said subject, its evolution and contemporary trends. The issues of women's reproductive rights and pregnant women's rights have been covered. Focus also lies on rights of sex workers and prostitutes. Existing global laws for eliminating all kinds of discrimination against women have been discussed including the recent protocols and declarations. International laws regarding elimination of violence against women and their protection during armed conflicts and emergencies have been covered in brief. An overview is also provided herein about the world conference on women and the "Beijing Platform of Action" with focus on its review during the follow up periods till date. Role of institutions like UN women and UNIFEM for promoting human rights of women has been described. Similarly, the constitution and role of "National Commission for Women" in India and other major initiatives of Government of India with respect to protection and promotion of women's rights have been reflected upon briefly.

Focus also lies on the specific Indian law which is enforced nationally for the protection of women against sexual harassment at workplace. In addition, the law which is implemented in India for protecting women against all types of domestic violence has been analysed and critically evaluated. The Indian law for prohibiting indecent representation of women is discussed. The law for prohibiting dowry is discussed alongwith its possible misuse. Besides, the law for protecting the rights of Muslim women on divorce is dealt. The act and rule for the prevention of practice of

Sati in India is described. This book also presents readers with a summary of focal points of all major national laws concerning the protection of rights of women and its promotion in long term. The publication is user friendly and systematic in its presentation.

August 2012

B. Ramaswamy

1

Introduction to Women's Rights : A Historical Perspective

Women's rights are entitlements and freedoms claimed for women and girls of all ages in many societies. In some places these rights are institutionalised or supported by law, local custom, and behaviour, whereas in others they may be ignored or suppressed. They differ from broader notions of human rights through claims of an inherent historical and traditional bias against the exercise of rights by women and girls in favour of men and boys. Issues commonly associated with notions of women's rights include (though are not limited to) the right: to bodily integrity and autonomy; to vote (suffrage); to hold public office; to work; to fair wages or equal pay; to own property; to education; to serve in the military or be conscripted; to enter into legal contracts; and to have marital, parental and religious rights.

History of women's Rights : A Global Historical Perspective

Greece

The status of women in ancient Greece varied from city state to city state. Records exist of women in ancient Delphi, Gortyn, Thessaly, Megara and Sparta owning land, the most prestigious form of private property at the time. In ancient Athens, women had no legal personhood and were assumed to be part of the Oikos headed by the male Kyrios. Until marriage, women were under the guardianship of their father or other male relative, once married the husband became a woman's kyrios. As women were barred from conducting legal proceedings, the kyrios would do so on their behalf. Athenian women had limited right to property and therefore were not considered full citizens, as citizenship and the entitlement to civil and political rights was defined in relation to property and the means to life. However, women could acquire rights over property through gifts, dowry and inheritance, though her kyrios had the right to dispose of a woman's property. Athenian women could enter into a contract worth less than the value of a "medimnos of barley" (a measure of grain), allowing women to engage in petty trading. Women slaves, were not eligible for full citizenship in ancient Athens, though in rare circumstances they could become citizens if freed. The only permanent barrier to citizenship, and hence full political and civil rights, in ancient Athens was gender. No woman ever acquired citizenship in ancient Athens, and therefore women were excluded in principle and practice from ancient Athenian democracy. By contrast, Spartan women enjoyed a status, power, and respect that was unknown in the rest of the classical world. Although Spartan women were formally excluded from military and political life they enjoyed considerable status as mothers of Spartan warriors. As men engaged in military activity, women took responsibility for running estates. Following protracted warfare in the 4th century BC. Spartan women owned approximately between 35% and 40% of all Spartan land and property. By the Hellenistic Period, some of the wealthiest Spartans were women. They controlled their own properties, as well as the properties of male relatives who were away with the army. Spartan women rarely married before the age of 20, and unlike Athenian women who wore heavy, concealing clothes and were rarely seen outside the house, Spartan women wore short dresses and went where they pleased. Girls as well as boys received education, and young women as well as young men may have participated in the Gymnopaedia (Festival of Nude Youths). Plato acknowledged that extending civil and political rights to women would substantively alter the nature of the household and the state. Aristotle, who had been taught by Plato, denied that women were slaves or subject to property, arguing that "nature has distinguished between the female and the slave", but he considered wives to be "bought". He argued that women's main economic activity is that of safeguarding the household property created by men. According to Aristotle the labour of women added no value because "the art of household management is not identical with the art of getting wealth, for the one uses the material which the other provides". Contrary to these views, the Stoic philosophers argued for equality of the sexes, sexual inequality being in their view contrary to the laws of nature. In doing so, they followed the Cynics, who argued that men and women should wear the same clothing and receive the same kind of education. They also saw marriage as a moral companionship between equals rather than a biological or social necessity, and practiced these views in their lives as well as their teachings. The Stoics adopted the views of the Cynics and added them to their own theories of human nature, thus putting their sexual egalitarianism on a strong philosophical basis.

Rome

Father Knows Best: Under Roman Law all legitimate children male or female fell under Patria Potestas. Patria Potestas was technically absolute, and early on included the right to kill children but during the Late Republic customs changed, and during the Empire legal rules changed in reflection. The unique thing about Patria Potestas was that it had no age limits, according to Gaius a man could be consul, have a wife and children of his own and future prominence but as long as his father was alive was still under his potestas (power) and so could own nothing. Patria Potestas only ended with either the death of the father, or emancipation by him. Early in the Republic Manus Marriage ended the potestas for women, but during the middle and later Republic that form of marriage became rare, eventually disappearing completely.

Marriage Under Law : Rome had only two forms of marriage, and both had exactly the opposite view of legal effects. Manus Marriage was the earlier form of marriage and placed the woman under her husbands manus legally standing in the position of a daughter. Under this type of marriage women could own nothing, and had little if any legal protections. On the other hand, a woman assumed the position of her husbands daughter in Manus Marriage making her agnatically instead of cognatically related to her children.

Marriage Sine Manu was the second form of marriage that replaced Manus, and was the opposite of Manus. Women married Sine Manu experienced no legal changes, so if her father was alive at time of marriage she continued to be his dependent and before the reign of Marcus Aurelius he could even force an end to the marriage. The lack of any legal change of status for the women meant that (provided their father had either died or emancipated them) they could own property, conduct most forms of business, and divorce her husband (without any reason needed). Legally speaking the only lack of independence a woman in Rome experienced in a marriage without Manus was from her father. The only legal issue related to marriage was dowry. A dowry was not required by law, but was usually provided by a father or if a father was nonexistent it would be whatever the bride wished to come out of her own estate. It was administered by the husband, but in the event of a divorce he was required to provide either the dowry or the equivalent of it back to his wife. In the case of adultery husbands got to keep portions of the dowry.

Politics: Legally speaking women were banned from politics. As with freedmen and slaves of the Imperial Family women of the imperial family gained some benefits from the fall of the Republic, but because the nature of the Principate was to hide dictatorship, such power had to be subtle and kept out of the public eye when possible. The ban on women and politics was they could not vote or run for office (sine suffragio) enlist in the army, or represent somebody else in court, women speaking their minds was not considered politics and so some women like Hortensia managed to make appearances in politics without violating the law.

Inheritance Rights: Everyone under the potestas of another had equal rights of inheritance under Roman Law, and wills that did otherwise ran risks of being challenged and invalidated as negligent.

Stoic Influence: Stoic philosophies had a strong effect on the development of law in ancient Rome. The Roman stoic thinkers Seneca and Musonius Rufus developed theories of just relationships (not to be confused with equality in society, or even equality) arguing that nature gives men and women equal capacity for virtue and equal obligations to act virtuously (a vague concept). Therefore they argued that men and women have an equal need for philosophical education. Stoic theories entered Roman law first through the Roman lawyer and senator Marcus Tullius Cicero and the influence of stoicism and philosophy increased while the status of women improved under the Empire.

Women's Rights in Religious Scriptures

Qur'an

The Quran, revealed to Muhammad over the course of 23 years, provided guidance to the Islamic community and modified existing customs in Arab society. From 610 and 661, known as the early reforms under Islam, the Quran introduced fundamental reforms to customary law and introduced rights for women in marriage, divorce and inheritance. By providing that the wife, not her family, would receive a dowry from the husband, which she could administer as her personal property, the Quran made women a legal party to the marriage contract.

While in customary law, inheritance was limited to male descendents, the Quran introduced rules on inheritance with certain fixed shares being distributed to designated heirs, first to the nearest female relatives and then the nearest male relatives. According to Annemarie Schimmel "compared to the pre-Islamic position of women, Islamic legislation meant an enormous progress; the woman has the right, at least according to the letter of the law, to administer the wealth she has brought into the family or has earned by her own work."

The general improvement of the status of Arab women included prohibition of female infanticide and recognising women's full personhood. Women were generally given greater rights than women in pre-Islamic Arabia and medieval Europe. Women were not accorded with such legal status in other cultures until centuries later. According to Professor William Montgomery Watt, when seen in such historical context, Muhammad "can be seen as a figure who testified on behalf of women's rights."

Women's Rights in the Middle Ages

According to English Common Law, which developed from the 12th Century onward, all property which a wife held at the time of a marriage became a possession of her husband. Eventually English courts forbade a husband's transferring property without the consent of his wife, but he still retained the right to manage it and to receive the money which it produced. French married women suffered from restrictions on their legal capacity which were removed only in 1965. In the 16th century, the Reformation in Europe allowed more women to add their voices, including the English writers Jane Anger, Aemilia Lanyer, and the prophetess Anna Trapnell. English and American Quakers believed that men and women were equal. Many Quaker women were preachers. Despite relatively greater freedom for Anglo-Saxon women, until the mid-19th century, writers largely assumed that a patriarchal order was a natural order that had always existed. This perception was not seriously challenged until the 18th century when Jesuit missionaries found matrilineality in native North American peoples.

Women's Rights in the 18th and 19th Century Europe

The Debutante (1807) by Henry Fuseli; The woman, victim of male social conventions, is tied to the wall, made to sew and guarded by governesses. The picture reflects Mary Wollstonecraft's views in *A Vindication of the Rights of Woman*, published in 1792.

Starting in the late 18th century, and throughout the 19th century, rights, as a concept and claim, gained increasing political, social and philosophical importance in Europe. Movements emerged which demanded freedom of religion, the abolition of slavery, rights for women, rights for those who did not own property and universal suffrage. In the late 18th Century the question of women's rights became central to political debates in both France and Britain. At the time some of the greatest thinkers of the Enlightenment, who defended democratic principles of equality and challenged notions that a privileged few should rule over the vast majority of the population, believed that these principles should be applied only to their own gender and their own race. The philosopher Jean Jacques Rousseau for example thought that it was the order of nature for woman to obey men. He wrote "Women do wrong to complain of the inequality of man-made laws" and claimed that "when she tries to usurp our rights, she is our inferior".

In 1791 the French playwright and political activist Olympe de Gouges published the *Declaration of the Rights of Woman and the Female Citizen*, modelled on the *Declaration of the Rights of Man and of the Citizen* of 1789. The Declaration is ironic in formulation and exposes the failure of the French Revolution, which had been devoted to equality. It states that: "This revolution will only take effect when all women become fully aware of their deplorable condition, and of the rights they have lost in society". The Declaration of the Rights of Woman and the Female Citizen follows the seventeen articles of the Declaration of the Rights of Man and of the Citizen point for point and has been described by Camille Naish as "almost a parody... of the original document". The first article of the Declaration of the Rights of Man and of the Citizen proclaims that "Men are born and remain free and equal in rights. Social distinctions may be based only on common utility." The first article of Declaration of the Rights of Woman and the Female Citizen replied: "Woman is born free and remains equal to man in rights. Social distinctions may only be based on common utility". De Gouges expands the sixth article of the Declaration of the Rights of Man and of the Citizen, which declared the rights of citizens to take part in the formation of law, to:

> "All citizens including women are equally admissible to all public dignities, offices and employments, according to their capacity, and with no other distinction than that of their virtues and talents".

De Gouges also draws attention to the fact that under French law women were fully punishable, yet denied equal rights.

Mary Wollstonecraft, a British writer and philosopher, published A Vindication of the Rights of Woman in 1792, arguing that it was the education and upbringing of women that created limited expectations. Wollstonecraft attacked gender oppression, pressing for equal educational opportunities, and demanded "justice!" and "rights to humanity" for all. Wollstonecraft, along with her British contemporaries Damaris Cudworth and Catherine Macaulay started to use the language of rights in relation to women, arguing that women should have greater opportunity because like men, they were moral and rational beings.

A Punch cartoon from 1867 mocking John Stuart Mill's attempt to replace the term 'man' with 'person', i.e. give women the right to vote. Caption: Mill's Logic: Or, Franchise for Females. "Pray clear the way, there, for these - a - persons."

In his 1869 essay 'The Subjection of Women' the English philosopher and political theorist John Stuart Mill described the situation for women in Britain as follows:

"We are continually told that civilisation and Christianity have restored to the woman her just rights. Meanwhile the wife is the actual bondservant of her husband; no less so, as far as the legal obligation goes, than slaves commonly so called."

Then a member of parliament, Mill argued that women should be given the right to vote, though his proposal to replace the term 'man' with 'person' in the second Reform Bill of 1867 was greeted with laughter in the House of Commons and defeated by 76 to 196 votes. His arguments won little support amongst contemporaries but his attempt to amend the reform bill generated greater attention for the issue of women's suffrage in Britain. Initially only one of several women's rights campaign, suffrage became the primary cause of the British women's movement at the beginning of the 20th Century. At the time the ability to vote was restricted to wealthy property owners within British jurisdictions. This arrangement implicitly excluded women as property law and marriage law gave men ownership rights at marriage or inheritance until the 19th century. Although male suffrage broadened during the century, women were explicitly prohibited from voting nationally and locally in the 1830s by a Reform Act and the Municipal Corporations Act. Millicent Fawcett and Emmeline Pankhurst led the public campaign on women's suffrage and in 1918 a bill was passed allowing women over the age of 30 to vote.

Women's Suffrage : The Right to Vote

During the 19th century women began to agitate for the right to vote and participate in government and law making. The ideals of women's suffrage developed alongside that of universal suffrage and today women's suffrage is considered a right (under the Convention on the Elimination of All Forms of Discrimination Against Women). During the 19th century the right to vote was gradually extended in many countries and women started to campaign for their right to vote. In 1893 New Zealand became the first country to give women the right to vote on a national level. Australia gave women the right to vote in 1902. A number of Nordic countries gave women the right to vote in the early 20th century – Finland (1906), Norway (1913), Denmark and Iceland (1915). With the end of the First World War many other countries followed – the Netherlands (1917), Austria, Canada, Czechoslovakia, Georgia, Poland and Sweden (1918), Germany and Luxembourg (1919), and the United States (1920) . Spain gave women the right to vote in 1931, France in 1944, Belgium, Italy, Romania and Yugoslavia in 1946. Switzerland gave women the right to vote in 1971, and Liechtenstein in 1984.

In Latin America some countries gave women the right to vote in the first half of the 20th century – Ecuador (1929), Brazil (1932), El Salvador (1939), Dominican Republic (1942), Guatemala (1956) and Argentina (1946). In India, under colonial rule, universal suffrage was granted in 1935. Other Asian countries gave women the right to vote in the mid 20th century – Japan (1945), China (1947) and Indonesia (1955). In Africa women generally got the right to vote along with men through universal suffrage – Liberia (1947), Uganda (1958) and Nigeria (1960). In many countries in the Middle East universal suffrage was acquired after the Second World War, although in others, such as Kuwait, suffrage is very limited. On 16 May 2005, the Parliament of Kuwait extended suffrage to women by a 35–23 vote.

Women's Property Rights

During the 19th century women in the United States and Britain began to challenge laws that denied them the right to their property once they married. Under the common law doctrine of coverture husbands gained control of their wives' real estate and wages. Beginning in the 1840s, state legislatures in the United States and the British Parliament began passing statutes that protected women's property from their husbands and their husbands' creditors. These laws were known as the Married Women's Property Acts. Courts in the 19th-century United States also continued to require privy examinations of married women who sold their property. A privy examination was a practice in which a married woman who wished to sell her property had to be separately examined by a judge or justice of the peace outside of the presence of her husband and asked if her husband was pressuring her into signing the document.

Modern Movements for Women's Rights

In the subsequent decades women's rights again became an important issue in the English speaking world. By the 1960s the movement was called "feminism" or "women's liberation." Reformers wanted the same pay as men, equal rights in law, and the freedom to plan their families or not have children at all. Their efforts were met with mixed results.

In the UK, a public groundswell of opinion in favour of legal equality had gained pace, partly through the extensive employment of women in what were traditional male roles during both world wars. By the 1960s the legislative process was being readied, tracing through MP Willie Hamilton's select committee report, his equal pay for equal work bill, the creation of a Sex Discrimination Board, Lady Sear's draft sex anti-discrimination bill, a government Green Paper of 1973, until 1975 when the first British Sex Discrimination Act, an Equal Pay Act, and an Equal Opportunities Commission came into force. With encouragement from the UK government, the other countries of the EEC soon followed suit with an agreement to ensure that discrimination laws would be phased out across the European Community.

In the USA, the National Organisation for Women (NOW) was created in 1966 with the purpose of bringing about equality for all women. NOW was one important group that fought for the Equal Rights Amendment (ERA). This amendment stated that "equality of rights under the law shall not be denied or abridged by the United States or any state on account of sex." But there was disagreement on how the proposed amendment would be understood. Supporters believed it would guarantee women equal treatment. But critics feared it might deny women the right to be financially supported by their husbands. The amendment died in 1982 because not enough states had ratified it. ERAs have been included in subsequent Congresses, but have still failed to be ratified.

Birth Control and Reproductive Rights of Women

In the 1870s feminists advanced the concept of voluntary motherhood as a political critique of involuntary motherhood and expressing a desire for women's emancipation. Advocates for voluntary motherhood disapproved of contraception, arguing that women should only engage in sex for the purpose of procreation and advocated for periodic or permanent abstinence.

Cover of the 1919 Birth Control Review, published by Margaret Sanger. In relation to "How shall we change the law?" Sanger wrote "...women appeal in vain for instruction concerning contraceptives. Physicians are willing to perform abortions where they are pronounced necessary, but they refuse to direct the use of preventives which would make the abortions unnecessary... "I can't do it - the law does not permit it."

In the early 20th Century birth control was advanced as alternative to the then fashionable terms family limitation and voluntary motherhood. The phrase "birth control" entered the English language in 1914 and was popularised by Margaret Sanger, who was mainly active in the US but had gained an international reputation by the 1930s. The British birth control campaigner Marie Stopes made contraception acceptable in Britain during the 1920 by framing it in scientific terms. Stopes assisted emerging birth control movements in a number of British colonies. The birth control movement advocated for contraception so as to permit sexual intercourse as desired without the risk of pregnancy. By emphasising control the birth control movement argued that women should have control over their reproduction and the movement had close ties to the feminist movement. Slogans such as "control over our own bodies" criticised male domination and demanded women's liberation, a connotation that is absent from the family planning, population control and eugenics movements. In the 1960s and 1970s the birth control movement advocated for the legalisation of abortion and large scale education campaigns about contraception by governments. In the 1980s birth control and population control organisations co-operated in demanding rights to contraception and abortion, with an increasing emphasis on "choice".

Birth control has become a major theme in feminist politics who cited reproduction issues as examples of women's powerlessness to exercise their rights. The societal acceptance of birth control required the separation of sex from procreation, making birth control a highly controversial subject in the 20th Century. In a broader context birth control has become an arena for conflict between liberal and conservative values, raising questions about family, personal freedom, state intervention, religion in politics, sexual morality and social welfare. Reproductive rights, that is rights relating to sexual reproduction and reproductive health, were first discussed as a subset of human rights at the United Nation's 1968 International Conference on Human Rights. Reproductive rights are not recognised in international human rights law and is an umbrella term that may include some or all of the following rights: the right to legal or safe abortion, the right to control one's reproductive functions, the right to access quality reproductive healthcare, and the right to education and access in order to make reproductive choices free from coercion, discrimination, and violence. Reproductive rights may also be understood to include education about contraception and sexually transmitted infections, and freedom from coerced sterilisation and contraception, protection from gender-based practices such as female genital cutting, or FGC, and male genital mutilation, or MGM. Reproductive rights are understood as rights of both men and women, but are most frequently advanced as women's rights.

Women's access to legal abortions is restricted by law in most countries in the world. Where abortion is permitted by law, women may only have limited access to safe abortion services. Only a small number of countries prohibit abortion in all cases. In most countries and jurisdictions, abortion is allowed to save the pregnant woman's life, or where the pregnancy is the result of rape or incest. According to Human Rights Watch "Abortion is a highly emotional subject and one that excites deeply held opinions. However, equitable access to safe abortion services is first and foremost a human right. Where abortion is safe and legal, no one is forced to have one. Where abortion is illegal and unsafe, women are forced to carry unwanted pregnancies to term or suffer serious health consequences and even death. Approximately 13% of maternal deaths worldwide are attributable to unsafe abortion—between 68,000 and 78,000 deaths annually." According to Human Rights Watch "the denial of a pregnant woman's right to make an independent decision regarding abortion violates or poses a threat to a wide range of human rights." Other groups however, such as the Catholic Church, the Christian right and most Orthodox Jews, regard abortion not as a right but as a 'moral evil'.

United Nations and World Conferences on Women

In 1946 the United Nations established a Commission on the

Status of Women. Originally as the Section on the Status of Women, Human Rights Division, Department of Social Affairs, and now part of the Economic and Social Council (ECOSOC). Since 1975 the UN has held a series of world conferences on women's issues, starting with the World Conference of the International Women's Year in Mexico City. These conferences created an international forum for women's rights, but also illustrated divisions between women of different cultures and the difficulties of attempting to apply principles universally. Four World Conferences have been held, the first in Mexico City (International Women's Year, 1975), the second in Copenhagen (1980) and the third in Nairobi (1985). At the Fourth World Conference on Women in Beijing (1995), The Platform for Action was signed. This included a commitment to achieve "gender equality and the empowerment of women". In 2010, UN Women is founded by merging of Division for the Advancement of Women, International Research and Training Institute for the Advancement of Women, Office of the Special Adviser on Gender Issues Advancement of Women and United Nations Development Fund for Women by General Assembly Resolution 63/311.

Natural Law and Women's Rights

17th century natural law philosophers in Britain and America, such as Thomas Hobbes, Jean-Jacques Rousseau and John Locke, developed the theory of natural rights in reference to ancient philosophers such as Aristotle and the Christian theologise Aquinas. Like the ancient philosophers, 17th century natural law philosophers defended slavery and an inferior status of women in law. Relying on ancient Greek philosophers, natural law philosophers argued that natural rights were not derived from god, but were "universal, self-evident, and intuitive", a law that could be found in nature. They believed that natural rights were self-evident to "civilised man" who lives "in the highest form of society". Natural rights derived from human nature, a concept first established by the ancient Greek philosopher Zeno of Citium in *Concerning Human Nature*. Zenon argued that each rational and civilised male Greek citizen had a "divine spark" or "soul" within him that existed independent of the body. Zeno founded the Stoic philosophy and the idea of a human nature was adopted by other Greek philosophers, and later natural law philosophers and western humanists. Aristotle developed the widely adopted idea of rationality, arguing that man was a "rational animal" and as such a natural power of reason. Concepts of human nature in ancient

Greece depended on gender, ethnic, and other qualifications and 17th Century natural law philosophers came to regard women along with children, slaves and non-whites, as neither "rational" nor "civilised". Natural law philosophers claimed the inferior status of women was "common sense" and a matter of "nature". They believed that women could not be treated as equal due to their "inner nature". The views of 17th Century natural law philosophers were opposed in the 18th and 19th Century by Evangelical natural theology philosophers such as William Wilberforce and Charles Spurgeon, who argued for the abolition of slavery and advocated for women to have rights equal to that of men. Modern natural law theorist, and advocates of natural rights, claim that all people have a human nature, regardless of gender, ethnicity or other qualifications, therefore all people have natural rights.

Human Rights and Women's Rights

Convention on the Elimination of All Forms of Discrimination Against Women

The Universal Declaration of Human Rights, adopted in 1948, enshrines "the equal rights of men and women", and addressed both the equality and equity issues. In 1979 the United Nations General Assembly adopted the Convention on the Elimination of All Forms of Discrimination against Women (CEDAW) for legal implementation of the Declaration on the Elimination of Discrimination against Women. Described as an international bill of rights for women, it came into force on 3 September 1981. The UN member states that have not ratified the convention are Iran, Nauru, Palau, Somalia, Sudan, Tonga, and the United States. Niue and the Vatican City, which are non-member states, have also not ratified it.

The Convention defines discrimination against women in the following terms:

> Any distinction, exclusion or restriction made on the basis of sex which has the effect or purpose of impairing or nullifying the recognition, enjoyment or exercise by women, irrespective of their marital status, on a basis of equality of men and women, of human rights and fundamental freedoms in the political, economic, social, cultural, civil or any other field.

It also establishes an agenda of action for putting an end to sex-based discrimination for which states ratifying the Convention are required to enshrine gender equality into their domestic legislation, repeal all discriminatory provisions in their laws, and enact new provisions to guard against discrimination against women. They must also establish tribunals and public institutions to guarantee women effective protection against discrimination, and take steps to eliminate all forms of discrimination practiced against women by individuals, organisations, and enterprises.

United Nations Security Council Resolution 1325

On October 31 2000, the United Nations Security Council unanimously adopted United Nations Security Council Resolution 1325, the first formal and legal document from the United Nations Security Council that requires all states respect fully international humanitarian law and international human rights law appicable to the rights and protection of women and girls during and after the armed conflicts.

Maputo Protocol

The Protocol to the African Charter on Human and Peoples' Rights on the Rights of Women in Africa, better known as the Maputo Protocol, was adopted by the African Union on 11 July 2003 at its second summit in Maputo,Mozambique. On 25 November 2005, having been ratified by the required 15 member nations of the African Union, the protocol entered into force. The protocol guarantees comprehensive rights to women including the right to take part in the political process, to social and political equality with men, and to control of their reproductive health, and an end to female genital mutilation.

Rape and Sexual Violence against Women

Rape, sometimes called sexual assault, is an assault by a person involving sexual intercourse with or sexual penetration of another person without that person's consent. Rape is generally considered a serious sex crime as well as a civil assault. When part of a widespread and systematic practice rape and sexual slavery are now recognised as crime against humanity and war crime. Rape is also now recognised as an element of the crime of genocide when committed with the intent to destroy, in whole or in part, a targeted group.

Rape as an Element of the Crime of Genocide

In 1998, the International Criminal Tribunal for Rwanda established by the United Nations made landmark decisions that rape is a crime of genocide under international law. The trial of Jean-Paul Akayesu, the mayor of Taba Commune in Rwanda, established precedents that rape is an element of the crime of genocide. The Akayesu judgement includes the first interpretation and application by an international court of the 1948 Convention on the Prevention and Punishment of the Crime of Genocide. The Trial Chamber held that rape, which it defined as "a physical invasion of a sexual nature committed on a person under circumstances which are coercive", and sexual assault constitute acts of genocide insofar as they were committed with the intent to destroy, in whole or in part, a targeted group, as such. It found that sexual assault formed an integral part of the process of destroying the Tutsi ethnic group and that the rape was systematic and had been perpetrated against Tutsi women only, manifesting the specific intent required for those acts to constitute genocide.

Judge Navanethem Pillay said in a statement after the verdict: "From time immemorial, rape has been regarded as spoils of war. Now it will be considered a war crime. We want to send out a strong message that rape is no longer a trophy of war." An estimated 500,000 women were raped during the 1994 Rwandan Genocide.

Rape and Sexual Enslavement as Crime against Humanity

The Rome Statute Explanatory Memorandum, which defines the jurisdiction of the International Criminal Court, recognises rape, sexual slavery, enforced prostitution, forced pregnancy, enforced sterilisation, "or any other form of sexual violence of comparable gravity" as crime against humanity if the action is part of a widespread or systematic practice. The Vienna Declaration and Programme of Action also condemn systematic rape as well as murder, sexual slavery, and forced pregnancy, as the "violations of the fundamental principles of international human rights and humanitarian law." and require a particularly effective response.

Rape was first recognised as crime against humanity when the International Criminal Tribunal for the former Yugoslavia issued arrest warrants based on the Geneva Conventions and Violations of the Laws or Customs of War. Specifically, it was recognised that Muslim women in Foca (southeastern Bosnia and Herzegovina) were subjected to systematic and widespread gang rape, torture and sexual enslavement by Bosnian Serb soldiers, policemen, and members of paramilitary groups after the takeover of the city in April 1992. The indictment was of major legal significance and was the first time that sexual assaults were investigated for the purpose of prosecution under the rubric of torture and enslavement as a crime against humanity. The indictment was confirmed by a 2001 verdict by the International Criminal Tribunal for the former Yugoslavia that rape and sexual enslavement are crimes against humanity. This ruling challenged the widespread acceptance of rape and sexual enslavement of women as intrinsic part of war. The International Criminal Tribunal for the former Yugoslavia found three Bosnian Serb men guilty of rape of Bosniac (Bosnian Muslim) women and girls (some as young as 12 and 15 years of age), in Foca, eastern Bosnia and Herzegovina. Furthermore two of the men were found guilty of the crime against humanity of sexual enslavement for holding women and girls captive in a number of de facto detention centres. Many of the women subsequently disappeared.

Timeline of Women's Rights

Women's Rights Before 19th Century

- 622: Arabia: The Constitution of Medina is declared, which outlines many of Muhammad's early reforms under Islam, including an improved legal status for women in Islam, who were generally given greater rights than women in pre-Islamic Arabia and medieval Europe.
- 1718: Sweden: Female taxpaying members of the cities' guilds are allowed to vote and stand for election during the age of liberty; this right is banned (for local elections) in 1758 and (general elections) in 1771.
- 1754: Germany: Dorothea Erxleben the first woman doctor.
- 1776: France: Female tailors are allowed into the guild of tailors.
- 1778: Sweden: Barnamordsplakatet; unmarried women are allowed to leave their home town to give birth anonymously and have the birth registered anonymously, to refrain from answering any questions about the birth and, if they choose to keep their child, to have their unmarried status not mentioned in official documents to avoid social embarrassment.
- 1788: France: noble widows are known to have voted to the French States-General in 1788-89 in the absence of a male guardian. United States of America (to stand for election).
- 1789: France is the first country in Europe where it is suggested that women are to be in the Assembly of the Estates, there are several demands to include women in the reforms of the right to vote.
- 1790: France: Equal inheritance rights (later abolished).
- 1792: France : The reformed laws of marriage and divorce greatly favours women's equal rights in France, but all of

these laws are abolished by Napoleon Bonaparte's Code Napoleon in 1804.

- 1792: France : Local women-units of the defense army are founded in several cities; although the military was never officially open to women, about eight thousand women were estimated to have served openly in the French army in local troops (but not in the battle fields) between 1792 and 1794, but women were officially barred from the army in 1795.
- 1793: France : The question of women's right to vote is discussed in the parliament; women's right to vote is acknowledged as a principle, but it is still put aside with the view that the time is not right to make this a reality and is therefore postponed.

Women's Rights During 19th century

- 1810: Sweden : Unmarried women are allowed to be declared of legal majority by royal dispensation.
- 1821: USA : The first Women's university is founded.
- 1829: India : Sati is banned.
- 1833: USA : The first co-educational university, Oberlin, open to both sexes is founded in Ohio.
- 1839: Great Britain: it is made possible for mothers to be made guardian for children at divorce. STEL Mississippi in USA: Married women are allowed separate economy from their hubands.
- 1841: Bulgaria: The first girls school makes education for women available.
- 1842: Sweden: Elementary school compulsory by law for both boys and girls.
- 1845: Sweden: Equal inheritance for sons and daughters (in the absence of a will).
- 1846: Sweden: Professions within the trades are opened on the same terms as men for all unmarried women.
- 1847: Belgium: Elementary school for both genders.
- 1848: The state of New York in the United States : Separate economy and independence allowed for married women.
- 1849: Elizabeth Blackwell becomes the first female doctor in USA, and in 1858 also in Great Britain.
- 1850: Iceland : Legal majority for (unmarried) women in Iceland.

- 1851: Guatemala: Women who fulfill the demands of personal economic wealth are granted citizenship.
- 1853: Sweden: Women formally allowed to teach at universities.
- 1854: Norway: Equal inheritance rights. Massachusetts in USA: Married women granted separate economy and legal majority.
- 1857: Denmark: Women (if unmarried) are declared to be of legal majority in Denmark; no longer minors in law. Great Britain: formal Divorce, not just legal separation, is made possible.
- 1858: Sweden : Legal majority for unmarried women·
- 1859: Sweden: Several professions of lower officials are opened to women. Canada: Married women granted the right to own property.
- 1861: Sweden: The profession of dentist is open to women in Sweden; Rosalie Fougelberg becomes the first woman dentist and the personal dentist of the queen in 1867 (though Amalia Assur was first, but with a special permission). USA: Lucy Hobbs Taylor becomes the first woman dentist. France: Julie-Victoire Daubié becomes the first female student.
- 1863: Norway: Unmarried women granted legal majority (at the same age as men in 1869).
- 1864: Finland: Legal majority for women. Sweden: Unmarried female industry workers are given the same rights as men. Sweden: Husbands are forbidden to abuse their wives· Bohemia: taxpaying women and women in "learned profession" made eligable to the legislative body in 1864.
- 1865: Italy : Legal majority for unmarried women is granted by the new constitution. Switzerland: Women are allowed to study.
- 1867: Russia: Women allowed to study in Russia (at the same terms as men in 1905) and in Finland (at the same terms as men in 1901).
- 1868: The United States formally allows women to study, although several universities had already been open to women earlier.
- 1869: Arabella Mansfield becomes the first woman to enter the practice of law in the U.S.

- 1870: Great Britain: Legal majority for unmarried women; this law is improved in 1874, 1882, and in 1893. Sweden: Women are allowed to study (at the same terms as men 1873)· the first female student is Betty Pettersson. India: The murder of female infants is banned.
- 1871: Japan: The first female students are granted scholarships to the United States.
- 1872: Sweden: Arranged marriages are forbidden. Canada: Women with dependent children who have no husband may have homestead land in accordance with the Public Lands of the Dominion Statute. Japan: geishas are made independent.
- 1873: Britain: Mothers are granted guardianshp for children at divorce. Custody of Infants Act 1873. Japan: Schools for the education of women to various professions are founded.
- 1874: The Netherlands: Aletta Jacobs becomes the first woman allowed to study medicine. Italy: The universities open to women. Sweden: Married women are granted economical equality and legal majority. France: The first female trade union. Japan: Elementary education for both genders, the profession of school teacher is opened to both sexes.
- 1875: Denmark: Women allowed to study·
- 1876: Great Britain: Women formally allowed to study.
- 1877: Chile: Women are allowed to study.
- 1878: Finland: Equality in inheritance· Great Britain: Abuse is recognised as grounds for divorce.
- 1879: Brazil: Women allowed to study.
- 1880: France: Women are allowed to study. Belgium: Women are allowed to study. Australia : Women are allowed to study. Canada:Women are allowed to study.
- 1882: Great Britain: Married women are granted separate economy and legal majority (Married Women's Property Act 1882). USA: Women are granted legal majority in the entire USA. France: Elementary school for both genders.
- 1883: Romania: women allowed to study (Coeducation at the universities).
- 1884: Norway: women allowed to study. Germany: Legal majority for unmarried women. Mexico: Legal majority for unmarried women. Ontario: married women are given control over their own property.

- 1885: France: Divorce is again allowed (after having been abolished since 1814).
- 1886: Britain: Josephine Butler puts a stop to the prostitution regemen. Mexico: The first women attend university.
- 1888: Spain: women are allowed to study with a written approval from a male guardian. Norway: Legal majority for married women.
- 1889: Sweden: women electable to social boards in schools and poor-care.
- 1891: India: Females younger than 12 are banned from marrying (Child marriage).
- 1891: U.S.: Marie Owens hired as a police officer in Chicago.
- 1895: South Carolina in the United States: Separate economy allowed for married women. Upper Canada: Women allowed to work as barristers.
- 1896: Austria-Hungary (and thereby also the future Czech Republic and Slovakia) : women allowed to study. The profession of lawyer are opened to both sexes in USA as a whole - but the first female lawyer in an American state was recorded already in 1869.
- 1898: Haiti: women allowed to study.
- 1899: Denmark: Legal majority for married women.

Women's Rights During the 20th century

- 1900: Belgium: Legal majority for women in Belgium. Iceland: legal majority for married women. Egypt and Tunisia: Girls schools are founded. Japan: foundation of a women's university. France: The profession of lawyer are opened to both sexes.
- 1901: Sweden: Women are given four weeks maternity leave·
- 1902: China: Foot binding is abolished, after having handicapped women's feet since ca 1010.
- 1904: France : Legal majority for women. Mexico: Divorce is legalised.
- 1906: Finland (to stand for election). Sweden : municipal suffrage, since 1862 granted to unmarried women and widows, are allowed also for married women.
- 1907: Japan : the first coeducational university. Norway (to stand for election). Finland (first female Members of Parliament).

- 1908: Married women in France granted legal majority and economic equality, and the women of Germany are allowed to study.
- 1909: Sweden : women granted eligibility to municipal councils.
- 1917: Netherlands (to stand for election).
- 1918: Soviet Russia: the first Soviet Constitution explicitly declares the equal rights of men and women.
- 1919: Italy : Married women granted legal majority. Great Britain: The Sex Disqualification (Removal) Act 1919.
- 1920: China: The first female students are accepted in the Peking University, soon followed by universities all over China. Canada (to stand for election, with some restrictions/ conditions).
- 1920: Sweden: reformed marriage act grants the spouses equal rights.
- 1921: Belgium (to stand for election). Full equal rights for married women in Sweden.
- 1922: Belgium and Japan: women are allowed to be lawyers.
- 1926: Turkey: Women are granted legal majority, are admitted to the universities, and the harems and the veil are abolished.
- 1927: Mexico: Legal majority for married women.
- 1934: Turkey (to stand for election).
- 1935: Iran: Women are admitted to Tehran University.
- 1936: Iran: Reza Shah Pahlavi set the mandatory unveiling of women—a highly controversial policy which nonetheless was significant for the desegregation of women.
- 1937: Puerto Rico (to stand for election).
- 1938: Sweden: Contraception is allowed.
- 1939: Sweden: It becomes forbidden to fire a woman for marrying or having children.
- 1945: 'British Guiana'-Guyana (to stand for election).
- 1946: 'Burma'-Myanmar (to stand for election).
- 1947: Sweden: Equal salary for both sexes.
- 1948: Sweden: Maternity pay.
- 1953: Mexico (to stand for election).

- 1958: Sweden: Women allowed to become priests.
- 1960: Canada (to stand for election, with no restrictions/ conditions).
- 1961: El Salvador (to stand for election).
- 1963: Papua New Guinea (to stand for election).
- 1970: Democratic Republic of the Congo (to stand for election).
- 1973: Andorra, San Marino (to stand for election).
- 1975: The right to abortion is secured in Sweden, South Africa and USA.
- 1978: 'Rhodesia'-Zimbabwe (to stand for election).
- 1980: Sweden: Gender discrimination forbidden by law.
- 1986: Djibouti (to stand for election).
- 1991: Great Britain: England and Wales: Marital rape was made illegal by the case of *R v R*.

Legal Rights of Women A Historical Perspective

The Legal rights of women refers to the social and human rights of women. One of the first women's rights declarations was the Declaration of Sentiments. The dependent position of women in early law is proved by the evidence of most ancient systems.

Mosaic law

In the Mosaic law, for monetary matters, women's and men's rights were almost exactly equal. A woman was entitled to her own private property, including land, livestock, slaves, and servants. A woman had the right to inherit whatever anyone bequeathed to her as a death gift, and in the absence of sons would inherit everything. A woman could likewise bequeath her belongings to others as a death gift. Upon dying intestate, a woman would be inherited by her children if she had them, her husband if she was married, or her father if she were single. A woman could sue in court and did not need a male to represent her.

In some situations, women actually had more rights than men. For example, captive women had to be ransomed prior to any male captives. Even though sons inherited property, they had a responsibility to support their mother and sisters from the estate, and had to ensure that both mother and sisters were taken care of prior to their being able to benefit from the inheritance, and if that wiped out the estate, the boys had to supplement their income from elsewhere.

When it came to specific religious or sacramental activities, women had fewer opportunities or privileges than men. For example, in monetary or capital cases women could not serve as witnesses. A woman could not serve as a kohen in the Temple. A woman could not serve as queen, the monarch had to be male. A divorce could only be granted by the husband, upon which time she would receive the Ketubah and the return of significant portions of her dowry. The vow of an unmarried girl between the ages of 12 years and 12 years and six months might be nullified by her father and the vow of a wife which affected marital obligations may be annulled by her husband; the guilt or innocence of a wife accused of adultery might be tested through the Sotah process, although this only was successful if the husband was innocent of adultery, and daughters could inherit only in the absence of sons.

Egyptian Law on Women's Rights

In Ancient Egypt, legally, a woman shared the same rights and status as a man - at least, theoretically. An Egyptian woman was entitled to her own private property, which could include land, livestock, slaves and servants, etc. She had the right to inherit whatever anyone bequeathed to her, as well as bequeathing her belongings to others. She could divorce her husband (upon which all possessions belonging to her - including the dowry - were reverted to her sole ownership), and sue in court. Most notably, a woman could do these legal matters without a male to represent her. However, on the whole, men vastly outnumbered women in most trades, including government administrators; the average woman still centered her time around the home and family. A few women became pharaohs, and women held important positions in government and trade.

Roman Law on Women's Rights

Women in ancient Rome were citizens, but could not run for political office or vote. Roman women had little political freedom in society, but substantial freedom outside of politics, and some were outspoken and took an interest in the politics of their day. The status of a woman would vary from a fish monger with very little money to a woman of great wealth and daughter and married to prominent politicians like Caecilia Metella, and those are the women more likely to have left a mark. Women had full capacity for themselves, but none for others, although some emperors recognised a woman's relationship to her own sons and daughters.

Christian Laws and Influences on Women's Rights

The following are a few of the matters in which Christianity appears to have made alterations, generally but perhaps not always improvements, in the law. As a rule the influence of the church was exercised in favor of the abolition of the disabilities imposed by the older law upon celibacy and childlessness, of increased facilities for entering a professed religious life, and of due provision for the wife. The church also supported the political power of those who were friendly toward the clergy. The appointment of mothers and grandmothers as tutors was sanctioned by Justinian. The restrictions on the marriage of senators and other men of high rank with women of low rank were extended by Constantine, but it was almost entirely removed by Justinian. Second marriages were discouraged, especially by making it legal to impose a condition that a widow's right to property should cease on re-marriage, and the Leonine Constitutions at the end of the 9th century made third marriages punishable. The same constitutions made the benediction of a priest a necessary part of the ceremony of marriage. The criminal law also changed its perspectives on women. Adultery was punished with death by Constantine, but the penalty was reduced by Justinian to banishment to a convent. A woman condemned for adultery could not re-marry. A marriage between a Christian and a Jew rendered the parties guilty of adultery. Severe laws were enacted against offences of unchastity, especially procurement and incest. It was a capital crime to carry off or offer violence to a nun. Women were subject to penalties for wearing dress or ornaments (except rings) imitating those reserved for the emperor and his family. Actresses and women of bad fame were not to wear the dress of virgins dedicated to Heaven. If a consul had a wife or mother living with him, he was allowed to incur greater expense than if he lived alone. The interests of working women were protected by enactments for the regulation of the gynoecia, or workshops for spinning, dyeing, etc. The canon law, looking with disfavour on the female independence prevailing in the later Roman law, tended rather in the opposite direction . The Decretum Gratiani specially inculcated subjection of the wife to the husband, and obedience to his will in all things. The chief differences between canon and Roman law were in the law of marriage, especially in the introduction of publicity and of the formalities of the ring and the kiss. The benediction of a priest was made a necessary part of the ceremony, as indeed it had been made by the civil power, as has been already stated, in the post-Justinian period of Roman law.

Islamic Law on Women's Rights

In the early Middle Ages, an early effort to improve the status of women occurred during the early reforms under Islam, when women were given greater rights in marriage, divorce and inheritance. Women were not accorded with such legal status in other cultures, including the West, until centuries later. The Oxford Dictionary of Islam states that the general improvement of the status of Arab women included prohibition of female infanticide and recognising women's full personhood. "The dowry, previously regarded as a bride-price paid to the father, became a nuptial gift retained by the wife as part of her personal property." Under Islamic law, marriage was no longer viewed as a "status" but rather as a "contract", in which the woman's consent was imperative. "Women were given inheritance rights in a patriarchal society that had previously restricted inheritance to male relatives." Annemarie Schimmel states that "compared to the pre-Islamic position of women, Islamic legislation meant an enormous progress; the woman has the right, at least according to the letter of the law, to administer the wealth she has brought into the family or has earned by her own work." Some have claimed that women generally had more legal rights under Islamic law than they did under Western legal systems until more recent times. English Common Law transferred property held by a wife at the time of a marriage to her husband, which contrasted with the Sura: "Unto men (of the family) belongs a share of that which Parents and near kindred leave, and unto women a share of that which parents and near kindred leave, whether it be a little or much - a determinate share" (Qur'an 4:7), albeit maintaining that husbands were solely responsible for the maintenance and leadership of his wife and family. "French married women, unlike their Muslim sisters, suffered from restrictions on their legal capacity which were removed only in 1965."

Education as per Islamic Law

Women in Islam played an important role in the foundations of many Islamic educational institutions, such as Fatima al-Fihri's founding of the University of Al Karaouine in 859. This continued through to the Ayyubid dynasty in the 12th and 13th centuries, when 160 mosques and madrasahs were established in Damascus, 26 of which were funded by women through the Waqf (charitable trust or trust law) system. Half of all the royal patrons for these institutions were also women. According to the Sunni scholar Ibn Asakir in the 12th century, there were opportunities for female education in the medieval Islamic world, writing that women could study, earn ijazahs (academic degrees), and qualify as scholars and teachers. This was especially the case for learned and scholarly families, who wanted to ensure the highest possible education for both their sons and daughters. Ibn Asakir had himself studied under 80 different female teachers in his time. Female education in the Islamic world was inspired by Muhammad's wives: Khadijah, a successful business woman, and Aisha, a renowned hadith scholar and military leader. According to a hadith attributed to Muhammad, he praised the women of Medina because of their desire for religious knowledge:

> "How splendid were the women of the ansar; shame did not prevent them from becoming learned in the faith."

While it was not common for women to enroll as students in formal classes, it was common for women to attend informal lectures and study sessions at mosques, madrasahs and other public places. While there were no legal restrictions on female education, some men did not approve of this practice, such as Muhammad ibn al-Hajj (d. 1336) who was appalled at the behaviour of some women who informally audited lectures in his time:

> "[Consider] what some women do when people gather with a shaykh to hear [the recitation of] books. At that point women come, too, to hear the readings; the men sit in one place, the women facing them. It even happens at such times that some of the women are carried away by the situation; one will stand up, and sit down, and shout in a loud voice. [Moreover] her 'awra will appear; in her house, their exposure would be forbidden — how can it be allowed in a mosque, in the presence of men?"

Employment as per Islamic Law

The labor force in the Caliphate were employed from diverse ethnic and religious backgrounds, while both men and women were involved in diverse occupations and economic activities. Women were employed in a wide range of commercial activities and diverse occupations in the primary sector (as farmers for example), secondary sector (as construction workers, dyers, spinners, etc.) and tertiary sector (as investors, doctors, nurses, presidents of guilds, brokers, peddlers, lenders, scholars, etc.). Muslim women also held a monopoly over certain branches of the textile industry, the largest and most specialised and market-oriented industry at the time, in occupations such as spinning, dyeing, and embroidery. In comparison, female property rights and wage labour were relatively uncommon in Europe until the Industrial Revolution in the 18th and 19th centuries.

Scandinavia

The early law of the northern parts of Europe is interesting from the different ways in which it treated women. The position of women varied greatly. Before Christianity, women in Scandinavia had a relatively free and independent position. Unmarried women in general, referred to as *maer* and *mey*, were secured their right to independence: at the age of 20, a woman reached the right of legal majority and had the right to decide about her own place of residence and stand by herself in a juridical sense before the law. The one exception to her independence was the right to choose marriage partner, which was a matter for the whole family. The idea was that the proper way of providing for a woman was by giving her a marriage portion. But, once she is married into a separate community, neither she nor her children are deemed to have any further claim on the parent group. The same rights applied to widows. The right to inherit in itself applied to both the paternal aunt, paternal niece and paternal granddaughter of the deceased, who were all named as "odalkvinna" A woman with no son, if unmarried, could also inherit the position of head of the family from her father or her brother, and was in such a case, as a Baugrygr, specifically awarded all rights normally performed by a male head of the family. The Baugrygr, however, only kept this position while unmarried, otherwise leaving the position to her spouse or son.

These liberties changed after the introductions of Christianity, and from the late 13th-century, they are no longer mentioned. Women were thereafter under perpetual tutelage, whether married or unmarried. In the code of Christian V, at the end of the 17th century, it was enacted that if a woman married without the consent of her tutor he might have, if he wished, administration of her goods during her life. The provision made by the Scandinavian laws under the name of morning-gift was perhaps the parent of the modern settled property.

Women's Rights in the British Isles

Women's Rights in Ireland

The Brehon law of Ireland excepted women from the ordinary course of the law. They could distrain or contract only in certain named cases, and distress upon their property was regulated by special rules. In general, every woman had to have a male guardian. Women seem not to have been entitled to the slightest possession of land under the Brehon law, but rather had assigned to them a certain number of their father's cattle as their marriage-portion.

However, their legal status was not as low as in many Germanic cultures; and it seems that the status of Irish women improved somewhat with time, especially after the introduction of Christianity. For instance, beginning in the eighth century, female heirs inherited real estate if they had no brothers. These women became known as "heiresses" and, while only a small minority of women living at this time, they could exercise a considerable amount of political and legal influence. If an heiress married a landless husband, she was seen as his legal guardian, leading to a very unusual case of complete gender role reversal. However, most women did not own land and remained more or less dependent on their husbands; under the ancient Brehon laws one could not be counted as a free citizen unless one owned land independently. The holding of political offices, similarly, seems to have been only suitable for men; nowhere in Irish historical tracts is any female High Queen or chieftain mentioned, and warfare and political affairs were generally all-male.

Even with these legal restrictions placed upon women, they retained some legal capacity. The arrival of St. Patrick and the introduction of Christian Roman law affected the medieval Irish view of marriage. By the eighth century, the preferred form of marriage was one between social equals, under which a woman was technically legally depedent on her husband and had half his honor price, but could exercise considerable authority in regard to the transfer of property. Such women were called "women of joint dominion". Adult sons appear to have gained rights under the new Christian laws as well, as surviving texts seem to indicate that sons could impugn bad contracts that would harm his inheritance. Daughters, however, continued to have little or no legal independence, although after the eighth century they could no longer be forced into marriage by their parents.

Women's Rights in England

The laws of Athelstan contained a peculiarly brutal provision for the punishment of a female slave convicted of theft: She was to be burned alive by eighty other female slaves. Other laws were directed against the practice of witchcraft by women. Burning was the punishment specially appropriated to women convicted of treason or witchcraft. A case of sentence to execution by burning for treason occurred as late as 1784.

Monogamy was enforced both by the civil and ecclesiastical law. Second and third marriages involved penance. A glimpse of cruelty in the household is afforded by the provision, occurring no less than three times in the ecclesiastical legislation, that if a woman scourged her female slave to death, she must do penance.

Traces of wife-purchase were still seen in the law of Athelberht of Kent, which stated that if a man carried off a freeman's wife, he must, at his own expense, procure another wife for the husband. (See also bride kidnapping.) The codes contain few provisions as to the property of married women, but those few appear to prove that they were in a better position than at later dates.

The development of the bride price no doubt was in the same direction. It was the sum paid by the husband to the wife's family for the purchase of part of the family property, while the morning-gift was paid to the bride herself. In its English form, morning-gift occurs in the laws of Canute; in its Latinised form of *morgangiva*, it occurs in the Leges Henrici Primi.

The old common and statute law of England placed women in a special position. A woman was exempt from legal duties more particularly attaching to men and not performable by a deputy. She could not hold a proper feud, i.e., one of which the tenure was by military service. The same principle appears in the rule that she could not be endowed of a castle maintained for the defense of the realm and not for the private use of the owner. She could receive homage, but not render it in the form used by men.

She could be the constable, either of a castle or a villa, but not the sheriff, except in the one case of Westmorland, where an hereditary office was exercised in the 17th century by Anne, countess of Dorset, Pembroke and Montgomery.

In certain cases a woman could transmit rights that she could not enjoy. Edward III's claim to the crown of France rested on such a power of transmission. However, the claim was a breach of the French constitutional law, which rejected the claim of a woman.

By Magna Carta a woman could not accuse a man of murder except of that of her husband. This disability no doubt arose from the fact that in trial by battle she naturally did not appear in person but through a champion.

In some old statutes, very curious sumptuary regulations as to women's dress occur. By the sumptuary laws of Edward III in 1363 (37 Edw. III, cc. 8-14), women were, in general, to be dressed according to the position of their fathers or husbands. It is worthy of notice that at the times of passing these sumptuary laws, the trade interests of women were protected by the legislature.

In some cases, the wives and daughters of tradesmen were allowed to assist in the trades of their husbands and fathers. Some trading corporations, such as the East India Company, recognised no distinction of sex in their members.

At common law a woman could own both real and personal property. However, in the case of a married woman the husband had a life interest in any real property: this continued even after the wife's death, and was known as tenancy "by the curtsey". Personal property passed into the ownership of the husband absolutely, with the exception of certain items of adornment or household use known as paraphernalia.

These rules were circumvented by the rules of equity, as enforced by the Court of Chancery. Property designed for the benefit of a married woman was vested in trustees, and her rights under that trust remained her own and did not vest in the husband.

Women's Rights in Scotland

In Scotland, as early as Regiam Majestatem (14th century), women were the object of special legal regulation. In that work, the mercheta mulieris (probably a tax paid to the lord on the marriage of his tenant's daughter) was fixed at a sum differing according to the rank of the woman. Numerous ancient laws dealt with trade and sumptuary matters. By the Leges Quatuor Burgorum, female brewsters making bad ale were to forfeit eightpence and be put on the cucking-stool, and were to set an ale-wand outside their houses under a penalty of fourpence. The same laws also provided that a married woman committing a trespass without her husband's knowledge might be chastised like an under-age child.

Women's Rights in Wales

The second part of the Welsh Law Codes begins with "the laws of women", such as the rules governing marriage and the division of property if a married couple should separate. The position of women under Welsh law differed significantly from that of their Norman-English contemporaries. A marriage could be established in two basic ways. The normal way was that the woman would be given to a man by her kindred; the abnormal way was that the woman could elope with a man without the consent of her kindred. In the latter case, her kindred could compel her to return if she was still a virgin, but if she was not, she could not be compelled to return. If the relationship lasted for seven years, she had the same entitlements as if she had been given by her kin.

A number of payments are connected with marriage. *Amobr* was a fee payable to the woman's lord on the loss of her virginity, whether on marriage or otherwise. *Cowyll* was a payment due to the woman from her husband on the morning after the marriage, marking her transition from virgin to married woman. *Agweddi* was the amount of the common pool of property owned by the couple that was due to the woman if the couple separated before the end of seven years. The total of the agweddi depended on the woman's status by birth, regardless of the actual size of the common pool of property. If the marriage broke up after the end of seven years, the woman was entitled to half the common pool.

If a woman found her husband with another woman, she was entitled to a payment of six score pence the first time and a pound the second time; on the third occasion she was entitled to divorce him. If the husband had a concubine, the wife was allowed to strike her without having to pay any compensation, even if it resulted in the concubine's death. A woman could only be beaten by her husband for three things: for giving away something that she was not entitled to give away, for being found with another man, or for wishing a blemish on her husband's beard. If he beat her for any other cause, she was entitled to the payment of *sarhad*. If the husband found her with another man and beat her, he was not entitled to any further compensation. Women were not allowed to inherit land, except under special circumstances, but the rule for the division of moveable property when one of a married couple died was the same for both sexes. The property was divided into two equal halves, with the surviving partner keeping one half and the dying partner being free to give bequests from the other half.

Women's Rights as per the Edwardian Era Laws

In 1911, under English law, the earliest age at which a girl could contract a valid marriage was 12; boys had to be 14. Under the lnfants Settlement Act 1855, a valid settlement could be made by a woman at 17 with the approval of the court, while the age for a man was 20; by the Married Women's Property Act 1907, any settlement by a husband of his wife's property was not valid unless executed by her if she was of full age, or confirmed by her after she attained full age.

An unmarried woman was liable for the support of illegitimate children till they attain the age of 16. She was generally assisted, in the absence of agreement, by an affiliation order granted by magistrates. A married woman having separate property was, under the Married Women's Property Acts 1882 and 1908, liable for the support of her parents, husband, children and grandchildren becoming chargeable to any union or parish.

In common law, the father, rather than the mother, was entitled to the custody of a legitimate child up to the age of 16, and could only forfeit such right by misconduct. But the Court of Chancery, wherever there was trust property and the infant could be made a ward of court, took a less rigid view of the paternal rights and looked more to the interest of the child, and consequently in some cases to the extension of the mother's rights in common law.

Legislation tended in the same direction. By the Custody of Infants Act 1873, the Court of Chancery was empowered to enforce a provision in a separation deed, giving up the custody or control of a child to the mother. The Judicature Act 1873 enacted that, in questions relating to the custody and education of infants, the rules of equity should prevail.

The most remarkable disabilities under which women were still placed in 1910 were the exclusion of female heirs from succession to real estate, except in the absence of a male heir; and the fact that a husband could obtain a divorce for the adultery of his wife, while a wife could obtain it only for her husband's adultery if coupled with some other cause, such as cruelty or desertion.

Almost all existing disabilities were lifted by the Sex Disqualification (Removal) Act 1919.

Women's Rights in Spain and Aquitania

Women in Christian Spain and Southern France, those regions part of the Visigothic Kingdom (418–721) and its various successor states (Asturias, León, Castile, Navarra, Aragon, Aquitania (Occitania) and Languedoc) Visigothic Law and Roman Law combined to allow women more rights then their contemporaries would enjoy until the 20th century. Particularly with the Liber Judiciorum as codified 642/643 and expanded on in the Code of Recceswinth in 653, women could inherit land and title and manage it independently from their husbands or male relations, dispose of their property in legal wills if they had no heirs, and women could represent themselves and bear witness in court by age 14 and arrange for their own marriages by age 20. In Spain these laws were further codified between 1252-1284 by Alfonso X of Castile with the Siete Partidas.

Women's Rights as per Hindu Law

In the East, up until 16th century, women were generally treated almost as untouchables and had very few rights. They were subjected to highly degrading practises like purdah (living separately from men or in seclusion, see also sex segregation); sati, the killing of the wife on the dead husband's funeral pyre; child marriage, when girls of between 5 and 10 years old were married off, without their consent or knowledge; dowry, the giving of expensive gifts by the bride's family to the groom's family in agreement to the wedding; etc.

Women in ancient India used to be very respected. There is no exclusion of women according to the Vedas. Motherhood is considered the greatest glory of Hindu women. The Taittiriya Upanishad teaches, "Matridevo bhava" - "Let your mother be god to you." In this mantra of Brahmacharya Sukta, it is emphasised that girls too should train themselves as students and only then enter into married life. The Sukta specifically emphasizes that girls should receive the same level of training as boys.

2

Women's Reproductive Rights and Pregnant Women's Rights

Women's Reproductive Rights

Reproductive rights are legal rights and freedoms relating to reproduction and reproductive health. The World Health Organisation defines reproductive rights as follows:

Reproductive rights rest on the recognition of the basic right of all couples and individuals to decide freely and responsibly the number, spacing and timing of their children and to have the information and means to do so, and the right to attain the highest standard of sexual and reproductive health. They also include the right of all to make decisions concerning reproduction free of discrimination, coercion and violence.

Reproductive rights began to develop as a subset of human rights at the United Nation's 1968 International Conference on Human Rights. The resulting non binding Proclamation of Teheran was the first international document to recognise one of these rights when it stated that: "Parents have a basic human right to determine freely and responsibly the number and the spacing of their children." States, though, have been slow in incorporating these rights in internationally legally binding instruments. Thus, while some of these rights have already been recognised in hard law, that is, in legally binding international human rights instruments, others have been mentioned only in non binding recommendations and, therefore, have at best the status of soft law in international law, while a further group is yet to be accepted by the international community and therefore remains at the level of advocacy.

According to Knudsen, issues related to reproductive rights are some of the most vigorously contested rights' issues worldwide, regardless of the population's socioeconomic level, religion or culture. Reproductive rights may include some or all of the following: the right to legal or safe abortion, the right to birth control, the right to access quality reproductive healthcare, and the right to education and access in order to make reproductive choices free from coercion, discrimination, and violence. Reproductive rights may also include the right to receive education about contraception and sexually transmitted infections, and freedom from coerced sterilisation, abortion, and contraception, and protection from gender-based practices such as female genital mutilation (FGM) and male genital mutilation (MGM).

Pregnant Patients' Rights

Pregnant patients' rights refers to pregnant women's rights regarding medical care during the pregnancy and childbirth. It refers specifically to a patient's rights within a medical setting and should not be confused with pregnancy discrimination.

The International Conference on Population and Development (ICPD), convened in Cairo by the United Nations in September 1994, adopted a Programme of Action which set goals for all countries to reach by 2015. Among these goals, the Programme of Action urges countries to make available education and services for medical care during pregnancy and delivery and during the postnatal period. It also urged the availability of referral for further diagnosis and treatment for complications of pregnancy and delivery.

In the United States, medical services during pregnancy and especially during labour and delivery began to increase drastically in the 1930s. In the 1950s, advocacy groups raised concern about medical services that were possibly unnecessary or even harmful to the mother, child, or both, and began to urge that pregnant women have the right to refuse such services. In 1987, Angela Carder, a pregnant cancer patient, died along with her baby at George Washington University Medical Center after a court-ordered Caesarian section. As a result of this case, beginning in the early 1990s, hospitals began to set policies stating that decisions regarding pregnant patients would be made by the patient herself, her family, and her doctors.

Pregnant Patients' Rights in the US

Pregnant patients' rights regarding medical care during the pregnancy and childbirth are specifically a patient's rights within a medical setting and should not be confused with pregnancy discrimination. A great deal of discussion regarding pregnant patients' rights has taken place in the United States.

History

In Western countries, medical services used during labor and delivery have increased since the 1930s. Starting in the 1950s, with the natural childbirth movement gaining strength, concern increased over typical hospital practices during childbirth. These medical services included medications and procedures that were not always necessary, some of which had potential to harm the mother, the baby, or both. Various health-related and consumer organisations groups began to advocate for a pregnant woman's right to be informed about medical services related to pregnancy and childbirth and for her right to refuse such services.

In the United States, the American College of Obstetricians and Gynecologists (ACOG) acknowledged the legal obligation of physicians to obtain informed consent for procedures related to pregnancy and childbirth in 1974.

Decision-making Regarding Pregnant Patients' Care

A 1987 study found that in the preceding decade, at least 22 hospitals in the United States sought direction from the courts regarding care for pregnant patients. Fifteen court orders were sought, all but one without careful study of the legal facts of the case.

In a landmark 1990 case, George Washington University Medical Center (GWUMC) announced a new policy regarding pregnant patients' rights as part of the out-of-court settlement of a case in which a pregnant patient, Angela Carder, died. The new policy stated that decisions regarding medical care for pregnant patients would be made by the patient herself, her doctors, and her family, not by the courts. Although the settlement applied only to GWUMC, the new policy, considered the most comprehensive of its kind at the time, was expected to influence other institutions.

Specific Rights Advocated

Advocates endorse a pregnant patient's right to participate in medical decisions that may affect her well-being and that of her child. Specifically, these include but are not limited to the right to know the effects and risks to both the woman and the child associated with a drug or procedure, as well as the right to know about additional and alternative treatments.

Some groups, such as the American Hospital Association in its "Patient's Bill of Rights", advocate additional rights, including rights to the following:

- To receive medical assistance regardless of where the patient gives birth (whether at home, in a hospital, etc.).
- To refuse drug treatment of any kind.
- To be accompanied during labor and birth by a person or persons she cares for and to whom she looks for emotional support.
- To labor at her own pace without intervention if she chooses.
- To choose her own birthing position.
- To keep her baby at her bedside immediately after birth if the baby does not require specialised care, and to feed the baby according to a schedule she decides rather than according to a standard hospital regimen.

References

1. Ammer, Christine (2005). "Pregnant patient's rights". *Encyclopedia of Women's Health*, The (Fifth ed.). New York: Facts on File, Inc.. pp. 320-321.
2. Haire, Doris (2000). "The Pregnant Patient's Bill of Rights". Alliance for the Improvement of Maternity Services. http://www.aimsusa.org/ppbr.htm. Retrieved 2007-08-13.
3. Thornton, Terry E.; Lynn Paltrow (1991). "The Rights of Pregnant Patients: Carder Case Brings Bold Policy Initiatives". *Health Span* 8 (5). http://advocatesforpregnantwomen.org/main/publications/articles_and_reports/the_rights_of_pregnant_ patients_carder_case_brings_bold_policy_initiatives.php. Retrieved 2007-08-13.
4. Greenhouse, Linda (November 29, 1990). "Hospital Sets Policy on Pregnant Patients' Rights". *The New York Times*. http://query.nytimes.com/gst/fullpage.html?sec=health&res= 9C0CE7DE1139F93AA15752C1A966958260. Retrieved 2007-08-13.

3

Sex Workers' and Prostitutes' Rights

Sex workers' rights encompass a variety of aims being pursued globally by individuals and organisations that specifically involve the human rights and labor rights of sex workers. Sex worker activists and advocates argue that sex workers should have the same basic human rights and labour rights as other working people. Since the mid-1970s sex workers across the world have organised, demanding the decriminalisation of prostitution, equal protection under the law, improved working condition and the right to travel and receive social benefits such as pensions.

Sex Workers' Rights Movement

The sex workers' right movement emerged in the 1970s as the prostitutes' rights movement. A key event occurred in 1975 when 150 prostitutes took over the main church in Lyons, France, to protest about the unsolved murders of local prostitutes, exorbitant police fines and multiple arrests. The movement spread to other parts of France as prostitutes joined the strike and took over other churches. In Paris, prostitutes demanded their full rights as citizens and called for the introduction of a non-punitive tax system that would provide them with the right to pension and welfare benefits like "every other French woman". They also demanded to be nationalised as civil servants of sex. The prostitutes challenged the notion that those who sold sex were deviant and claimed that sexual commerce was a "job determined by the sexual needs of one part of society" – the client who always went unpunished. The strike lasted seven days and ended with the police invading the churches. The strike drew worldwide attention to the conditions under which prostitutes worked and spurred the creation of the French Collective of Prostitutes and the sex workers' rights movement in France. Similar groups subsequently formed in many parts of the world, including early on in Latin America and India, as well as England, Australia, Germany, Italy, Denmark, Canada and in major US cities.

The popular slogan used by the prostitutes' rights movement in the US "outlaw poverty not prostitution" highlighted that economic hardship made it necessity for many women across the world to sell sex. In the UK, the English Collective of Prostitutes called laws punishing prostitution "laws which punish women for refusing poverty". Aside from prostitute unions numerous international conventions and platforms were organised, including the International Congresses of Whores (1985 in Amsterdam and 1986 in Brussels). Adding to this numerous publications by sex workers have appeared in print. Since the mid-1970s, sex workers across the world have organised, demanding the decriminalisation of prostitution, equal protection under the law, improved working condition, the right to pay taxes, travel and receive social benefits such as pensions.

In the 1990s, the sex workers' rights movement broadened its scope, including transgender, developing world, lesbian, gay, bisexual, heterosexual, migrants, men and women sex workers. Sex workers' rights organisation continue to form throughout Africa, Latin America and Asia. In Mexico City the La Union Unica has organised not just sex workers but all who participate and profit from the sex industry, including taxi drivers, bartenders and hotel workers. The sex workers' rights movement has advanced the recognition of prostitution as a profession. In New South Wales, Australia, an official sex worker union was formed in 1996 under the auspieces of the Australian Liquor, Hospitality and Miscellaneous Workers' Union. In Paraguay the national workers' union has recognised sex workers as legitimate workers, meaning they can retire and receive full pension benefits.

Development of a Rights-based Approach

The World Charter for Prostitutes' Rights was adopted in 1985 by the International Committee for Prostitutes' Rights (ICPR) to protect the rights of prostitutes worldwide. The World Charter emerged out of the prostitutes' rights movement and was established through the two World Whores Congresses held in Amsterdam (1985) and Brussels (1986) which epitomised a worldwide prostitutes' rights movement and politics. The Charter established a human rights based approach which has subsequently been further elaborated by the prostitutes' rights movement. In 1999, the Santa Monica Mirror credited the World Charter, among others, for having "articulated a global political movement seeking recognition and social change". In 2003, a writer in the journal "*Humanist*" noted that the World Charter had become "a template used by human rights groups all over the world". In the late 1990s the term "sex worker" was popularised as an alternative to "whore" or "prostitute".

World Charter for Prostitutes' Rights (1985)

The World Charter for Prostitutes' Rights calls for the decriminalisation of "all aspects of adult prostitution resulting from individual decisions". The World Charter also supports that prostitutes should be guaranteed "all human rights and civil liberties", including the freedom of speech, travel, immigration, work, marriage, and motherhood, and the right to unemployment insurance, health insurance and housing. Furthermore the World Charter calls for protection of "work standards", including the abolition of laws which impose any systematic zoning of prostitution, and calls for prostitutes having the freedom to choose their place of work and residence, and to "provide their services under the conditions that are absolutely determined by themselves and no one else". The World Charter also calls for prostitutes to pay regular taxes "on the same basis as other independent contractors and employees", and to receive the same benefits for their taxes.

European Conference on Sex Work, Human Rights, Labour and Migration

The first European Conference on Sex Work, Human Rights, Labour and Migration was held in Brussels, 15–17 October 2005. The conference endorsed The Declaration of the Rights of Sex Workers in Europe and the final day of the conference was held in the European Parliament. MEP Monica Frassoni (Italian Green Party) hosted the final day, during which MEP Vittorio Agnoletto of the Confederal Group of the European United Left became the first signatory to the Declaration.

The conference was held 20 years after the Second World War. Congress took place in the European Parliament and was organised in response to what the organisers called “increasing repressive legislative policies and state practices against sex workers across Europe”. The objectives of the conference were to re-establish sex workers’ rights back on the European agenda and change the human trafficking debate into a debate on labour, migration and human rights. The conference also endorsed a Sex Workers in Europe Manifesto and presented recommendations for better prostitution policies to the European Parliament. Conference organisers also thought to establish alliance with international labour, migration and human rights organisations.

The Declaration of the Rights of Sex Workers in Europe (2005)

The Declaration was finalised at the conference and is based on international human rights instruments. The process of establishing the Declaration was initiated by SIGN (the Sexwork Initiative Group Netherlands) and the Declaration was established based on a year long consultation with sex workers across Europe and international human rights, labour and migration experts. Based on the results of this consultation, a draft Declaration was established for consideration at the conference. The Declaration highlights what the International Committee on the Rights of Sex Workers in Europe calls "current violations of the rights of sex workers in Europe which occured across health and social care, housing, employment, education, administrative law and criminal justice system". Furthermore the Declaration highlights "actions required to ensure that the rights of sex workers are respected in Europe".

According to the Declaration different approaches to the sex industry have been adopted across Europe (regarding female, male and transgender sex workers, and including migrant sex workers). These approaches range from acceptance of sex work as labour and the introduction of labour rights for sex workers to the criminalisation of a wide range of practices associated with sex work. This criminalisation may affect the sex worker, sex workers' partners or clients. The Declaration states that "legislative measures that restrict the fundamental rights and freedoms of sex workers proliferate at local, national and international levels, claiming to be in the interests of combating organised crime and promoting public health". The Declaration argues that this contradicts advice given by UNAIDS and the World Health Organisation stating that legislation restricting the rights of sex workers undermine public health policies by driving the sex industry underground. As well as the European Parliament's Resolution on Violence Against Women, which called for the decriminalisation of prostitution and a guarantee that prostitutes enjoy the rights of other citizens. The Declaration states that "many measures are in violation of the obligation of States under international human rights law to respect, promote and protect the human rights of all persons within their territory, without discrimination, and including the right to privacy, to a family life, to legally leave and return to one's country, to be free from torture, inhuman or degrading treatment and from arbitrary detention, and in favour of the freedom of expression, information, freedom of association, and movement". The Declaration notes that "there is not one country within Europe – including those with regulated sex industries – where sex workers have not reported discrimination and violations of their human rights".

The Declaration reiterates that under international law it is a fundamental human right that "all persons are equal before the law and are entitled without discrimination to the equal protection of the law". The Declaration identifies human, labour and migrant rights that sex workers should be entitled to under international law, hence synthesising rights that have been agreed in international treaties and covenants for all citizens. The Declaration furthermore proposes steps and policies to ensure the protection of those rights for sex workers. The Declaration cites 17 regional or international human rights and labour rights treaties, including the International Covenant on Civil and Political Rights, the International Covenant on Economic, Social and Cultural Rights, the Convention on the Elimination of All Forms of Discrimination Against Women, the International Convention on the Protection of the Rights of All Migrant Workers and Members of Their Families, the Convention Relating to the Status of Refugees, the Universal Declaration of Human Rights and the EU Charter of Fundamental Rights.

According to the Declaration "all individuals within Europe, including sex workers are entitled to the following rights", which "European governments are obliged to respect, protect and fulfil":

- the right to life, liberty and security of person
- the right to be free from arbitrary interference with one's private and family life, home or correspondence and from attacks on honour and reputation
- the right to the highest attainable standard of physical and mental health
- the right to freedom of movement and residence
- the right to be free from slavery, forced labour and servitude
- the right to equal protection of the law and protection against discrimination and any incitement to discrimination under

any of the varied and intersecting status of gender, race, citizenship, sexual orientation etc.

- the right to marry and found a family
- the right to work, to free choice of employment and to just and favourable conditions of work
- the right to peaceful assembly and association
- the right to leave any country, including one's own, and to return to one's own country
- the right to seek asylum and to non-refoulement
- the right to participate in the cultural and public life of society

Under the right to work, to free choice of employment and to just and favourable conditions of work, the Declaration effectively calls for the decriminalisation of sex work, stating that "the lack of acknowledgement of sex work as labour or a profession has adverse consequences on the working conditions of sex workers and denies them access to protection provided by national and European labour legislation". The Declaration also demands that "sex workers should be entitled to equitable employment and social security benefits".

Forced Prostitution

Forced prostitution is a form of sexual slavery that is considered more profitable than the drug trade and arms trade. Laws in Sweden, Norway and Iceland, where it is illegal to pay for sex, but not to be a prostitute, define all forms of prostitution as exploitative or de facto slavery. Sex workers' rights advocates have issued numerous critiques of these laws as another form of prohibition and stigmatisation that serve mainly to marginalise sex workers. Sex workers' rights organisations argue that decriminalisation and extension of labor rights to sex workers is more effective in ensuring their economic, mental and medical health than any form of prohibition.

Sex Workers' Rights and HIV Debate

According to Achieving Universal Access – the UK's strategy for halting and reversing the spread of HIV in the developing world sex workers and other groups such as prisoners are most affected by AIDS. "They are more likely to be living HIV than the general population, are less able to deal with the impact of the epidemic and are most likely to be failed by existing policies, programmes, support and services." According to the strategy document sex workers are among the most marginalised and discriminated against in society, and that as a result of criminalisation it is often difficult to reach sex workers with interventions such as condom promotion.

In July 2006 UNAIDS undertook a global consultation on Sex Work and HIV/AIDS prevention and treatment. At this consultation sex workers and public health experts called for better conditions for sex workers, highlighting the impact of violence, police repression and criminalisation have in general on HIV prevention efforts. Participants overwhelmingly favoured a rights-based approach to sex work. However, participants from the US and Sweden expressed support for a model of combating the existence of the sex industry itself rather than HIV. During the International AIDS Conference in Toronto, Canada (August 2006) the UNFPA promoted a rights-based approach in a document on HIV and sex work. The document entitled UNFPA IAC Briefing Note on HIV and Sex Work stated that in 2006 the UNAIDS Committee of Cosponsoring Organisations Executive Heads had agreed to a holistic, global approach to sex work – "one that went well beyond providing condoms, to including a package of health and social service, sustainable livelihoods, respect for human rights, and addressing gender concerns." The document also stated that the UN system-wide approach on HIV and sex work will be rights-based but that UNFPA and the other UNAIDS Co-Sponsors do not have a position on the legalisation of sex work, which was a matter for individual UN member states. However, the document states that all UNAIDS Co-Sponsors support the human rights of sex workers, including the right to access services free of stigma and discrimination, and to be protected from violence. The UNAIDS Guidance Note: HIV and Sex Work published in 2007 did however not reflect the rights-based approach.[20]

In the Guidance Note, UNAIDS placed strong emphasis on strategies to reduce the number of women who sell sex by encouraging sex workers to leave the industry and preventing women from taking up sex work. The Guidance Note advocate the reduction of demand for sex work as an HIV prevention strategy by criminalising or otherwise repressing the purchase of sexual services. This approach (sometimes called the "Swedish model") has been condemned by some human rights advocates who argue that it can increase the risk of HIV for sex workers by driving sex workers underground and limiting their ability to choose working conditions and clients. [21] The Canadian HIV/AIDS Legal Network criticised the Guidance Note, stating that it is inconsistent with previous UN statements on the central importance of the rights of sex workers in programs and policies related to sex work and HIV. "The Guidance Note fails to consider seriously the precarious human rights situation of sex workers, and the way abusive and violent policies and ill-conceived national laws undermine sex workers' rights. It also fails to discuss the human rights of sex workers as workers, including their right to work, their right to a livelihood of their choosing, and their right to workplace safety."

In June 2008 at the United Nations General Assembly High Level Meeting on HIV/AIDS sex workers commended UN Secretary General Ban Ki Moon for promoting the "Report of the Commission on AIDS in Asia", which calls for the decriminalisation of sex work, and called upon governments to "avoid programmes that accentuate AIDS related stigma and can be counterproductive. Such programmes may include 'crack-downs' on red-light areas and arrest of sex workers".

International Day to End Violence Against Sex Workers

International Day to End Violence Against Sex Workers is observed annually on 17 December by sex workers, their advocates, friends, families and allies.

First celebrated in 2003, the International Day to End Violence Against Sex Workers is the brainchild of Dr. Annie Sprinkle and the Sex Workers Outreach Project USA (SWOP-USA), an American Sex Worker's Rights organisation.

Originally conceived as a memorial and vigil for the victims of the Green River Killer in Seattle Washington, it has evolved into an annual international event.

The day calls attention to AIDS, hate crimes committed against sex workers all over the globe as well as the need to remove the stigma and discrimination that is perpetuated by custom and prohibitionist laws that has made violence against sex-workers acceptable.

The red umbrella has become an important symbol for Sex Workers Rights and it is increasingly being used on December 17: "First adopted by Venetian sex workers for an anti-violence march in 2002, red umbrellas have come to symbolise resistance against discrimination for sex workers worldwide."

World Charter for Prostitutes' Rights

Bronze statue Belle in Amsterdam's red-light district De Wallen, in front of the Oude Kerk. It was unveiled in March 2007 with the inscription "Respect sex workers all over the world."

The World Charter for Prostitutes' Rights is a declaration of rights adopted in 1985 to protect the rights of prostitutes worldwide. It was adopted by the International Committee for Prostitutes' Rights (ICPR).

The Charter

The distinction between voluntary and forced prostitution was developed by the prostitutes' rights movement in response to feminists and others who saw all prostitution as abusive. The World Charter for Prostitutes' Rights calls for the decriminalisation of "all aspects of adult prostitution resulting from individual decisions." The World Charter also states that prostitutes should be guaranteed "all human rights and civil liberties," including the freedom of speech, travel, immigration, work, marriage, and motherhood, and the right to unemployment insurance, health insurance and housing. Furthermore the World Charter calls for protection of "work standards," including the abolition of laws which impose any systematic zoning of prostitution, and calls for prostitutes having the freedom to choose their place of work and residence, and to "provide their services under the conditions that are absolutely determined by themselves and no one else." The World Charter also calls for prostitutes to pay regular taxes "on the same basis as other independent contractors and employees," and to receive the same benefits for their taxes.

In an article announcing the adoption of the World Charter, the United Press International reported: "Women from the world's oldest profession, some wearing exotic masks to protect their identity, appealed on Friday at the world's first international prostitutes' convention for society to stop treating them like criminals."

Development of a Human Rights Approach

The World Charter emerged out of the prostitutes' rights movement starting in the mid 1970s. It was established through the two World Whores Congresses held in Amsterdam (1985) and Brussels (1986) which epitomised a worldwide prostitutes' rights movement and politics. The Charter established a human rights based approach which has subsequently been further elaborated by the prostitutes' rights movement.

In 1999, the Santa Monica Mirror commented on the popularisation of the term "sex worker" as an alternative to "whore" or "prostitute" and credited the World Charter, among others, for having "articulated a global political movement seeking recognition and social change."

In 2000, the Carnegie Council published a report commenting on the results of the World Charter, fifteen years after its adoption. The report concluded that the human rights approach embodied in the World Charter had proved "extremely useful for advocates seeking to reduce discrimination against sex workers." For example, human rights advocates in Australia utilised the language of human rights to resist "mandatory health tests" for sex workers and to require that information regarding health be kept confidential. However, the report also found that efforts to define prostitution as a human rights abuse had led some governments to take action to abolish the sex industry.

And in 2003, a writer in the journal "*Humanist*" noted that the World Charter had become "a template used by human rights groups all over the world."

Reaction

The World Charter was initially met with scepticism and ridicule. *Time* reported: "Just what were all those hookers doing in the hallowed halls of the European Parliament in Brussels last week? The moral outrage echoing in the corridors may have suggested that a re-creation of Sodom and Gomorrah was being staged. Reason: about 125 prostitutes, including three men, were attending the Second World Whores Congress." *The Philadelphia Daily News* asked, "Does it contain a layoff clause?" Another writer referred to it derisively as "a Magna Carta for whores."

The Charter remains controversial, as many feminists consider prostitution to be one of the most serious problems facing women, particularly in developing countries. In Jessica Spector's 2006 book *Prostitution and Pornography*, Vednita Carter and Evelina Giobbe offer the following critique of the Charter:

> "Pretending prostitution is a job like any other job would be laughable if it weren't so serious. Leading marginalised prostituted women to believe that decriminalisation would materially change anything substantive in their lives as prostitutes as dangerous and irresponsible. There are no liberating clauses in the World Charter. Pimps are not 'third party managers."

Notes and References

1. Press Release 17 December 2003 by the Urban Justice Center "Candlelight Vigil Calls for an End to Violence Against Sex Worker: International Memorial Day Focuses Attention on Violence Against Sex Workers"
2. December 17 International Day to End Violence Against Sex Workers.
3. Article 17 December 2003 by the Shannon Kiely for *The McGill Daily* "Sex workers and supporters unite"
4. Kamala Kempadoo, Jo Doezema (1998). *Global Sex Workers*, pp. 19–20. Routledge.
5. Melissa Hope Ditmore (2006). *Encyclopedia of Prostitution and Sex Work*, p. 625. Greenwood Publishing Group.
6. Kempadoo, Kamala; Jo Doezema (1998). *Global Sex Workers. Routledge*. pp. 37. http://books.google.com/books?id= fiJztJAgUTMC& dq = forced+prostitution&source=gbs_ summary_ s&cad=0.
7. World Charter for Prostitutes' Rights.
8. "Prostitutes Appeal For Decriminalisation". *St. Petersburg Times*. 1986-02-16. http://news.google.com/newspapers?id=c9sOAAAAIBAJ&sjid=1HwDA AAAIBAJ&pg=6964,44854&dq =world+charter+for+ prostitutes+rights.
9. Kempadoo, Kamala; Jo Doezema (1998). *Global Sex Workers*. Routledge. pp. 19–20.http://books.google.com/books?id=fiJztJAgUTMC &dq=forced+ prostitution &source=gbs_summary_s&cad=0.
10. "World Notes Belgium". *Time*. 2006-10-13. http://www.time.com/time/magazine/article/0,9171,962548,00.html.
11. Penelope Saunders (2000-08-06). "Fifteen Years after the World Charter for Prostitutes' Rights". Carnegie Council. http://www.cceia.org/resources/publications/dialogue/2_03/articles/629.html/:pf_printable.
12. Amalia Cabezos (July 28 – August. 4, 1999). "Hookers in the House of the Lord". *Santa Monica Mirror*. http://www.smmirror.com/Volume1/issue6/hooker.html.
13. Kimberly Klinger (Jan-Feb, 2003). "Prostitution humanism and a woman's choice — Perspectives on Prostitution". *Humanist*. http://findarticles.com/p/articles/mi_m1374/is_1_63/ai_96417149/pg_2.
14. "Does It Contain A Layoff Clause?". *Philadelphia Daily News*. 1985-02-15. http://nl.newsbank.com/nl-search/we/Archives?p_product=DN&s_site=philly&p_multi=PI.
15. "House of ill repute". *The Daily Pennsylvanian*. 1996-03-06. http://media.www.dailypennsylvanian.com/media/storage/paper882/news/1996/03/06/Resources/Column.House.Of.Ill.Repute-2174331.shtml.
16. Jessica Spector (editor) (2006). *Prostitution and Pornography: Philosophical Debate about the Sex Industry*, p. 35. Stanford University Press. .

4

Eliminating Discrimination Against Women

Convention on the Elimination of All Forms of Discrimination Against Women

The Convention on the Elimination of all Forms of Discrimination against Women (CEDAW) is an international convention adopted in 1979 by the United Nations General Assembly. Described as an international bill of rights for women, it came into force on 3 September 1981. The United States is the only developed nation that has not ratified the CEDAW. Several countries have ratified the Convention subject to certain declarations, reservations, and objections.

The Convention

Signed	: 18 December 1979
Location :	: New York City
Effective :	: 3 September 1981
Condition	: 20 ratifications
Parties	: 186 (Complete List)

The Convention defines discrimination against women in the following terms:

Any distinction, exclusion or restriction made on the basis of sex which has the effect or purpose of impairing or nullifying the recognition, enjoyment or exercise by women, irrespective of their marital status, on a basis of equality of men and women, of human rights and fundamental freedoms in the political, economic, social, cultural, civil or any other field.

It also establishes an agenda of action for putting an end to sex-based discrimination:

States must take measures to seek to eliminate prejudices and customs based on the idea of the inferiority or the superiority of one sex or on stereotyped role for men and women.

States ratifying the Convention are required to enshrine gender equality into their domestic legislation, repeal all discriminatory provisions in their laws, and enact new provisions to guard against discrimination against women. However, special protection for maternity is not regarded as gender discrimination (Article 4). Appropriate measures, including legislation, to suppress all forms of trafficking in women and forced prostitution are also not regarded as gender discrimination (Article 6). Equal opportunity in education for female students is required, and coeducation is encouraged. (Article 10). States ratifying the Convention must also establish tribunals and public institutions to guarantee women effective protection against discrimination, and take steps to eliminate all forms of discrimination practiced against women by individuals, organisations, and enterprises [Article 2, (e)].

Members and Ratification

The seven UN member states that have not ratified or acceded to the convention are Iran, Nauru, Palau, Somalia, Sudan, Tonga, and the United States. These are either Islamic states (Iran, Somalia, Sudan) or small Pacific Island nations (Nauru, Palau, Tonga), or the United States. Niue and the Vatican City have also not signed it. The United States has signed, but not yet ratified.

In 2007, after much pressure from women's organisations such as the National Alliance of Taiwan Women's Associations, Taiwan's Legislative Yuan ratified the stipulations of CEDAW into its own domestic policy. It is still awaiting CEDAW's approval of its ratification.

Committee on the Elimination of Discrimination against Women

Convention oversight is the task of the Committee on the Elimination of Discrimination against Women, which is made up of 23 experts on women's issues from different UN member states. The Committee meets twice a year to review reports on compliance with the Convention's provisions that the signatory nations are required to submit every four years.

The Committee is one of the eight UN-related human rights treaty bodies.

The Committee's members, described as "experts of high moral standing and competence in the field covered by the Convention", are elected to serve four-year terms in staggered elections held every two years. Its officers are : A chairperson, three vice-chairpersons, and a rapporteur. Efforts are made to ensure balanced geographical representation and the inclusion of the world's different forms of civilisation and legal systems.

Committee members and experts also attend an annual luncheon, hosted by the NGO Committee on the Status of Women, NY (NGO CSW/NY), where key issues are discussed and the efforts of the committee are honored.

As of January 2011, the members are:

Name	*State*	*Term Expires*
Silvia Pimentel (Chairperson)	Brazil	2012
Victoria Popescu (Vice-Chairperson)	Romania	2012
Zohra Rasekh (Vice-Chairperson)	Afghanistan	2012
Nicole Ameline (Vice-Chairperson)	France	2012
Violet Tsisiga Awori (Rapporteur)	Kenya	2012
Magalys Arocha Dominguez	Cuba	2012
Barbara Evelyn Bailey	Jamaica	2012
Niklas Bruun	Finland	2012
Indira Jaising	India	2012
Soledad Murillo de la Vega	Spain	2012
Zou Xiaoqiao	China	2012
Ayse Feride Acar	Turkey	2014
Olinda Bareiro-Bobadilla	Paraguay	2014
Meriem Belmihoub-Zerdani	Algeria	2014
Naela Mohamed Gabr	Egypt	2014
Ruth Halperin-Kaddari	Israel	2014
Yoko Hayashi	Japan	2014
Ismat Jahan	Bangladesh	2014
Violeta Neubauer	Slovenia	2014
Pramila Patten	Mauritius	2014
Maria Helena Lopes de Jesus Pires	Timor Leste	2014
Patricia Schulz	Switzerland	2014
Dubravka Šimonovic	Croatia	2014

Optional Protocol

The Optional Protocol to the Convention on the Elimination of All Forms of Discrimination against Women is a side-agreement to the Convention which allows its parties to recognise the competence of the Committee on the Elimination of Discrimination against Women to consider complaints from individuals.

The Optional Protocol was adopted by the UN General Assembly on 6 October 1999 and entered into force on 22 December 2000. Currently it has 79 signatories and 102 parties.

Controversy

The neutrality of this article is disputed. Please see the discussion on the talk page. Please do not remove this message until the dispute is resolved. (September 2010)

In an article in *Moment* Magazine in February 2011, Paula Kweskin, in discussing so-called "honor" killings taking place in the Palestinian Authority, writes that two-thirds of all murders in the Palestinian Authority and Gaza are "honor" killings. These crimes go unpunished and laws grant impunity to those who kill based on "family honor." In interviews and press releases on their websites, many NGOs, including Badil, the Palestinian Center for Human Rights, and the Women's Center for Legal Aid and Counseling, have decried "honor" killings and the lack of legal protection for Palestinian women; yet these NGOs are silent when given a forum at CEDAW to address these problems.

The CEDAW has been controversial for statements seen by a number of states and NGOs as promoting Western-style radical feminism. Often referenced is a 2000 report which said that in Belarus, "the Committee is concerned by the continuing prevalence of sex-role stereotypes and by the reintroduction of such symbols as a Mothers' Day and a Mothers' Award, which it sees as encouraging women's traditional roles." Other controversial positions of CEDAW include supporting the decriminalisation of prostitution in specific countries, criticising Slovenia because only 30% of children are in daycare, and pressuring numerous states to decriminalise abortion. Other requests are seen by groups as a backdoor to forcing states parties to adopt an Equal Rights Amendment or comparable national legislation, which is seen as a violation of the CEDAW treaty mandate and the sovereignty of states parties. Australian and (defunct) New Zealand anti-feminist groups‹See Tfd›[weasel words] voiced similar concerns in the early eighties.

More recently, the controversy concerning CEDAW has centered around the question of easy access to abortion and contraception. According to C-FAM (the Catholic Family and Human Rights Institute), at UN meetings officials pressed the delegation from Colombia to liberalise its abortion laws and to inaugurate campaigns encouraging contraceptive use and "reproductive health awareness".

Many Islamic countries view the CEDAW as culturally biased towards the Western nations and have consequently placed reservations on the elements that they see as in fundamental contradiction with Islamic Sharia law.

Women and Human Rights as per CEDAW

Among the International human Rights treaties. CEDAW takes an important place in bringing the female half of humanity into the focus of human rights concerns. The spirit of the convention is rooted in the goals of the United Nations: to reaffirm faith in fundamental human rights in the dignity and worth of the human person, in the equal rights of men and women. The present document spells out the meaning of equality and how it can be achieved in so doing, the Convention establishes not only an international bill of rights for women, but also an agenda for action by countries to guarantee the enjoyment of those rights.

Text Convention on the Elimination of All Forms of Discrimination against Women

G.A. res. 34/180, 34 U.N. GAOR Supp. (No. 46) at 193, U.N. Doc. A/34/46, entered into force Sept. 3, 1981.

The States Parties to the present Convention

Noting that the Charter of the United Nations reaffirms faith in fundamental human rights, in the dignity and worth of the human person and in the equal rights of men and women,

Noting that the Universal Declaration of Human Rights affirms the principle of the inadmissibility of discrimination and proclaims that all human beings are born free and equal in dignity and rights and that everyone is entitled to all the rights and freedoms set forth therein, without distinction of any kind, including distinction based on sex,

Noting that the States Parties to the International Covenants on Human Rights have the obligation to ensure the equal rights of men and women to enjoy all economic, social, cultural, civil and political rights,

Considering the international conventions concluded under the auspices of the United Nations and the specialised agencies promoting equality of rights of men and women,

Noting also the resolutions, declarations and recommendations adopted by the United Nations and the specialised agencies promoting equality of rights of men and women,

Concerned, however, that despite these various instruments extensive discrimination against women continues to exist,

Recalling that discrimination against women violates the principles of equality of rights and respect for human dignity, is an obstacle to the participation of women, on equal terms with men, in the political, social, economic and cultural life of their countries, hampers the growth of the prosperity of society and the family and makes more difficult the full development of the potentialities of women in the service of their countries and of humanity,

Concerned that in situations of poverty women have the least access to food, health, education, training and opportunities for employment and other needs,

Convinced that the establishment of the new international economic order based on equity and justice will contribute significantly towards the promotion of equality between men and women,

Emphasising that the eradication of apartheid, all forms of racism, racial discrimination, colonialism, neo-colonialism, aggression, foreign occupation and domination and interference in the internal affairs of States is essential to the full enjoyment of the rights of men and women,

Affirming that the strengthening of international peace and security, the relaxation of international tension, mutual co-operation among all States irrespective of their social and economic systems, general and complete disarmament, in particular nuclear disarmament under strict and effective international control, the affirmation of the principles of justice, equality and mutual benefit in relations among countries and the realisation of the right of peoples under alien and colonial domination and foreign occupation to self-determination and independence, as well as respect for national sovereignty and territorial integrity, will promote social progress and development and as a consequence will contribute to the attainment of full equality between men and women,

Convinced that the full and complete development of a country, the welfare of the world and the cause of peace require the maximum participation of women on equal terms with men in all fields,

Bearing in mind the great contribution of women to the welfare of the family and to the development of society, so far not fully recognised, the social significance of maternity and the role of both parents in the family and in the upbringing of children, and aware that the role of women in procreation should not be a basis for discrimination but that the upbringing of children requires a sharing of responsibility between men and women and society as a whole,

Aware that a change in the traditional role of men as well as the role of women in society and in the family is needed to achieve full equality between men and women,

Determined to implement the principles set forth in the Declaration on the Elimination of Discrimination against Women and, for that purpose, to adopt the measures required for the elimination of such discrimination in all its forms and manifestations,

Have agreed on the following:

PART I

Article I

For the purposes of the present Convention, the term "discrimination against women" shall mean any distinction, exclusion or restriction made on the basis of sex which has the effect or purpose of impairing or nullifying the recognition, enjoyment or exercise by women, irrespective of their marital status, on a basis of equality of men and women, of human rights and fundamental freedoms in the political, economic, social, cultural, civil or any other field.

Article 2

States Parties condemn discrimination against women in all its forms, agree to pursue by all appropriate means and without delay a policy of eliminating discrimination against women and, to this end, undertake:

(a) To embody the principle of the equality of men and women in their national constitutions or other appropriate legislation if not yet incorporated therein and to ensure, through law and other appropriate means, the practical realisation of this principle;

(b) To adopt appropriate legislative and other measures, including sanctions where appropriate, prohibiting all discrimination against women;

(c) To establish legal protection of the rights of women on an equal basis with men and to ensure through competent national tribunals and other public institutions the effective protection of women against any act of discrimination;

(d) To refrain from engaging in any act or practice of discrimination against women and to ensure that public authorities and institutions shall act in conformity with this obligation;

(e) To take all appropriate measures to eliminate discrimination against women by any person, organisation or enterprise;

(f) To take all appropriate measures, including legislation, to modify or abolish existing laws, regulations, customs and practices which constitute discrimination against women;

(g) To repeal all national penal provisions which constitute discrimination against women.

Article 3

States Parties shall take in all fields, in particular in the political, social, economic and cultural fields, all appropriate measures, including legislation, to ensure the full development and advancement of women, for the purpose of guaranteeing them the exercise and enjoyment of human rights and fundamental freedoms on a basis of equality with men.

Article 4

1. Adoption by States Parties of temporary special measures aimed at accelerating de facto equality between men and women shall not be considered discrimination as defined in the present Convention, but shall in no way entail as a consequence the maintenance of unequal or separate standards; these measures shall be discontinued when the objectives of equality of opportunity and treatment have been achieved.
2. Adoption by States Parties of special measures, including those measures contained in the present Convention, aimed at protecting maternity shall not be considered discriminatory.

Article 5

States Parties shall take all appropriate measures:

(a) To modify the social and cultural patterns of conduct of men and women, with a view to achieving the elimination of prejudices and customary and all other practices which are based on the idea of the inferiority or the superiority of either of the sexes or on stereotyped roles for men and women;

(b) To ensure that family education includes a proper understanding of maternity as a social function and the recognition of the common responsibility of men and women in the upbringing and development of their children, it being understood that the interest of the children is the primordial consideration in all cases.

Article 6

States Parties shall take all appropriate measures, including legislation, to suppress all forms of traffic in women and exploitation of prostitution of women.

PART II

Article 7

States Parties shall take all appropriate measures to eliminate discrimination against women in the political and public life of the country and, in particular, shall ensure to women, on equal terms with men, the right:

(a) To vote in all elections and public referenda and to be eligible for election to all publicly elected bodies;

(b) To participate in the formulation of government policy and the implementation thereof and to hold public office and perform all public functions at all levels of government;

(c) To participate in non-governmental organisations and associations concerned with the public and political life of the country.

Article 8

States Parties shall take all appropriate measures to ensure to women, on equal terms with men and without any discrimination, the opportunity to represent their Governments at the international level and to participate in the work of international organisations.

Article 9

1. States Parties shall grant women equal rights with men to acquire, change or retain their nationality. They shall ensure

in particular that neither marriage to an alien nor change of nationality by the husband during marriage shall automatically change the nationality of the wife, render her stateless or force upon her the nationality of the husband.

2. States Parties shall grant women equal rights with men with respect to the nationality of their children.

PART III

Article 10

States Parties shall take all appropriate measures to eliminate discrimination against women in order to ensure to them equal rights with men in the field of education and in particular to ensure, on a basis of equality of men and women:

(a) The same conditions for career and vocational guidance, for access to studies and for the achievement of diplomas in educational establishments of all categories in rural as well as in urban areas; this equality shall be ensured in pre-school, general, technical, professional and higher technical education, as well as in all types of vocational training;

(b) Access to the same curricula, the same examinations, teaching staff with qualifications of the same standard and school premises and equipment of the same quality;

(c) The elimination of any stereotyped concept of the roles of men and women at all levels and in all forms of education by encouraging coeducation and other types of education which will help to achieve this aim and, in particular, by the revision of textbooks and school programmes and the adaptation of teaching methods;

(d) The same opportunities to benefit from scholarships and other study grants;

(e) The same opportunities for access to programmes of continuing education, including adult and functional literacy programmes, particulary those aimed at reducing, at the earliest possible time, any gap in education existing between men and women;

(f) The reduction of female student drop-out rates and the organisation of programmes for girls and women who have left school prematurely;

(g) The same opportunities to participate actively in sports and physical education;

(h) Access to specific educational information to help to ensure the health and well-being of families, including information and advice on family planning.

Article 11

1. States Parties shall take all appropriate measures to eliminate discrimination against women in the field of employment in order to ensure, on a basis of equality of men and women, the same rights, in particular:

   (a) The right to work as an inalienable right of all human beings;

   (b) The right to the same employment opportunities, including the application of the same criteria for selection in matters of employment;

   (c) The right to free choice of profession and employment, the right to promotion, job security and all benefits and conditions of service and the right to receive vocational training and retraining, including apprenticeships, advanced vocational training and recurrent training;

   (d) The right to equal remuneration, including benefits, and to equal treatment in respect of work of equal value, as well as equality of treatment in the evaluation of the quality of work;

   (e) The right to social security, particularly in cases of retirement, unemployment, sickness, invalidity and old age and other incapacity to work, as well as the right to paid leave;

   (f) The right to protection of health and to safety in working conditions, including the safeguarding of the function of reproduction.

2. In order to prevent discrimination against women on the grounds of marriage or maternity and to ensure their effective right to work, States Parties shall take appropriate measures:

   (a) To prohibit, subject to the imposition of sanctions, dismissal on the grounds of pregnancy or of maternity leave and discrimination in dismissals on the basis of marital status;

   (b) To introduce maternity leave with pay or with comparable social benefits without loss of former employment, seniority or social allowances;

(c) To encourage the provision of the necessary supporting social services to enable parents to combine family obligations with work responsibilities and participation in public life, in particular through promoting the establishment and development of a network of child-care facilities;

(d) To provide special protection to women during pregnancy in types of work proved to be harmful to them.

3. Protective legislation relating to matters covered in this article shall be reviewed periodically in the light of scientific and technological knowledge and shall be revised, repealed or extended as necessary.

Article 12

1. States Parties shall take all appropriate measures to eliminate discrimination against women in the field of health care in order to ensure, on a basis of equality of men and women, access to health care services, including those related to family planning.
2. Notwithstanding the provisions of paragraph I of this article, States Parties shall ensure to women appropriate services in connection with pregnancy, confinement and the post-natal period, granting free services where necessary, as well as adequate nutrition during pregnancy and lactation.

Article 13

States Parties shall take all appropriate measures to eliminate discrimination against women in other areas of economic and social life in order to ensure, on a basis of equality of men and women, the same rights, in particular:

(a) The right to family benefits;

(b) The right to bank loans, mortgages and other forms of financial credit;

(c) The right to participate in recreational activities, sports and all aspects of cultural life.

Article 14

1. States Parties shall take into account the particular problems faced by rural women and the significant roles which rural women play in the economic survival of their families, including their work in the non-monetised sectors of the economy, and shall take all appropriate measures to ensure

the application of the provisions of the present Convention to women in rural areas.

2. States Parties shall take all appropriate measures to eliminate discrimination against women in rural areas in order to ensure, on a basis of equality of men and women, that they participate in and benefit from rural development and, in particular, shall ensure to such women the right:

   (a) To participate in the elaboration and implementation of development planning at all levels;

   (b) To have access to adequate health care facilities, including information, counselling and services in family planning;

   (c) To benefit directly from social security programmes;

   (d) To obtain all types of training and education, formal and non-formal, including that relating to functional literacy, as well as, inter alia, the benefit of all community and extension services, in order to increase their technical proficiency;

   (e) To organise self-help groups and co-operatives in order to obtain equal access to economic opportunities through employment or self employment;

   (f) To participate in all community activities;

   (g) To have access to agricultural credit and loans, marketing facilities, appropriate technology and equal treatment in land and agrarian reform as well as in land resettlement schemes;

   (h) To enjoy adequate living conditions, particularly in relation to housing, sanitation, electricity and water supply, transport and communications.

PART IV

Article 15

1. States Parties shall accord to women equality with men before the law.

2. States Parties shall accord to women, in civil matters, a legal capacity identical to that of men and the same opportunities to exercise that capacity. In particular, they shall give women equal rights to conclude contracts and to administer property and shall treat them equally in all stages of procedure in courts and tribunals.

3. States Parties agree that all contracts and all other private instruments of any kind with a legal effect which are directed at restricting the legal capacity of women shall be deemed null and void.
4. States Parties shall accord to men and women the same rights with regard to the law relating to the movement of persons and the freedom to choose their residence and domicile.

Article 16

1. States Parties shall take all appropriate measures to eliminate discrimination against women in all matters relating to marriage and family relations and in particular shall ensure, on a basis of equality of men and women:
   (a) The same right to enter into marriage;
   (b) The same right freely to choose a spouse and to enter into marriage only with their free and full consent;
   (c) The same rights and responsibilities during marriage and at its dissolution;
   (d) The same rights and responsibilities as parents, irrespective of their marital status, in matters relating to their children; in all cases the interests of the children shall be paramount;
   (e) The same rights to decide freely and responsibly on the number and spacing of their children and to have access to the information, education and means to enable them to exercise these rights;
   (f) The same rights and responsibilities with regard to guardianship, wardship, trusteeship and adoption of children, or similar institutions where these concepts exist in national legislation; in all cases the interests of the children shall be paramount;
   (g) The same personal rights as husband and wife, including the right to choose a family name, a profession and an occupation;
   (h) The same rights for both spouses in respect of the ownership, acquisition, management, administration, enjoyment and disposition of property, whether free of charge or for a valuable consideration.
2. The betrothal and the marriage of a child shall have no legal effect, and all necessary action, including legislation, shall

be taken to specify a minimum age for marriage and to make the registration of marriages in an official registry compulsory.

PART V

Article 17

1. For the purpose of considering the progress made in the implementation of the present Convention, there shall be established a Committee on the Elimination of Discrimination against Women (hereinafter referred to as the Committee) consisting, at the time of entry into force of the Convention, of eighteen EXPERTS and, after ratification of or accession to the Convention by the thirty-fifth State Party, of twenty-three experts of high moral standing and competence in the field covered by the Convention. The experts shall be elected by States Parties from among their nationals and shall serve in their personal capacity, consideration being given to equitable geographical distribution and to the representation of the different forms of civilisation as well as the principal legal systems.
2. The members of the Committee shall be elected by secret ballot from a list of persons nominated by States Parties. Each State Party may nominate one person from among its own nationals.
3. The initial election shall be held six months after the date of the entry into force of the present Convention. At least three months before the date of each election the Secretary-General of the United Nations shall address a letter to the States Parties inviting them to submit their nominations within two months. The Secretary-General shall prepare a list in alphabetical order of all persons thus nominated, indicating the States Parties which have nominated them, and shall submit it to the States Parties.
4. Elections of the members of the Committee shall be held at a meeting of States Parties convened by the Secretary-General at United Nations Headquarters. At that meeting, for which two thirds of the States Parties shall constitute a quorum, the persons elected to the Committee shall be those nominees who obtain the largest number of votes and an absolute majority of the votes of the representatives of States Parties present and voting.
5. The members of the Committee shall be elected for a term

of four years. However, the terms of nine of the members elected at the first election shall expire at the end of two years; immediately after the first election the names of these nine members shall be chosen by lot by the Chairman of the Committee.

6. The election of the five additional members of the Committee shall be held in accordance with the provisions of paragraphs 2, 3 and 4 of this article, following the thirty-fifth ratification or accession. The terms of two of the additional members elected on this occasion shall expire at the end of two years, the names of these two members having been chosen by lot by the Chairman of the Committee.
7. For the filling of casual vacancies, the State Party whose expert has ceased to function as a member of the Committee shall appoint another expert from among its nationals, subject to the approval of the Committee.
8. The members of the Committee shall, with the approval of the General Assembly, receive emoluments from United Nations resources on such terms and conditions as the Assembly may decide, having regard to the importance of the Committee's responsibilities.
9. The Secretary-General of the United Nations shall provide the necessary staff and facilities for the effective performance of the functions of the Committee under the present Convention.

Article 18

1. States Parties undertake to submit to the Secretary-General of the United Nations, for consideration by the Committee, a report on the legislative, judicial, administrative or other measures which they have adopted to give effect to the provisions of the present Convention and on the progress made in this respect:
   (a) Within one year after the entry into force for the State concerned;
   (b) Thereafter at least every four years and further whenever the Committee so requests.
2. Reports may indicate factors and difficulties affecting the degree of fulfilment of obligations under the present Convention.

Article 19

1. The Committee shall adopt its own rules of procedure.
2. The Committee shall elect its officers for a term of two years.

Article 20

1. The Committee shall normally meet for a period of not more than two weeks annually in order to consider the reports submitted in accordance with article 18 of the present Convention.
2. The meetings of the Committee shall normally be held at United Nations Headquarters or at any other convenient place as determined by the Committee.

Article 21

1. The Committee shall, through the Economic and Social Council, report annually to the General Assembly of the United Nations on its activities and may make suggestions and general recommendations based on the examination of reports and information received from the States Parties. Such suggestions and general recommendations shall be included in the report of the Committee together with comments, if any, from States Parties.
2. The Secretary-General of the United Nations shall transmit the reports of the Committee to the Commission on the Status of Women for its information.

Article 22

The specialised agencies shall be entitled to be represented at the consideration of the implementation of such provisions of the present Convention as fall within the scope of their activities. The Committee may invite the specialised agencies to submit reports on the implementation of the Convention in areas falling within the scope of their activities.

PART VI

Article 23

Nothing in the present Convention shall affect any provisions that are more conducive to the achievement of equality between men and women which may be contained:

(a) In the legislation of a State Party; or

(b) In any other international convention, treaty or agreement in force for that State.

Article 24

States Parties undertake to adopt all necessary measures at the national level aimed at achieving the full realisation of the rights recognised in the present Convention.

Article 25

1. The present Convention shall be open for signature by all States.
2. The Secretary-General of the United Nations is designated as the depositary of the present Convention.
3. The present Convention is subject to ratification. Instruments of ratification shall be deposited with the Secretary-General of the United Nations.
4. The present Convention shall be open to accession by all States. Accession shall be effected by the deposit of an instrument of accession with the Secretary-General of the United Nations.

Article 26

1. A request for the revision of the present Convention may be made at any time by any State Party by means of a notification in writing addressed to the Secretary-General of the United Nations.
2. The General Assembly of the United Nations shall decide upon the steps, if any, to be taken in respect of such a request.

Article 27

1. The present Convention shall enter into force on the thirtieth day after the date of deposit with the Secretary-General of the United Nations of the twentieth instrument of ratification or accession.
2. For each State ratifying the present Convention or acceding to it after the deposit of the twentieth instrument of ratification or accession, the Convention shall enter into force on the thirtieth day after the date of the deposit of its own instrument of ratification or accession.

Article 28

1. The Secretary-General of the United Nations shall receive

and circulate to all States the text of reservations made by States at the time of ratification or accession.

2. A reservation incompatible with the object and purpose of the present Convention shall not be permitted.
3. Reservations may be withdrawn at any time by notification to this effect addressed to the Secretary-General of the United Nations, who shall then inform all States thereof. Such notification shall take effect on the date on which it is received.

Article 29

1. Any dispute between two or more States Parties concerning the interpretation or application of the present Convention which is not settled by negotiation shall, at the request of one of them, be submitted to arbitration. If within six months from the date of the request for arbitration the parties are unable to agree on the organisation of the arbitration, any one of those parties may refer the dispute to the International Court of Justice by request in conformity with the Statute of the Court.
2. Each State Party may at the time of signature or ratification of the present Convention or accession thereto declare that it does not consider itself bound by paragraph I of this article. The other States Parties shall not be bound by that paragraph with respect to any State Party which has made such a reservation.
3. Any State Party which has made a reservation in accordance with paragraph 2 of this article may at any time withdraw that reservation by notification to the Secretary-General of the United Nations.

Article 30

The present Convention, the Arabic, Chinese, English, French, Russian and Spanish texts of which are equally authentic, shall be deposited with the Secretary-General of the United Nations.

IN WITNESS WHEREOF the undersigned, duly authorised, have signed the present Convention.

Optional Protocol Entered into Force on 22 December 2000

In a landmark decision for women, the General Assembly, acting without a vote, adopted on 6 October 1999 a 21-article

Optional Protocol to the Convention on the Elimination of all Forms of Discrimination against Women and called on all States parties to the Convention to become party to the new instrument as soon as possible.

By ratifying the Optional Protocol, a State recognizes the competence of the Committee on the Elimination of Discrimination against Women -- the body that monitors States parties' compliance with the Convention -- to receive and consider complaints from individuals or groups within its jurisdiction.

The Protocol contains two procedures: (1) A communications procedure allows individual women, or groups of women, to submit claims of violations of rights protected under the Convention to the Committee. The Protocol establishes that in order for individual communications to be admitted for consideration by the Committee, a number of criteria must be met, including those domestic remedies must have been exhausted. (2) The Protocol also creates an inquiry procedure enabling the Committee to initiate inquiries into situations of grave or systematic violations of women's rights. In either case, States must be party to the Convention and the Protocol. The Protocol includes an "opt-out clause", allowing States upon ratification or accession to declare that they do not accept the inquiry procedure. Article 17 of the Protocol explicitly provides that no reservations may be entered to its terms.

The Optional Protocol entered into force on 22 December 2000, following the ratification of the tenth State party to the Convention. The entry into force of the Optional Protocol puts it on an equal footing with International Covenant on Civil and Political Rights, the Convention on the Elimination of All Forms of Racial Discrimination, and the Convention against Torture and other Forms of Cruel, Inhuman or Degrading Treatment or Punishment, which all have communications procedures. The inquiry procedure is the equivalent of that under the Convention against Torture.

Optional Protocol to the Convention on the Elimination of Discrimination against Women

G.A. res. 54/4, annex, 54 U.N. GAOR Supp. (No. 49) at 5, U.N. Doc. A/54/49 (Vol. I) (2000), entered into force Dec. 22, 2000.

The States Parties to the present Protocol,

Noting that the Charter of the United Nations reaffirms faith in fundamental human rights, in the dignity and worth of the human person and in the equal rights of men and women,

Also noting that the Universal Declaration of Human Rights Resolution 217 A (III). proclaims that all human beings are born free and equal in dignity and rights and that everyone is entitled to all the rights and freedoms set forth therein, without distinction of any kind, including distinction based on sex,

Recalling that the International Covenants on Human Rights Resolution 2200 A (XXI), annex. and other international human rights instruments prohibit discrimination on the basis of sex,

Also recalling the Convention on the Elimination of All Forms of Discrimination against Women ("the Convention"), in which the States Parties thereto condemn discrimination against women in all its forms and agree to pursue by all appropriate means and without delay a policy of eliminating discrimination against women,

Reaffirming their determination to ensure the full and equal enjoyment by women of all human rights and fundamental freedoms and to take effective action to prevent violations of these rights and freedoms,

Have agreed as follows:

Article 1

A State Party to the present Protocol ("State Party") recognizes the competence of the Committee on the Elimination of Discrimination against Women ("the Committee") to receive and consider communications submitted in accordance with Article 2.

Article 2

Communications may be submitted by or on behalf of individuals or groups of individuals, under the jurisdiction of a State Party, claiming to be victims of a violation of any of the rights set forth in the Convention by that State Party. Where a communication is submitted on behalf of individuals or groups of individuals, this shall be with their consent unless the author can justify acting on their behalf without such consent.

Article 3

Communications shall be in writing and shall not be anonymous. No communication shall be received by the Committee if it concerns a State Party to the Convention that is not a party to the present Protocol.

Article 4

1. The Committee shall not consider a communication unless it has ascertained that all available domestic remedies have

been exhausted unless the application of such remedies is unreasonably prolonged or unlikely to bring effective relief.

2. The Committee shall declare a communication in admissible where:

   (a) The same matter has already been examined by the Committee or has been or is being examined under another procedure of international investigation or settlement;

   (b) It is incompatible with the provisions of the Convention;

   (c) It is manifestly ill-founded or not sufficiently substantiated;

   (d) It is an abuse of the right to submit a communication;

   (e) The facts that are the subject of the communication occurred prior to the entry into force of the present Protocol for the State Party concerned unless those facts continued after that date.

Article 5

1. At any time after the receipt of a communication and before a determination on the merits has been reached, the Committee may transmit to the State Party concerned for its urgent consideration a request that the State Party take such interim measures as may be necessary to avoid possible irreparable damage to the victim or victims of the alleged violation.
2. Where the Committee exercises its discretion under paragraph 1 of the present article, this does not imply a determination on admissibility or on the merits of the communication.

Article 6

1. Unless the Committee considers a communication inadmissible without reference to the State Party concerned, and provided that the individual or individuals consent to the disclosure of their identity to that State Party, the Committee shall bring any communication submitted to it under the present Protocol confidentially to the attention of the State Party concerned.
2. Within six months, the receiving State Party shall submit to the Committee written explanations or statements clarifying the matter and the remedy, if any, that may have been provided by that State Party.

Article 7

1. The Committee shall consider communications received under the present Protocol in the light of all information made available to it by or on behalf of individuals or groups of individuals and by the State Party concerned, provided that this information is transmitted to the parties concerned.
2. The Committee shall hold closed meetings when examining communications under the present Protocol.
3. After examining a communication, the Committee shall transmit its views on the communication, together with its recommendations, if any, to the parties concerned.
4. The State Party shall give due consideration to the views of the Committee, together with its recommendations, if any, and shall submit to the Committee, within six months, a written response, including information on any action taken in the light of the views and recommendations of the Committee.
5. The Committee may invite the State Party to submit further information about any measures the State Party has taken in response to its views or recommendations, if any, including as deemed appropriate by the Committee, in the State Party's subsequent reports under Article 18 of the Convention.

Article 8

1. If the Committee receives reliable information indicating grave or systematic violations by a State Party of rights set forth in the Convention, the Committee shall invite that State Party to cooperate in the examination of the information and to this end to submit observations with regard to the information concerned.
2. Taking into account any observations that may have been submitted by the State Party concerned as well as any other reliable information available to it, the Committee may designate one or more of its members to conduct an inquiry and to report urgently to the Committee. Where warranted and with the consent of the State Party, the inquiry may include a visit to its territory.
3. After examining the findings of such an inquiry, the Committee shall transmit these findings to the State Party concerned together with any comments and recommendations.

4. The State Party concerned shall, within six months of receiving the findings, comments and recommendations transmitted by the Committee, submit its observations to the Committee.
5. Such an inquiry shall be conducted confidentially and the cooperation of the State Party shall be sought at all stages of the proceedings.

Article 9

1. The Committee may invite the State Party concerned to include in its report under Article 18 of the Convention details of any measures taken in response to an inquiry conducted under Article 8 of the present Protocol.
2. The Committee may, if necessary, after the end of the period of six months referred to in Article 8.4, invite the State Party concerned to inform it of the measures taken in response to such an inquiry.

Article 10

1. Each State Party may, at the time of signature or ratification of the present Protocol or accession thereto, declare that it does not recognise the competence of the Committee provided for in Articles 8 and 9.
2. Any State Party having made a declaration in accordance with paragraph 1 of the present article may, at any time, withdraw this declaration by notification to the Secretary-General.

Article 11

A State Party shall take all appropriate steps to ensure that individuals under its jurisdiction are not subjected to ill treatment or intimidation as a consequence of communicating with the Committee pursuant to the present Protocol.

Article 12

The Committee shall include in its annual report under article 21 of the Convention a summary of its activities under the present Protocol.

Article 13

Each State Party undertakes to make widely known and to give publicity to the Convention and the present Protocol and to facilitate access to information about the views and recommendations of the Committee, in particular, on matters involving that State Party.

Article 14

The Committee shall develop its own rules of procedure to be followed when exercising the functions conferred on it by the present Protocol.

Article 15

1. The present Protocol shall be open for signature by any State that has signed, ratified or acceded to the Convention.
2. The present Protocol shall be subject to ratification by any State that has ratified or acceded to the Convention. Instruments of ratification shall be deposited with the Secretary-General of the United Nations.
3. The present Protocol shall be open to accession by any State that has ratified or acceded to the Convention.
4. Accession shall be effected by the deposit of an instrument of accession with the Secretary-General of the United Nations.

Article 16

1. The present Protocol shall enter into force three months after the date of the deposit with the Secretary-General of the United Nations of the tenth instrument of ratification or accession.
2. For each State ratifying the present Protocol or acceding to it after its entry into force, the present Protocol shall enter into force three months after the date of the deposit of its own instrument of ratification or accession.

Article 17

No reservations to the present Protocol shall be permitted.

Article 18

1. Any State Party may propose an amendment to the present Protocol and file it with the Secretary-General of the United Nations. The Secretary-General shall thereupon communicate any proposed amendments to the States Parties with a request that they notify her or him whether they favour a conference of States Parties for the purpose of considering and voting on the proposal. In the event that at least one third of the States Parties favour such a conference, the

Secretary-General shall convene the conference under the auspices of the United Nations. Any amendment adopted by a majority of the States Parties present and voting at the conference shall be submitted to the General Assembly of the United Nations for approval.

2. Amendments shall come into force when they have been approved by the General Assembly of the United Nations and accepted by a two-thirds majority of the States Parties to the present Protocol in accordance with their respective constitutional processes.
3. When amendments come into force, they shall be binding on those States Parties that have accepted them, other States Parties still being bound by the provisions of the present Protocol and any earlier amendments that they have accepted.

Article 19

1. Any State Party may denounce the present Protocol at any time by written notification addressed to the Secretary-General of the United Nations. Denunciation shall take effect six months after the date of receipt of the notification by the Secretary-General.
2. Denunciation shall be without prejudice to the continued application of the provisions of the present Protocol to any communication submitted under Article 2 or any inquiry initiated under Article 8 before the effective date of denunciation.

Article 20

The Secretary-General of the United Nations shall inform all States of:

(a) Signatures, ratifications and accessions under the present Protocol;

(b) The date of entry into force of the present Protocol and of any amendment under Article 18;

(c) Any denunciation under Article 19.

Article 21

1. The present Protocol, of which the Arabic, Chinese, English, French, Russian and Spanish texts are equally authentic, shall be deposited in the archives of the United Nations.
2. The Secretary-General of the United Nations shall transmit

certified copies of the present Protocol to all States referred to in Article 25 of the Convention.

Declaration on the Elimination of Discrimination against Women

The Declaration on the Elimination of Discrimination against Women is a human rights proclamation issued by the United Nations General Assembly, outlining that body's views on women's rights. It was adopted by the General Assembly on 7 November 1967. The Declaration was an important precursor to the legally binding Convention on the Elimination of All Forms of Discrimination Against Women.

Summary

The Declaration follows the structure of the Universal Declaration of Human Rights, with a preamble followed by eleven articles.

Article 1 declares that discrimination against women is "fundamentally unjust and constitutes an offence against human dignity". "Discrimination" is not defined.

Article 2 calls for the abolition of laws and customs which discriminate against women, for equality under the law to be recognised, and for states to ratify and implement existing UN human rights instruments against discrimination.

Article 3 calls for public education to eliminate prejudice against women.

Article 4 calls for women to enjoy full electoral rights, including the right to vote and the right to seek and hold public office.

Article 5 calls for women to have the same rights as men to change their nationality.

Article 6 calls for women to enjoy full equality in civil law, particularly around marriage and divorce, and calls for child marriages to be outlawed.

Article 7 calls for the elimination of gender discrimination in criminal punishment.

Article 8 calls on states to combat all forms of traffic in women and exploitation of prostitution of women.

Article 9 confers an equal right to education regardless of gender.

Article 10 calls for equal rights in the workplace, including non-discrimination in employment, equal pay for equal work, and paid maternity leave.

Article 11 calls on states to implement the principles of the Declaration.

References

1. Declarations, Reservations and Objections to CEDAW.
2. Member states.
3. Government Information Office, Republic of China (Taiwan). "Taiwan Aims to Sign Up Against Discrimination." September 8, 2006.
4. http://www.ngocsw.org/about/how-we-work.
5. Optional Protocol to the Convention on the Elimination of All Forms of Discrimination against Women, Article 1.
6. "Optional Protocol to Women's Convention Comes into Force". 2000-12-21. http://www.un.org/womenwatch/daw/cedaw/protocol/wom1242.htm. Retrieved 2008-07-15.
7. "Parties to the Optional Protocol to the Convention on the Elimination of All Forms of Discrimination against Women". UN OHCHR. http://treaties.un.org/Pages/ViewDetails.aspx?src=TREATY&mtdsg_no=IV-8-b&chapter=4&lang=en. Retrieved 2009-10-03.
8. NGOs Fail Palestinian Women at the UN
9. http://www.un.org/womenwatch/daw/cedaw/reports/a5538.pdf.
10. http://fota.cdnetworks.net/pdfs/2009-02-b-80-Nations-Pressured-by-CEDAW-Comm-summ.pdf.
11. Concerned Women for America - Exposing CEDAW.
12. "UN Committee Pressures Slovakia over its Concordat with the Catholic Church". http://www.c-fam.org/publications/id.664/pub_detail.asp.
13. "Declarations, Reservations and Objections to CEDAW". UN Division for the Advancement of Women. http://www.un.org/womenwatch/daw/cedaw/reservations-country.htm. Retrieved 2008-01-09.

13\. United Nations General Assembly Resolution 2263, 7 November, 1967.

14\. Declaration on the Elimination of Discrimination against Women, Article 1.

5

Laws Protecting Women in Emergency and Armed Conflict

Declaration on Elimination of Violence Against Women

The Declaration on the Elimination of Violence Against Women was adopted without vote by the United Nations General Assembly in its resolution 48/104 of 20 December 1993. Contained within it is the recognition of "the urgent need for the universal application to women of the rights and principles with regard to equality, security, liberty, integrity and dignity of all human beings". The resolution is often seen as complementary to, and a strengthening of, the work of the Convention on the Elimination of All Forms of Discrimination against Women and Vienna Declaration and Programme of Action. It recalls and embodies the same rights and principles as those enshrined in such instruments as the Universal Declaration of Human Rights and Articles 1 and 2 provide the most widely used definition of violence against women.[5] As a consequence of the resolution, in 1999, the General Assembly, led by the representative from the Dominican Republic, designated 25 November as the International Day for the Elimination of Violence against Women.

Background

The international recognition that women have a right to a life free from violence is a recent one. Historically, their struggles with violence, and with the impunity that often protects the perpetrators, is linked with their fight to overcome discrimination. Since its founding the United Nations has concerned itself with the advancement of women's rights, but did not specifically target the high rates of female targeted violence until 1993. One of the aims of the resolution was to overturn the prevailing governmental stance that violence against women was a private, domestic matter not requiring state intervention. To mark International Women's Day on 8 March 1993, General Secretary, Boutros Boutros-Ghali, issued a statement in preparation of the declaration explicitly outlining the UN's role in the 'promotion' and 'protection' of women's rights:

> "The struggle for women's rights, and the task of creating a new United Nations, able to promote peace and the values which nurture and sustain it, are one and the same. Today - more than ever - the cause of women is the cause of all humanity."

Definition of Violence Against Women

Articles 1 and 2 of the resolution provide the most widely used definition of violence against women.

Article One: For the purposes of this Declaration, the term "violence against women" means any act of gender-based violence that results in, or is likely to result in, physical, sexual or psychological harm or suffering to women, including threats of such acts, coercion or arbitrary deprivation of liberty, whether occurring in public or in private life.

Article Two: Violence against women shall be understood to encompass, but not be limited to, the following:

(a) Physical, sexual and psychological violence occurring in the family, including battering, sexual abuse of female children in the household, dowry-related violence, marital rape, female genital mutilation and other traditional practices harmful to women, non-spousal violence and violence related to exploitation;

(b) Physical, sexual and psychological violence occurring within the general community, including rape, sexual abuse, sexual harassment and intimidation at work, in educational institutions and elsewhere, trafficking in women and forced prostitution;

(c) Physical, sexual and psychological violence perpetrated or condoned by the State, wherever it occurs.

Special Rapporteur on Violence Against Women

As a consequence of the declaration on 4 March 1994, the Commission on Human Rights adopted Resolution 1994/45 in which it decided to appoint Radhika Coomaraswamy as its first United

Nations Special Rapporteur on violence against women, including its causes and consequences. The Special Rapporteur has a mandate to collect and analyse data from governments, treaty bodies, specialised agencies, NGOs, and other interested parties, and to respond effectively to such information. Furthermore, they also have a role in making recommendations on an international, national and regional level, as well as liaising with other Special Rapporteurs, special representatives, working groups and independent experts of the Commission on Human Rights.

On 18 June 2009 the Human Rights Council appointed Rashida Manjoo as the third incumbent of the role after the tenure of her predecessor, Dr. Yakin Erturk, came to an end.

Problems

Many advocates of Women's Rights as Human Rights have expressed concerns that much of the ground gained by the declaration has been threatened by the rise of more conservative forces within the international community. In March 2003, during a meeting of the UN Commission on the Status of Women the delegate from Iran objected to the inclusion of a paragraph that called on governments to "condemn violence against women and refrain from invoking any custom, tradition, or religious consideration to avoid their obligations with respect to its elimination as set out in the Declaration of the Elimination of Violence against Women." Representatives from Egypt, Pakistan, Sudan and US also raised objections; making it the first ever diplomatic failure at the UN Commission on the Status of Women.

Campaigns

Each year, the International Day for the Elimination of Violence against Women marks the start of '16 Days of Activism Against Gender Violence'.[13] Human Rights organisations such as Center for Women's Global Leadership, Unifem, Women Won't Wait, Women for a Change, Women's Aid, and other groups join together to speak out against gender violence and to promote the rights and principles of the declaration.

On 10 April 2009, Amnesty International held a demonstration in Narayanghat, Nepal, to highlight the plight of women's rights activists after the Nepalese state failed to protect two activists from violent attacks and, finally, their murder. Despite ratifying the declaration, Nepal had failed to abide by Article 4-c which asserts the clear obligation of states to:

"Exercise due diligence to prevent, investigate and, in

accordance with national legislation, punish acts of violence against women, whether those acts are perpetrated by the State or by private persons."

Declaration on the Elimination of Violence against Women

G.A. res. 48/104, 48 U.N. GAOR Supp. (No. 49) at 217, U.N. Doc. A/48/49 (1993).

The General Assembly,

Recognising the urgent need for the universal application to women of the rights and principles with regard to equality, security, liberty, integrity and dignity of all human beings,

Noting that those rights and principles are enshrined in international instruments, including the Universal Declaration of Human Rights, the International Covenant on Civil and Political Rights, the International Covenant on Economic, Social and Cultural Rights, the Convention on the Elimination of All Forms of Discrimination against Women and the Convention against Torture and Other Cruel, Inhuman or Degrading Treatment or Punishment,

Recognising that effective implementation of the Convention on the Elimination of All Forms of Discrimination against Women would contribute to the elimination of violence against women and that the Declaration on the Elimination of Violence against Women, set forth in the present resolution, will strengthen and complement that process,

Concerned that violence against women is an obstacle to the achievement of equality, development and peace, as recognised in the Nairobi Forward-looking Strategies for the Advancement of Women, in which a set of measures to combat violence against women was recommended, and to the full implementation of the Convention on the Elimination of All Forms of Discrimination against Women,

Affirming that violence against women constitutes a violation of the rights and fundamental freedoms of women and impairs or nullifies their enjoyment of those rights and freedoms, and concerned about the long-standing failure to protect and promote those rights and freedoms in the case of violence against women,

Recognising that violence against women is a manifestation of historically unequal power relations between men and women, which have led to domination over and discrimination against women by men and to the prevention of the full advancement of women, and that violence against women is one of the crucial social mechanisms by which women are forced into a subordinate position compared with men,

Concerned that some groups of women, such as women belonging to minority groups, indigenous women, refugee women, migrant women, women living in rural or remote communities, destitute women, women in institutions or in detention, female children, women with disabilities, elderly women and women in situations of armed conflict, are especially vulnerable to violence,

Recalling the conclusion in paragraph 23 of the annex to Economic and Social Council resolution 1990/15 of 24 May 1990 that the recognition that violence against women in the family and society was pervasive and cut across lines of income, class and culture had to be matched by urgent and effective steps to eliminate its incidence,

Recalling also Economic and Social Council resolution 1991/18 of 30 May 1991, in which the Council recommended the development of a framework for an international instrument that would address explicitly the issue of violence against women,

Welcoming the role that women's movements are playing in drawing increasing attention to the nature, severity and magnitude of the problem of violence against women,

Alarmed that opportunities for women to achieve legal, social, political and economic equality in society are limited, inter alia, by continuing and endemic violence,

Convinced that in the light of the above there is a need for a clear and comprehensive definition of violence against women, a clear statement of the rights to be applied to ensure the elimination of violence against women in all its forms, a commitment by States in respect of their responsibilities, and a commitment by the international community at large to the elimination of violence against women,

Solemnly proclaims the following Declaration on the Elimination of Violence against Women and urges that every effort be made so that it becomes generally known and respected:

Article 1

For the purposes of this Declaration, the term "violence against women" means any act of gender-based violence that results in, or is likely to result in, physical, sexual or psychological harm or suffering to women, including threats of such acts, coercion or arbitrary deprivation of liberty, whether occurring in public or in private life.

Article 2

Violence against women shall be understood to encompass, but not be limited to, the following:

(a) Physical, sexual and psychological violence occurring in the family, including battering, sexual abuse of female children in the household, dowry-related violence, marital rape, female genital mutilation and other traditional practices harmful to women, non-spousal violence and violence related to exploitation;

(b) Physical, sexual and psychological violence occurring within the general community, including rape, sexual abuse, sexual harassment and intimidation at work, in educational institutions and elsewhere, trafficking in women and forced prostitution;

(c) Physical, sexual and psychological violence perpetrated or condoned by the State, wherever it occurs.

Article 3

Women are entitled to the equal enjoyment and protection of all human rights and fundamental freedoms in the political, economic, social, cultural, civil or any other field. These rights include, inter alia:

(a) The right to life;

(b) The right to equality;

(c) The right to liberty and security of person;

(d) The right to equal protection under the law;

(e) The right to be free from all forms of discrimination;

(f) The right to the highest standard attainable of physical and mental health;

(g) The right to just and favourable conditions of work;

(h) The right not to be subjected to torture, or other cruel, inhuman or degrading treatment or punishment.

Article 4

States should condemn violence against women and should not invoke any custom, tradition or religious consideration to avoid their obligations with respect to its elimination. States should pursue by all appropriate means and without delay a policy of eliminating violence against women and, to this end, should:

(a) Consider, where they have not yet done so, ratifying or acceding to the Convention on the Elimination of All Forms of Discrimination against Women or withdrawing reservations to that Convention;

(b) Refrain from engaging in violence against women;

(c) Exercise due diligence to prevent, investigate and, in accordance with national legislation, punish acts of violence against women, whether those acts are perpetrated by the State or by private persons;

(d) Develop penal, civil, labour and administrative sanctions in domestic legislation to punish and redress the wrongs caused to women who are subjected to violence; women who are subjected to violence should be provided with access to the mechanisms of justice and, as provided for by national legislation, to just and effective remedies for the harm that they have suffered; States should also inform women of their rights in seeking redress through such mechanisms;

(e) Consider the possibility of developing national plans of action to promote the protection of women against any form of violence, or to include provisions for that purpose in plans already existing, taking into account, as appropriate, such cooperation as can be provided by non-governmental organisations, particularly those concerned with the issue of violence against women;

(f) Develop, in a comprehensive way, preventive approaches and all those measures of a legal, political, administrative and cultural nature that promote the protection of women against any form of violence, and ensure that the re-victimisation of women does not occur because of laws insensitive to gender considerations, enforcement practices or other interventions;

(g) Work to ensure, to the maximum extent feasible in the light of their available resources and, where needed, within the framework of international cooperation, that women subjected to violence and, where appropriate, their children have specialised assistance, such as rehabilitation, assistance in child care and maintenance, treatment, counselling, and health and social services, facilities and programmes, as well as support structures, and should take all other appropriate measures to promote their safety and physical and psychological rehabilitation;

(h) Include in government budgets adequate resources for their activities related to the elimination of violence against women;

(i) Take measures to ensure that law enforcement officers and public officials responsible for implementing policies to prevent, investigate and punish violence against women receive training to sensitise them to the needs of women;

(j) Adopt all appropriate measures, especially in the field of education, to modify the social and cultural patterns of conduct of men and women and to eliminate prejudices, customary practices and all other practices based on the idea of the inferiority or superiority of either of the sexes and on stereotyped roles for men and women;

(k) Promote research, collect data and compile statistics, especially concerning domestic violence, relating to the prevalence of different forms of violence against women and encourage research on the causes, nature, seriousness and consequences of violence against women and on the effectiveness of measures implemented to prevent and redress violence against women; those statistics and findings of the research will be made public;

(l) Adopt measures directed towards the elimination of violence against women who are especially vulnerable to violence;

(m) Include, in submitting reports as required under relevant human rights instruments of the United Nations, information pertaining to violence against women and measures taken to implement the present Declaration;

(n) Encourage the development of appropriate guidelines to assist in the implementation of the principles set forth in the present Declaration;

(o) Recognise the important role of the women's movement and non-governmental organisations world wide in raising awareness and alleviating the problem of violence against women;

(p) Facilitate and enhance the work of the women's movement and non-governmental organisations and cooperate with them at local, national and regional levels;

(q) Encourage intergovernmental regional organisations of which they are members to include the elimination of violence against women in their programmes, as appropriate.

Article 5

The organs and specialised agencies of the United Nations system should, within their respective fields of competence, contribute to the recognition and realisation of the rights and the principles set forth in the present Declaration and, to this end, should, inter alia:

(a) Foster international and regional cooperation with a view to defining regional strategies for combating violence, exchanging experiences and financing programmes relating to the elimination of violence against women;

(b) Promote meetings and seminars with the aim of creating and raising awareness among all persons of the issue of the elimination of violence against women;

(c) Foster coordination and exchange within the United Nations system between human rights treaty bodies to address the issue of violence against women effectively;

(d) Include in analyses prepared by organisations and bodies of the United Nations system of social trends and problems, such as the periodic reports on the world social situation, examination of trends in violence against women;

(e) Encourage coordination between organisations and bodies of the United Nations system to incorporate the issue of violence against women into ongoing programmes, especially with reference to groups of women particularly vulnerable to violence;

(f) Promote the formulation of guidelines or manuals relating to violence against women, taking into account the measures referred to in the present Declaration;

(g) Consider the issue of the elimination of violence against women, as appropriate, in fulfilling their mandates with respect to the implementation of human rights instruments;

(h) Cooperate with non-governmental organisations in addressing the issue of violence against women.

Article 6

Nothing in the present Declaration shall affect any provision that is more conducive to the elimination of violence against women that may be contained in the legislation of a State or in any international convention, treaty or other instrument in force in a State.

Declaration on the Protection of Women and Children in Emergency and Armed Conflict

G.A. res. 3318 (XXIX), 29 U.N. GAOR Supp. (No. 31) at 146, U.N. Doc. A/9631 (1974).

The General Assembly,

Having considered the recommendation of the Economic and Social Council contained in its resolution 1861 (LVI) of 16 May 1974,

Expressing its deep concern over the sufferings of women and children belonging to the civilian population who in periods of emergency and armed conflict in the struggle for peace, self-determination, national liberation and independence are too often the victims of inhuman acts and consequently suffer serious harm,

Aware of the suffering of women and children in many areas of the world, especially in those areas subject to suppression, aggression, colonialism, racism, alien domination and foreign subjugation,

Deeply concerned by the fact that, despite general and unequivocal condemnation, colonialism, racism and alien and foreign domination continue to subject many peoples under their yoke, cruelly suppressing the national liberation movements and inflicting heavy losses and incalculable sufferings on the populations under their domination, including women and children,

Deploring the fact that grave attacks are still being made on fundamental freedoms and the dignity of the human person and that colonial and racist foreign domination Powers continue to violate international humanitarian law,

Recalling the relevant provisions contained in the instruments of international humanitarian law relative to the protection of women and children in time of peace and war,

Recalling, among other important documents, its resolutions 2444 (XXIII) of 19 December 1968, 2597 (XXIV) of 16 December 1969 and 2674 (XXV) and 2675 (XXV) of 9 December 1970, on respect for human rights and on basic principles for the protection of civilian populations in armed conflicts, as well as Economic and Social Council resolution 1515 (XLVIII) of 28 May 1970 in which the Council requested the General Assembly to consider the possibility of drafting a declaration on the protection of women and children in emergency or wartime,

Conscious of its responsibility for the destiny of the rising generation and for the destiny of mothers, who play an important role in society, in the family and particularly in the upbringing of children,

Bearing in mind the need to provide special protection of women and children belonging to the civilian population,

Solemnly proclaims this Declaration on the Protection of Women and Children in Emergency and Armed Conflict and calls for the strict observance of the Declaration by all Member States:

1. Attacks and bombings on the civilian population, inflicting incalculable suffering, especially on women and children, who are the most vulnerable members of the population, shall be prohibited, and such acts shall be condemned.
2. The use of chemical and bacteriological weapons in the course of military operations constitutes one of the most flagrant violations of the Geneva Protocol of 1925, the Geneva Conventions of 1949 and the principles of international humanitarian law and inflicts heavy losses on civilian populations, including defenceless women and children, and shall be severely condemned.
3. All States shall abide fully by their obligations under the Geneva Protocol of 1925 and the Geneva Conventions of 1949, as well as other instruments of international law relative to respect for human rights in armed conflicts, which offer important guarantees for the protection of women and children.
4. All efforts shall be made by States involved in armed conflicts, military operations in foreign territories or military operations in territories still under colonial domination to spare women and children from the ravages of war. All the necessary steps shall be taken to ensure the prohibition of measures such as persecution, torture, punitive measures, degrading treatment and violence, particularly against that part of the civilian population that consists of women and children.
5. All forms of repression and cruel and inhuman treatment of women and children, including imprisonment, torture, shooting, mass arrests, collective punishment, destruction of dwellings and forcible eviction, committed by belligerents in the course of military operations or in occupied territories shall be considered criminal.

6. Women and children belonging to the civilian population and finding themselves in circumstances of emergency and armed conflict in the struggle for peace, self-determination, national liberation and independence, or who live in occupied territories, shall not be deprived of shelter, food, medical aid or other inalienable rights, in accordance with the provisions of the Universal Declaration of Human Rights, the International Covenant on Civil and Political Rights, the International Covenant on Economic, Social and Cultural Rights, the Declaration of the Rights of the Child or other instruments of international law.

References

1. "RESOLUTIONS: General Assembly, 48th session". un.org. http://www.un.org/Depts/dhl/res/resa48.htm. Retrieved February 24, 2010. [dead link]
2. "A/RES/48/104 - Declaration on the Elimination of Violence against Women - UN Documents: Gathering a body of global agreements". un-documents.net. http://www.un-documents.net/a48r104.htm. Retrieved February 24, 2010.
3. "Convention on the Elimination of All Forms of Discrimination against Women". un.org. http://www.un.org/womenwatch/daw/cedaw/ . Retrieved February 24, 2010.
4. Vienna Declaration and Programme of Action, Part II, paragraph 38.
5. "UNECE Gender Statistics - About Violence Against Women". unece.org. http://www.unece.org/stats/gender/vaw/about.html. Retrieved February 24, 2010.
6. "Ending Impunity for Violence Against Women and Girls". United Nations Department of Public Information. March 2007. http://www.un.org/events/women/iwd/2007/pdf/background.pdf. Retrieved 2010-01-03.
7. "WomenWatch - International Women's Day 1993". un.org. http://www.un.org/womenwatch/feature/iwd/1993/. Retrieved 24 February 2010.
8. "Question of integrating the rights". unhchr.ch. http://www.unhchr.ch/Huridocda/Huridoca.nsf/TestFrame/401503e99f333b03802567360041e65c?Opendocument. Retrieved February 24, 2010.
9. "Special Rapporteur on violence against women, its causes and consequences". www2.ohchr.org. http://www2.ohchr.org/english/issues/women/rapporteur/. Retrieved February 24, 2010.
10. "Violence Against Women: South African legal expert takes over as new UN Special Rapporteur". unhchr.ch. http://www.unhchr.ch/huricane/huricane.nsf/view01/45FE9FE81A1861D0C125761F0031B4C9?opendocument. Retrieved February 24, 2010.

11. Reilly, Niamh (2008-02-12). "Violence against Women / Library / Issues and Analysis / Home - AWID". awid.org. http://www.awid.org/eng/Issues-and-Analysis/Library/Violence-against-Women. Retrieved February 24, 2010.
12. Freeburg, Emily (2003-04-23). "U.N. Pact Sinks on Issue of Violence Against Women". womensenews.org. http://www.womensenews.org/story/international-policyunited-nations/030424/un-pact-sinks-issue-violence-against-women. Retrieved February 24, 2010.
13. "UNFPA - 16 Forms of Gender Violence & 16 Ways to Stop It". unfpa.org. http://www.unfpa.org/public/News/events/16days/. Retrieved February 24, 2010.
14. "AIUK : Nepal: Two women human rights activists murdered after government fails to protect them from violent attacks". amnesty.org.uk. http://www.amnesty.org.uk/news_details.asp?NewsID=18151. Retrieved February 24, 2010.

6

World Conference on Women and Beijing Platform for Action

Beijing World Conference on Women

The United Nations convened the Fourth World Conference on Women (FWCW) on 4-15 September 1995 in Beijing, China. Delegates had prepared a Declaration and Platform for Action that aimed at achieving greater equality and opportunity for women. The three previous World Conferences were in Mexico City (International Women's Year, 1975), Copenhagen (1980) and Nairobi (1985).

The official name of the Conference was "The Fourth World Conference on Women: Action for Equality, Development and Peace". 189 governments and more than 5,000 representatives from 2,100 non-governmental organisations participated in the Conference.

The principal themes were the advancement and empowerment of women in relation to women's human rights, women and poverty, women and decision-making, the girl-child, violence against women and other areas of concern. The resulting documents of the Conference are The Beijing Declaration and Platform for Action.

The overriding message of the Fourth World Conference on Women was that the issues addressed in the Platform for Action are global and universal. Deeply entrenched attitudes and practices perpetuate inequality and discrimination against women, in public and private life, in all parts of the world. Accordingly, implementation requires changes in values, attitudes, practices and priorities at all levels. The Conference signaled a clear commitment to international norms and standards of equality between men and women; that measures to protect and promote the human rights of women and girl-children as an integral part of universal human rights must underlie all action; and that institutions at all levels must be reoriented to expedite implementation. Governments and the UN agreed to promote the "gender mainstreaming" in policies and programmes.

The Beijing Platform for Action

This outcome of the Beijing Conference is an agenda for women's empowerment. It aims at accelerating the implementation of the Nairobi Forward-Looking Strategies for the Advancement of Women. It deals with removing the obstacles to women's public participation in all spheres of public and private lives through a full and equal share in economic, social, cultural and political decision-making.

The *Platform for Action* sets out a number of actions that should lead to fundamental changes by the year 2000 - the Five Year Review of the Beijing Conference at a Special Session of the UN General Assembly (Beijing +5).

Implementing the Beijing Platform for Action is not mainly a responsibility of governments, but also of institutions in the public, private and non-governmental sectors at the community, national, subregional, regional and international levels. The Platform acknowledges that significant progress will depend on building strategic partnerships and involving all stakeholders in the efforts towards change.

The Beijing Declaration and Platform for Action were adopted by consensus on 15 September 1995. The Declaration embodies the commitment of the international community to the advancement of women and to the implementation of the Platform for Action, ensuring that a gender perspective is reflected in all policies and programmes at the national, regional and international levels. The Platform for Action sets out measures for national and international action for the advancement of women over the five years until 2000.

If implemented, the Platform for Action will enhance the social, economic and political empowerment of women, improve their health and their access to relevant education and promote their reproductive rights. The action plan sets time-specific targets, committing nations to carry out concrete actions in such areas as health, education, decision-making and legal reforms with the ultimate goal of eliminating all forms of discrimination against women in both public and private life.

The issue of global advocacy for abortion rights was

controversial, with the United States and the Holy See publicly disagreeing over the issue.

Mission Statement

The Platform for Action is an agenda for women's empowerment. It aims at accelerating the implementation of the Nairobi Forward-looking Strategies for the Advancement of Women and at removing all the obstacles to women's active participation in all spheres of public and private life through a full and equal share in economic, social, cultural and political decision-making. This means that the principle of shared power and responsibility should be established between women and men at home, in the workplace and in the wider national and international communities. Equality between women and men is a matter of human rights and a condition for social justice and is also a necessary and fundamental prerequisite for equality, development and peace. A transformed partnership based on equality between women and men is a condition for people-centred sustainable development. A sustained and long-term commitment is essential, so that women and men can work together for themselves, for their children and for society to meet the challenges of the twenty-first century.

The Platform for Action reaffirms the fundamental principle set forth in the Vienna Declaration and Programme of Action, adopted by the World Conference on Human Rights, that the human rights of women and of the girl child are an inalienable, integral and indivisible part of universal human rights. As an agenda for action, the Platform seeks to promote and protect the full enjoyment of all human rights and the fundamental freedoms of all women throughout their life cycle.

The Platform for Action emphasizes that women share common concerns that can be addressed only by working together and in partnership with men towards the common goal of gender equality around the world. It respects and values the full diversity of women's situations and conditions and recognizes that some women face particular barriers to their empowerment.

The Platform for Action requires immediate and concerted action by all to create a peaceful, just and humane world based on human rights and fundamental freedoms, including the principle of equality for all people of all ages and from all walks of life, and to this end, recognizes that broad- based and sustained economic growth in the context of sustainable development is necessary to sustain social development and social justice.

The success of the Platform for Action will require a strong commitment on the part of Governments, international organisations and institutions at all levels. It will also require adequate mobilisation of resources at the national and international levels as well as new and additional resources to the developing countries from all available funding mechanisms, including multilateral, bilateral and private sources for the advancement of women; financial resources to strengthen the capacity of national, subregional, regional and international institutions; a commitment to equal rights, equal responsibilities and equal opportunities and to the equal participation of women and men in all national, regional and international bodies and policy- making processes; and the establishment or strengthening of mechanisms at all levels for accountability to the world's women.

For the commonly understood meaning of the term "gender", see annex IV to the present report.

The Beijing Platform for Action (BFPA)

The Beijing Platform for Action (BPFA) was adopted at the Fourth United Nations World Conference on Women, held in Beijing in 1995. It is an internationally agreed plan for achieving equality for women across 12 critical areas – poverty, education and training, health, the economy, power and decision-making, human rights, armed conflict, institutional mechanisms, the environment, violence against women and the girl child.

Following the 1995 Fourth United Nations World Conference on Women, the United Nations General Assembly mandated the United Nations Commission on the Status of Women to integrate into its program a follow-up process to the Conference, regularly reviewing the critical areas of concern in the BPFA and to develop its role in mainstreaming a gender perspective in United Nations activities.

In 1996, the Commission adopted a multi-year program of work based on the 12 critical areas of concern identified in the BPFA for the period of 1997-2000. Subsequent work programs were adopted in 2001 and most recently in 2006 based on the BPFA and the Beijing +5 Outcome Document.

Beijing +15

The 54th session of the United Nations Commission on the Status of Women (CSW 54) marked the 15 year review of the BPFA also known as Beijing +15.

The Australian Government Office for Women led the

Australian delegation to CSW 54 in New York from 1-12 March 2010. The delegation comprised representatives from the Office for Women, the Equal Employment for Women in the Workplace Agency, AusAID, the Department of Education, Employment and Workplace Relations, and the Human Rights Commission.

Also included on the Australian Government delegation were three community representatives, two of whom are Indigenous women, Mary O'Reeri and Leanne Miller, and a community expert, Carole Shaw.

Australia contributes to the regional review of the Beijing Platform in the lead-up to CSW 54/Beijing +15 in New York in March 2010.

Australia was represented at the High Level Intergovernmental Meeting on Gender Equality held in Bangkok from 16-18 November 2009.

The meeting of Minister and senior officials was convened by the United Nations Economic and Social Commission for Asia and the Pacific (ESCAP) as part of the 15 year review process for the regional implementation of the Beijing Declaration and Platform for Action adopted at the Fourth World Conference on Women (Beijing, 1995) and the outcome of the twenty-third special session of the General Assembly (2000) for the ESCAP region.

Australia delivered a Country Statement, highlighting key achievements and remaining challenges in implementing the Beijing Platform for Action in Australia.

Ministers and senior officials from 40 countries reaffirmed their commitment to women's empowerment with the adoption of the Bangkok Declaration for Beijing +15 which will intensify the region's effort to improve the lives of women and girls.

This meeting was one of five regional reviews undertaken by all five United Nations regional commissions in the lead-up to the 54th session of the Commission on the Status of Women (CSW) which took place in New York from 1-12 March 2010. These regional reviews fed into the 54th CSW meeting which reviewed the global implementation of the Beijing Declaration and Platform for Action and what has been achieved in the 15 years since its adoption.

Australia's response to the UNESCAP Questionnaire on the implementation of the outcome of the Fourth World Conference on Women (Beijing 1995)

In April 2009 the Australian Government provided its response to the UNESCAP Questionnaire on the implementation of the outcome of the Fourth World Conference on Women (Beijing 1995) in preparation for the regional review and appraisals for the 15th anniversary of the adoption of the Beijing Declaration and Platform for Action in 2010. The Australian Government response outlines Australia's progress towards the 12 critical areas of concern of the Platform for Action between 2004 and 2009.

Since Australia's response was submitted to UNESCAP in April 2009 the Government has announced a number of key initiatives. These recent developments further support Australia's progress in the implementation of the Beijing Declaration and Platform for Action.

The BPFA review process

The BPFA has been reviewed on two previous occasions:

The 23rd Special Session of the UN General Assembly, in 2000: Women 2000: gender equality, development and peace for the twenty-first century (Beijing +5) during which Beijing Plus Five Political Declaration and the Outcome Documents were adopted.

The 49th session of the Commission on the Status of Women (Beijing +10) during which commitment to the Beijing Platform for Action and the Beijing Plus Five Outcome Document was reaffirmed and the Beijing Plus Ten and Beyond report was prepared.

Review years are critical times for assessing progress towards implementation of the BPFA internationally and determining the way ahead toward the goal of gender equality and women's empowerment.

Australia was actively involved in the Beijing +5 and Beijing +10 reviews. In the lead up to Beijing +10, the Office for Women undertook consultation with NGOs as part of a review of Australia's progress towards implementation of the Beijing Platform for Action and the Beijing Plus Five Outcome Document.

Beijing and its Follow-up

The Commission on the Status of Women has been responsible for organising and following up the world conferences on women in Mexico (1975), Copenhagen (1980), Nairobi (1985) and Beijing (1995). Over the past decade, the Commission has systematically reviewed progress in the implementation of the twelve critical areas of concern identified in the Beijing Platform for Action at its annual sessions, and has adopted action-oriented recommendations, in the form of agreed conclusions, to facilitate increased implementation at all levels.

The Commission acted as the Ad-hoc Preparatory Committee for the twenty-third special session of the General Assembly (Beijing+5). The outcome identified persistent gaps and challenges and provided new recommendations for action to ensure full implementation of the commitments made in Beijing in 1995.

The ten-year review of the Beijing Platform for Action was carried out by the Commission at its forty-ninth session in March 2005. The Commission adopted a Declaration on the occasion of the ten-year review. Member States reaffirmed the Beijing Declaration and Platform for Action and the outcome of the twenty-third special session of the General Assembly and pledged to ensure their full and accelerated implementation.

The fifteen-year review of the Beijing Platform for Action took place during the fifty-fourth session of the CSW.

Five-year Review of the implementation of the Beijing Declaration and Platform for Action (Beijing + 5) held in the General Assembly, 5 - 9 June 2000

(a) Introduction

1. The twenty-third special session of the General Assembly on "Women 2000: gender equality, development and peace for the twenty-first century" took place at the United Nations Headquarters in New York from 5 June to 9 June 2000 and adopted a Political Declaration and outcome document entitled "further actions and initiatives to implement the Beijing Declaration and Platform for Action". This briefing note summarizes the steps leading up to the special session and immediate implications of its outcome for the work of the Commission on the Status on Women, one of the main functional commissions of ECOSOC and the main intergovernmental body tasked with the responsibility of promoting the advancement of women and gender equality.
2. A broader assessment of the implications of the Political Declaration and "further actions and initiatives to implement the Beijing Declaration and Platform for Action" adopted by the General Assembly at its special session is available in the Report of the Secretary-General "Implementation of the Outcome of the Fourth World Conference on Women and of the Special Session of the General Assembly entitled "Women 2000: Gender Equality, Development and Peace in the Twenty-first Century" (A/55/341).

(b) The Preparatory Process

3. The General Assembly, in resolution 52/100, decided to convene a special session to review progress in the implementation of the Nairobi Forward-looking Strategies for the Advancement of Women and the Beijing Declaration and Platform for Action. The special session was to take place five years after the Fourth World Conference on Women (FWCW) which was held in Beijing in 1995. In accordance with the General Assembly resolution 52/231 the Commission on the Status of Women, with its ten member Bureau, was to act as the preparatory committee (prepcom) for the special session and the Division for the Advancement of Women, under the guidance of the Special Adviser on Gender Issues and the Advancement of Women, serve as the substantive Secretariat.

4. The Bureau of the prepcom was composed of the following members, Asith Bhattacharjee (India), Patricia Flor (Germany), Misako Kaji (Japan), Christine Kapalata (United Republic of Tanzania), Sonia R. Leonce-Carryl (Saint Lucia), Monica Martinez (Ecuador), Kristen Mlacak (Canada), Rasa Ostrauskaite (Lithuania), Dubravka Simonovic (Croatia). Ms. Irma Engelbrecht of South Africa, was elected Chairperson of prepcom at its second session in March 1999, she was replaced by Ms. Roselyn Odere of Kenya, who was elected by the prepcom at its resumed session on 30 June 1999. Ms. Odera chaired the third session of the prepcom in 2000. With the transfer of Ms. Odera by her government to another post in March 2000, the African group nominated Ms. Christine Kapalata as here replacement. She was elected at a formal meeting of the prepcom on 20 April, 2000 and the vacancy thus emerged was filled by the election of Ms. Aisha Afifi of Morocco by the African group.

A. Substantive Preparations

(i) The Intergovernmental Process

5. The CSW acting as the prepcom held formal and informal meetings during the Commission's forty-second session from 2-13 March 1998. At its first meeting, the prepcom considered and adopted draft resolution (E/CN.6/1998/11) entitled "Follow-up to the Fourth World Conference on Women and full implementation of the Beijing Declaration and Platform for Action" submitted by the Chairperson on the basis of informal consultations. (See the report of the Commission on the

Status of Women, E/1998/27). Subsequently, at its second session from 15 to 19 March 1999, the prepcom held formal meetings and recommended the adoption of the draft resolution, "Preparations for the special session of the GA entitled:, "Women 2000: Gender equality, development and peace for the twenty-first century" by the General Assembly through the ECOSOC."

6. In December 1999, during informal consultations, Member States agreed on the structure of the outcome document "further actions and initiatives to implement the Beijing Declaration and Platform for Action". The document was to be short and concise and would consist of four sections:
   - (i) Introduction;
   - (ii) Achievements and obstacles in the implementation of the twelve critical areas of the Platform for Action;
   - (iii) Current challenges affecting the full implementation of the Beijing Declaration and the Platform for Action;
   - (iv) Actions and initiatives to overcome obstacles and to achieve the full and accelerated implementation of the Beijing Platform for Action.

7. In January 2000, a concise draft outcome document (17 pages) was prepared by the Division for the Advancement of Women (DAW), and presented to the Bureau of the Commission on the Status of Women for their inputs and revisions. The action paragraphs in Chapter IV of the initial draft was structured along the three themes of the women's conferences, i.e. equality, development and peace. This document was later distributed to Member States for comments and inputs. Inputs from NGO's and the UN system were also considered in the preparation of the document.

8. During informal consultations in late January, the Bureau decided to change the structure of Chapter IV. Instead of the three themes, actions were to be presented according to national level and international level and under each level according to the various actors, including Governments, the United Nations system, international and regional organisations, non-governmental organisations and other actors of civil society. The Division for the Advancement of Women revised the document accordingly and the Member States were called on to provide their amendments to the document. The expanded document, reaching nearly 100 pages, formed the basis of subsequent negotiations.

9. At its third session from 7-17 March, 2000 and 20 April, 2000 (A/S-23/2), the prepcom negotiated the proposed outcome document in two parallel Working Groups. Working Group I, chaired by Kirsten Mlacak (Canada), negotiated the first three sections of the document and Working Group II, chaired by Asith K. Bhattacharjee (India), dealt with Section IV. The outstanding paragraphs of the Political Declaration (E/CN/6/2000/PC/L.5), on which considerable discussions had taken place during informal consultations in November 1999, were also negotiated during this session. A consensus was reached on the text of the Political Declaration, but work on the proposed outcome document was not finalised. As a result, negotiations had to continue during informal consultations before (8 May - 2 June 2000) and during the special session.

10. During its third session the prepcom held a panel discussion entitled "Outlook on gender equality, development and peace beyond the year 2000". This panel was organised in conjunction with a panel discussion on emerging issues within the context of the CSW session the same year. The discussions in the former panel focused on the differential impact of globalisation on women and men. Panelists noted that there was a need for compensatory policies that addressed the effects of restructuring, on the one hand, and policies that would restructure the women's agenda enhancing women's capacity to take full advantage of the global economic changes, on the other. Issues such as poverty, violence, armed conflict among others were also addressed (see moderator's summary in annex II of document A/S-23/2).

11. The issues that emanated from the panel discussions were complementary to the issues raised in the report of the Secretary-General on the review and appraisal of the implementation of the Beijing Platform for Action (E/CN.6/2000/PC/2) which was before the prepcom at this session. Review and appraisal of the implementation of the Beijing Platform for Action is further elaborated under item 3 of this section of the present report.

12. In accordance with resolution 54/142, the prepcom submitted, for approval, a draft provisional agenda of the twenty-third special session of the General Assembly which would have the special session review and appraise progress made in implementing the twelve critical areas of concern in the Beijing Platform for Action, and identify further actions and initiatives for overcoming obstacles to its implementation.

13. The prepcom also had before it a draft decision entitled "Organisational arrangements for the twenty-third special session of the General Assembly (contained in E/CN.6/2000/PC/L.6) and decided, pending adoption by the General Assembly, that the special session should be presided over by the President and Vice-Presidents of the fifty-fourth regular Assembly session. In addition, the decision contained provisions for the composition of the Bureau and the establishment of an Ad Hoc Committee of the Whole.

14. Two other draft decisions were recommended by the prepcom for adoption by the General Assembly: Arrangements regarding participation of non-governmental organisations at the twenty-third special session of the General Assembly (E/CN.6/2000/PC/L.3); and Draft decision II: Arrangements regarding accreditation of non-governmental organisations to the special session (E/CN.6/2000/PC/L.4).

15. The General Assembly decision (54/466) noted that given the availability of time, a limited number of NGOs that are in consultative status with the Economic and Social Council may also make statements in the debate in the plenary of the special session provided neither that their application for consultative status with the Council has been rejected, nor that their consultative status with the Council has been withdrawn or suspended. The decision on accreditation (54/467) allowed non-governmental organisations that were neither in consultative status with the Economic and Social Council, nor accredited to the Fourth World Conference on Women and its preparatory process, to apply for accreditation to the special session.

(ii) Regional Preparatory Meetings

16. In its resolution 54/142 of 17 December 1999 on preparations for the special session, the General Assembly encouraged all regional commissions and other intergovernmental regional organisations to carry out activities in support of the preparatory process, inter alia, through holding meetings to ensure a regional perspective on implementation and on further actions and initiatives, and to make their reports available in 2000 to the Commission on the Status of Women acting as the preparatory committee. The following preparatory meetings were held under the auspices of the five regional commissions (E/CN.6/PC/6 and addenda 1-6):

    (a) The regional meeting of the Economic and Social

Commission for Asia and the Pacific (ESCAP) took place in Bangkok, from 26-29 October, 1999 and identified 49 strategies and recommendations to further implement the Beijing Platform for Action;

(b) The regional meeting of the Economic Commission for Africa (ECA) was held in Addis Ababa, from 22-26 November, 1999 and issued a Declaration that reaffirmed the commitments of the ECA countries to the Beijing and Dakar Platforms for Action;

(c) The regional meeting of the Economic and Social Commission for West Asia (ESCWA) was held in Beirut, from 12-15 December, 1999 and resulted in a vision for equality between women and men in the region in the new millennium;

(d) The regional meeting of the Economic Commission for Europe (ECE) took place in Geneva, from 19-21 January, 2000 and adopted a series of agreed conclusions on further actions for the full implementation of the Platform;

(e) The regional meeting of the Economic Commission for Latin America and the Caribbean (ECLAC) was held in Lima, from 8-10 February, 2000 and adopted the Lima Consensus, which took into account the Port of Spain Declaration (October 1999), and reaffirmed commitment to the implementation of the Beijing Platform for Action. The Lima Consensus outlined 25 actions, and adopted three resolutions.

17. NGOs fully participated in the regional meetings. They held numerous activities to contribute to the assessment of implementation and development of regional strategies for further action.

(iii) Review and Appraisal of the Implementation of the Platform for Action

18. The review of the implementation of the Platform for Action has been a long and challenging process involving all actors at national, regional and global levels. After the FWCW, the Commission on the Status of Women adopted a work program for the years 1996-1999 in order to monitor the implementation of the strategic objectives set forth for each of the critical areas of concern in the Platform. Thus, during this period the Commission devoted itself to the review of

progress in this regard and adopted resolutions and agreed conclusions containing recommendations for accelerated implementation. These have been compiled and published by the Division for the Advancement of Women (sales No. 00IV6).

19. The Commission invited Governments to prepare national action plans in accordance with the Platform. As of 1 October 2000, the Division for the Advancement of Women has received 117 plans from Member States and observers and provided the CSW with their analysis (E/CN.6/1998/6 and E/CN.6/1999/2/Add.1).

20. Four years after the Beijing Conference, governments were asked to report on their actions to implement the Platform for Action in the 12 critical areas of concern. As of 1 October 2000, 153 Member States and 2 observers responded to the questionnaire prepared by the Secretariat in collaboration with the five regional commissions and sent out in October 1998. This response rate of over 80% per cent is of itself, indicative of the strong worldwide commitment to the goal of gender equality. An analysis of the main trends in the implementation of the Platform as contained in these reports was carried out and submitted by the Division for the Advancement of Women to the preparatory committee at its third session in March 2000 (E/CN.6/2000/PC/2). The responses to the questionnaire are available on the DAW website (http://www.un.org/womenwatch/daw/).

21. Review of the national reports show that profound changes in the status and role of women have occurred in the years since the start of the United Nations Decade for Women in 1976, some more markedly since the FWCW. Women have entered the labour force in unprecedented numbers, increasing the potential for their ability to participate in economic decision making at various levels, starting with the household. Women, individually and collectively, have been major actors in the rise of civil society throughout the world, stimulating pressure for increased awareness of the gender equality dimensions of all issues, and demanding a role in national and global decision making processes. Thus, the role of non-governmental organisations, especially women's organisations, in putting the concerns of women and gender equality on the national and international agenda was acknowledged by many Governments.

22. Despite much progress, responses from Member States

indicate that much more work needs to be done with regard to implementation of the Platform for Action. Two major areas - violence and poverty - continue to be major obstacles to gender equality worldwide. Globalisation has added new dimensions to both areas, creating new challenges for the implementation of the Platform, such as trafficking in women and girls, changing nature of armed conflict, growing gap between nations and genders, the detachment of macroeconomic policy from social protection concerns.

23. Overall, the analysis of the national reports on the implementation of the Platform for Action revealed that there had been no major breakthrough with regard to equal sharing of decision making in political structures at national and international levels. In most countries of the world, representation of women remains low. Even in countries where a "critical mass" in decision-making positions within the public sector has been achieved, there are few women on boards of directors of major business corporations. There is need for more careful monitoring of progress in ensuring women's equal participation in these positions of economic power.

(iv) Emerging Issues and Trends

24. In its resolution (E/1996/6), the Economic and Social Council requested the Commission to identify, in the follow-up to the Fourth World Conference on Women, emerging issues, trends and new approaches to issues affecting the situation of women or equality between women and men that required urgent consideration, and make substantive recommendations thereon. The General Assembly (A/Res/52/231), also requested a report on emerging issues to be submitted to the Commission on the Status of Women at its forty-fourth session, including additional material on further actions and initiatives for the preparation of the outlook beyond the year 2000.

25. In order to comply with these resolutions, an international workshop on "Beijing +5 – Future Actions and Initiatives" was convened by the Division for the Advancement of Women and hosted by the Economic and Social Commission for Western Asia (ESCWA) at the United Nations House in Beirut, Lebanon, from 8 to 10 November 1999. The workshop assessed the impact of trends of global change on gender equality, development and peace in terms of the

implementation of the Platform, and recommended measures to address the emerging challenges. Recommendations were formulated in respect of five categories: attitudes and practices; governance; alliances and coalitions; social and economic justice, and peace-building. The report of the workshop was before the prepcom at its third session (E/CN.6/2000/PC/4).

A. Organisational Preparations

26. Under the guidance of the Office of the Assistant Secretary-General, Department of General Assembly Affairs and Conference Services, an interdepartmental task force was established to coordinate the organisational preparations for the special session. The task force met on a monthly basis to decide on organisational aspects of the special session. On the basis of these meetings, an information note was issued outlining the arrangements related to all organisational matters, including the guidelines for the accreditation of delegates and NGO representatives; security measures; special events; media related matters as well as secretariat focal points responsible for various processes and services.

(c) The Special Session of the General-Assembly

A. General Assembly Plenary

27. The special session, during its plenary meetings, heard statements that focused on the progress made and the remaining obstacles to the implementation to the Platform for Action. The plenary was addressed by representatives of 148 Member States, including two Prime Ministers, four Vice-Presidents, Ministers and Vice-Ministers. Representatives of three non-member States, 16 observers, five heads of UN programmes and specialised agencies, five non-governmental organisations and the Chairperson of the Committee on the Elimination of Discrimination against Women (CEDAW) also addressed the plenary.

28. At the opening session, the Secretary-General emphasised the progress made since the Fourth World Conference in Beijing. Human rights of women had gained recognition, violence against women was now an illegal act in almost every country, and there had been worldwide mobilisation against harmful traditional practices. But the Secretary-General noted that much still remained to be done, including addressing new challenges such as HIV/AIDS and increased

armed conflict. While women entered the labour market in unprecedented numbers, the gender divide still persisted, women earned less, and were involved in informal and unpaid work. There has been no breakthrough in women's participation in decision making processes and little progress in the legislation in favour of women's rights to own land and other property. In his statement, the Secretary-General focused on the importance of education, stressing that it was both the entry point into the global economy and the best defense against its pitfalls. Once they were educated and integrated into the workforce, women would have more choices and be able to provide better nutrition, health care and education for their children.

29. In the statements to the plenary meetings of the special session, Governments strongly reiterated their commitment to the Beijing goals and called for international cooperation to fight against poverty and trafficking in women. Overwhelming support was expressed in favour of the Convention on the Elimination of All forms of Discrimination against Women and its Optional Protocol, the Convention on the Rights of the Child, the Convention against Transnational Organised Crime, as well as the Rome Statute of the International Criminal Court.

B. Ad Hoc Committee of the Whole

30. At the first plenary meeting of its twenty-third special session, the General Assembly established an Ad Hoc Committee of the Whole to consider agenda item 8 entitled "Review and appraisal of progress made in the implementation of the twelve critical areas of concern in the Beijing Platform for Action." In connection with its consideration of the agenda items 8 and 9, the Ad Hoc Committee had before it the report of the Commission on the Status of Women acting as the preparatory committee entitled "Women 2000: gender equality, development and peace for the twenty-first century" (A/S-23/2 and Add.1 and 2 (Parts I-IV and IV/corr.1). Ms. Christina Kapalata (United Republic of Tanzania), who served as Chairperson of the preparatory committee, was elected Chairperson of the Ad Hoc Committee (see Report of the Ad Hoc Committee of the Whole - A/S - 23/10/Rev.1).

31. Over the five-day period, the Ad Hoc Committee held 3 formal meetings to hear representatives of various UN agencies and the NGO community. Number of informal

meetings were also held to negotiate the proposed outcome document for further actions and initiatives for the full implementation of the Platform for Action. In this connection, the Committee's work proceeded in two parallel negotiations within the context of Working Group I and Working Group II. Contact groups were formed to address difficult issues such as health, globalisation, human rights and the girl child, family, armed conflict and issues of diversity. The initial negotiating groups included the G-77 and China, the European Union and associated countries and the JUSCANZ (Japan, United States, Canada, Australia and New Zealand). Where the G-77 and China did not have a group position they negotiated in smaller groups. The major groups that emerged included CARICOM (the Caribbean Community), SLAC (Some Latin American Countries) and SADC (Southern African Development Community). A number of individual delegations were also active in the negotiations.

32. At its 3rd meeting, on 10 June, the Ad Hoc Committee of the Whole considered its draft report (A/S - 23/AC.1/L.1 and Add.1-42) and 2 draft resolutions: Political Declaration and Further actions and initiatives to implement the Beijing Declaration and Platform for Action as submitted by the Chairperson in document A/S-23/AC.1/L.2.

C. The Non-governmental Dimension

NGO Participation

33. A total of 2,052 NGO participants representing 1,038 NGOs registered for the special session including 272 NGOs accredited in accordance with General Assembly decision 54/467. Almost 25 per cent of the participants were from the ECE region, 27.1 per cent from North America, 19.7 per cent from the ESCAP region, 11.6 per cent from the ECA region, 10.6 per cent from the ECLAC region and 1.9 per cent were from the ESCWA region. In addition, approximately 2400 participants of non-governmental organisations registered for activities held outside of the United Nations facilities.

34. NGOs organised 15 panel discussions during the special session. The Secretariat facilitated the organisation of the panels, the "live feed" of the opening and closing sessions of the plenary and daily NGO briefings. In collaboration with the U.S. Host Committee, NGOs also held numerous side events and activities at locations throughout New York City.

Side Events Organised by the Entities of the United Nations

35. Numerous side events organised by the United Nations system and other international organisations were held. The Bureau of the Commission on the Status of Women acting as the preparatory committee sponsored three high level panels organised by UN entities. A panel on "Mainstreaming a Gender Perspective in Peacekeeping Operations" was held by the Department of Peace Keeping Operations (DPKO), the Office of the Special Advisor on Gender Issues (OSAGI) and the Division for the Advancement of Women (DAW). It addressed the issue of gender mainstreaming in the peace process, including peacekeeping, peace building and conflict prevention. The panel on "Dialogue between NGOs and Governments: For a Gender-Sensitive Citizenship" was organised by the Regional Commissions. It discussed the emergence of women's groups and gender equality initiatives within the framework of an increasingly stronger civil society. The third panel on "The Role of Men and Boys in Ending Gender Based Violence" discussed the need to change dominant perceptions of masculinity to combat violence. The panel was organised by the OSAGI, the DAW, the United Nations Men's Group for Gender Equality, UNICEF and UNIFEM.

D. Outcome of the Special Session

36. On June 10, 2000 the General Assembly adopted by consensus the Political Declaration and "further Actions and Initiatives to Implement the Beijing Platform for Action". In his closing statement, the President of the General Assembly remarked that there had been no backward movement on Beijing language and that in several areas the Outcome Document moved the global agenda on gender equality forward.

37. Governments and the international community once more reaffirmed their commitment to the Platform for Action and a common development agenda with gender equality as an underlying principle. The outcome document recognised that the efforts towards ensuring women's advancement needed to combine a focus on women's conditions and basic needs with a holistic approach based on equal rights and partnerships, promotion and protection of all human rights and fundamental freedoms. It further recognised that policies, programmes and budgetary processes should adopt a gender perspective, be based on a clear research based knowledge

on the situation of women and girls and sex disaggregated data and be defined in terms of short and long term time-bound targets and measurable goals and follow up mechanisms to assess progress.

38. The special session reaffirmed the importance of gender mainstreaming in all areas and at all levels and the complementarity between mainstreaming and special activities targeting women. Certain areas were identified as requiring focussed attention. These included; education; social services and health; including sexual and reproductive health; the HIV/AIDS pandemic; violence against women and girls; the persistent and increasing burden of poverty on women; vulnerability of migrant women including exploitation and trafficking; natural disaster and environmental management; the development of strong, effective and accessible national machineries for the advancement of women; and the formulation of strategies to enable women and men to reconcile and share equally work and family responsibilities.

39. 199 actions to be taken at the national and international levels by Governments, the United Nations system, international and regional organisations, including international financial institutions, the private sector, non-governmental organisations and other actors of civil society were agreed on. A number of these actions set new targets and reconfirmed existing ones:

   (a) Closure of the gender gap in primary and secondary education by 2005, and free and compulsory and universal primary education for both girls and boys by 2015 (67c);

   (b) The achievement of a 50 per cent improvement in levels of adult literacy by 2015, especially for women through (95f);

   (c) The creation and maintenance of a non-discriminatory, as well as gender sensitive legal environment through reviewing legislation with a view to striving to remove discriminatory provisions as soon as possible, preferably by 2005 (68b);

   (d) Universal access to high quality primary health care, throughout the life cycle, including sexual and reproductive health care, not later than 2015 (79b);

40. In addition to further action on the twelve critical areas of concern the document addressed areas which have gained

importance since the Beijing Conference. Emphasis was placed on women's access to decision-making particularly in peace keeping processes, gender-sensitive approaches to HIV/AIDS and humanitarian crises, changing patterns of migratory flows, new technologies, violence against women, including trafficking and in armed conflict and the realisation of women's full enjoyment of economic, social, cultural, civil and political rights. Actions also addressed the challenges presented by globalisation to the implementation of the Beijing Declaration and Platform for Action.

41. Many of the actions identified specific groups of women as their primary target:

    (a) Older aging/women
    (b) adolescents/young women
    (c) refugees/asylum seekers
    (d) indigenous women
    (e) entrepreneurs/self employed
    (f) migrant women
    (g) rural women
    (h) disabled women
    (i) female household heads

42. As in the case of other conference reviews, the special session stressed the need for continued international cooperation to increase the flow of resources for the Platform's goals of gender equality, development and peace, in particular through reaffirmation and fulfillment of the internationally agreed target of 0.7 per cent of the gross national product of developed countries for overall official development assistance, and support for the Cologne initiative for the reduction of debt and the 20/20 initiative. The outcome document also emphasised the need to identify and implement development-oriented and durable solutions which integrate a gender perspective to the external debt and debt-servicing problems of developing countries, including least developed countries, in order to help these countries finance development programmes and projects, including the advancement of women.

Beyond the Special Session

43. The Political Declaration and the Outcome Document strongly

confirm that the Beijing Platform for Action remains the reference point for governmental commitment to women's advancement and gender equality. However, new areas of focus and action were highlighted by the special session. This predicates that the results of Beijing and Beijing + 5 need to be consolidated. In this context, the outcome of a number of intergovernmental processes since 8 June 2000 offer further guidelines; in particular the substantive session of Economic and Social Council (ECOSOC), the fifty fifth session of the General Assembly and the Security Council meeting on Women, Peace and Security.

44. In 2000, for the first time during its substantive session, ECOSOC's coordination segment focused on an integrated and coordinated follow-up to major United Nations conferences and summits. Building upon the coordination theme, the Council adopted agreed conclusions E/2000/2 "Assessment of the progress made within the United Nations system, through conference reviews, in the promotion of an integrated and coordinated implementation of and follow-up to major United Nations conferences and summits in the economic, social and related fields." These efforts by ECOSOC could reinforce the cross-cutting nature of the outcomes of the five-year reviews, including the Fourth World Conference on Women and the twenty-third special session of the General Assembly and ensure their full cooperation in follow-up activities of the United Nations and its system of organisations.

45. In its resolution (E/2000/26), the Council noted with concern the persistent problems in addressing the challenges of poverty eradication, gender inequalities, empowerment and advancement of women and employment as reflected in the outcome documents of the recent five-year reviews of the Fourth World Conference and the World Summit for Social Development. The Council therefore strongly encouraged Governments to pursue and strengthen their efforts to work towards achieving the goals of poverty eradication and reiterated the call to relevant organisations of the United Nations system and the international community to take consistent, coherent, coordinated and joint actions in support of national efforts to eradicate poverty.

46. At its fifty-fifth session, the General Assembly adopted resolution A/Res/55/71, "Follow-up to the Fourth World Conference on Women and full implementation of the Beijing

Declaration and Platform for Action and the outcome of the twenty-third special session of the General Assembly." Stressing the importance of the outcome of the five-year review of the Fourth World Conference on Women, the Assembly calls on Governments and the United Nations system to take effective action to achieve the full and effective implementation of the Beijing Declaration and Platform for Action and the outcome of the twenty-third special session of the General Assembly. The Assembly invited ECOSOC to continue to promote a coordinated follow-up to and implementation of the outcomes of the major United Conferences and summits and their reviews, ensure gender mainstreaming as an integral part of the activities of the follow-up and its work. The Assembly reaffirmed the need for the mobilisation of resources at the national and international levels, the promotion of an active and visible policy of mainstreaming a gender perspective by the United Nations, including through the work of the Special Adviser on Gender Issues and Advancement of Women and through the maintenance of gender units and focal points.

47. Recalling its previous resolution (54/283), the General Assembly adopted draft resolution A/Res/55/13, "Review of the problem of human immunodeficiency virus/acquired immunodeficiency syndrome in all its aspects" and decided to convene, as a matter of urgency, a special session of the General Assembly, from 25 to 27 June 2001 to address and review the problem of HIV/AIDS. Recalling the outcome document of the twenty-third special session, the Assembly decided to address the issue of the gender specific impact of HIV/AIDS, especially on women and girls during the special session.

48. On 31 October 2000, the Security Council adopted resolution 1325 (2000) on Women, Peace and Security. Recalling the commitments of the Beijing Declaration and Platform for Action (A/52/231) as well as those contained in the outcome document of the twenty-third special session of the General Assembly, in particular those concerning women and armed conflict, the Council reaffirmed the important role of women in the prevention and resolution of conflicts and in peace-building. The Council stressed the importance of their equal participation and full involvement in all efforts for the maintenance and promotion of peace and security, and the

need to increase their role in decision-making with regard to conflict prevention and resolution.

49. On the basis of guidance emanating from these fora, the Commission on the Status of Women, at its 45th. Session in March 2001, will adopt a new multi-year work programme for the years 2002-2006. At this session the Commission will also consider two thematic issues: (a) women, the girl child and human immunodeficiency virus/acquired immunodeficiency syndrome (HIV/AIDS); (b) gender and all forms of discrimination, in particular racism, racial discrimination, xenophobia and related intolerance.

50. The Division for the Advancement of Women held expert group meetings in conjunction with these two thematic agenda items. The expert group meeting on HIV-AIDS was held in Namibia on 13-17 November and the meeting on gender and racism was held in Croatia from 21 to 24 November. The Division for the Advancement of Women will prepare and forward a report on the outcome of each expert group meeting to the Commission at its next session. Aide-memoire of the two expert groups meetings are available on DAW website.

51. In accordance with ECOSOC decision 2000/237, the DAW is tasked with the preparations of a proposed multi-year work programme to be submitted to the CSW to consider and adopt at its session in March. Towards this end, the Division has undertaken a number of activities:

    (a) brainstorming meetings with representatives of NGO's (September 18, 2000); delegates (September 21); and academicians (September 22);

    (b) review the statements Member States delivered at the Beijing + 5 special session, the Millenium Assembly, and the General Assembly third committee deliberations;

    (c) review the multi-year work programme of other relevant functional commissions;

    (d) identify relevant international years and conferences of the United Nations system.

Ten-year Review and Appraisal

Ten-year Review and Appraisal of the implementation of the Beijing Declaration and Platform for Action and the outcome of the twenty-third special session of the General Assembly held during the forty-ninth session of the CSW, from 28 February to 11 March 2005.

Background

In the Political Declaration adopted in by the United Nations General Assembly at its twenty-third special session in June 2000, Member States agreed to "assess regularly further implementation of the Beijing Platform for Action with a view to bringing together all parties involved in 2005 to assess progress and consider new initiatives, as appropriate, ten years after the adoption of the Beijing Platform for Action".

A review and appraisal of the implementation of the Beijing Declaration and Platform for Action adopted at the Fourth World Conference on Women (Beijing, 1995), and the outcome of the twenty-third special session of the General Assembly (2000), was mandated in the multi-year programme of work of the Commission on the Status of Women for its forty-ninth session in March 2005. The Commission considered two themes:

- "Review of the implementation of the Beijing Platform for Action and the outcome documents of the twenty-third special session of the General Assembly"; and
- "Current challenges and forward-looking strategies for the advancement and empowerment of women and girls"

The review and appraisal by the Commission focused on implementation at national level and identify achievements, gaps and challenges and provided an indication of areas where actions and initiatives, within the framework of the Platform for Action and the outcome of the special session (Beijing+5), are most urgent to further implementation.

15-year review of the implementation of the Beijing Declaration and Platform for Action (1995) and the outcomes of the twenty-third special session of the General Assembly (2000)

From 1-12 March 2010, the Commission on the Status of Women undertook a fifteen-year review of the implementation of the Beijing Declaration and Platform for Action and the outcomes of the twenty-third special session of the General Assembly. Emphasis was placed on the sharing of experiences and good practices, with a view to overcoming remaining obstacles and new challenges, including those related to the Millennium Development Goals. Member States, representatives of non-governmental organisations and of

UN entities participated in the session. A series of parallel events provided additional opportunities for information exchange and networking.

National and regional review processes fed into the global review process.

The General Assembly marked the 15th anniversary of the adoption of the Beijing Declaration and Platform for Action in a commemorative meeting during CSW.

7

UN for Women's Rights

The United Nations Entity for Gender Equality and the Empowerment of Women, also known as UN Women, is a United Nations entity working for the empowerment of women and girls.

UN Women became operational in January 2011. Former president of Chile Michelle Bachelet is the inaugural Executive Director. As with UNIFEM previously, UN Women is a member of the United Nations Development Group.

History

The provisions set forth by resolution 63/311 on system-wide coherence, adopted by the United Nations General Assembly on 2 October, 2010, constituted the blueprint for UN Women. Seeking to strengthen the United Nation's institutional arrangements for gender equality and women empowerment, resolution 63/311 supported the consolidation of four distinct parts of the UN system that focused exclusively on gender equality and women's empowerment into a composite entity to be led by an Under-Secretary-General. Moreover, the resolution requested that the Secretary-General of the United Nations produce a proposal specifying the mission statement of the composite entity and its organisational arrangements, including an organisational chart, funding and the executive board to oversee its operational activities.

In response to the UN General Assembly resolution 63/311, in January 2006 the Secretary-General presented the report A/64/588, entitled "Comprehensive Proposal for the Composite Entity for Gender Equality and the Empowerment of Women." In his report, the Secretary-General resolved that, rather than relieving other parts of the United Nations system of their responsibility for contributing to the promotion of gender equality and women's empowerment, the new entity should seek to sharpen the focus and impact of the gender equality activities of the entire United Nations system. Additionally, Secretary-General Ban Ki-moon estimated that approximately $125 million per annum were needed for operating costs and "start-up" capacity at the country, regional, and headquarters levels. Moreover, an additional $375 million per annum were needed in the initial phase to respond to country level requests for programmatic support.

After years of negotiations between UN Member States, women's groups and civil society, on 2 July 2010 the United Nations General Assembly unanimously adopted resolution 64/289, thus creating UN Women by merging the Division for the Advancement of Women (DAW); the International Research and Training Institute for the Advancement of Women (INSTRAW, established in 1976); the Office of the Special Adviser on Gender Issues Advancement of Women (OSAGI, established in 1997), and the United Nations Development Fund for Women (UNIFEM, established in 1976). Secretary-General Ban Ki-moon announced at the founding of the movement that he is "grateful to Member States for having taken this major step forward for the world's women and girls. UN Women will significantly boost UN efforts to promote gender equality, expand opportunity, and tackle discrimination around the globe."

On September 14, 2010, it was announced that former President of Chile Michelle Bachelet was appointed as head of UN Women. Various countries supported the creation of the body and welcomed Bachelet as chief. During General Debate at the opening of the 65th General Assembly of the United Nations, world leaders commended the creation of the body and its intention to "empower women," as well as welcoming Bachelet's position as the inaugural head.

Structure and functioning

Resolution 64/289 determined that the entity should be headed by an Under-Secretary-General, to be appointed by the Secretary-General in consultation with Member States, for a term of four years, with the possibility of renewal for one term.

The organisation is governed by a multi-tiered intergovernmental governance structure in charge of providing normative and operational policy guidance. The General Assembly, Economic and Social Council, and the Commission on the Status of Women (CSW) constitute the governance structure that sets forth the normative policy guiding principles of the Entity. The intergovernmental governance structure in charge of providing operational policy guidance to UN Women includes the General Assembly, the Economic and Social Council and the organisation's Executive Board. The latter consist of forty-one members, elected by the Economic and Social Council for a term of three years and distributed as follows:

- Ten from the Group of African States
- Ten from the Group of Asian States
- Four from the Group of Eastern European States
- Six from the Group of Latin American and Caribbean States
- Five from the Group of Western European and Other States
- Six from contributing countries. Four seats will be selected by and from the top ten largest providers of voluntary core contributions to UN Women. The remaining two seats will be allocated to two developing countries not members of the Development Assistance Committee of the Organisation for Economic Cooperation and Development (DAC/OECD). These two countries will be selected by the developing countries not members of the Development Assistance Committee among the top ten providers of voluntary core contributions to the entity.

The resources required to fund all normative processes are obtained from the Entity's regular budget and approved by the General Assembly, whereas the budget for service operational processes and activities at all levels are funded from voluntary contributions and approved by the Executive Board of UN Women.

Current executive board composition

The Executive Board, elected on 10 November 2010, consists of:

- Africa: Angola, Cape Verde, Congo, Côte d'Ivoire, Democratic Republic of the Congo (DRC), Ethiopia, Lesotho, Libya, Nigeria and Tanzania
- Asia: Bangladesh, China, India, Indonesia, Japan, Kazakhstan, Malaysia, Pakistan, Republic of Korea and Timor-Leste
- Eastern Europe: Estonia, Hungary, Russian Federation and Ukraine
- Latin America and the Caribbean: Argentina, Brazil, Dominican Republic, El Salvador, Grenada and Peru

- Western Europe: Denmark, France, Italy, Luxembourg and Sweden
- Contributing Countries: Mexico, Norway, Saudi Arabia, Spain, United Kingdom and United States

Mandate

The mandate and functions of UN Women consist of the consolidated mandates and functions of the Office of the Special Adviser on Gender Issues and Advancement of Women, the Division for the Advancement of Women, the United Nations Development Fund for Women and the International Research and Training Institute for the Advancement of Women. In addition to the aforementioned mandates, the entity must lead, coordinate and promote the accountability of the United Nations system in its work on gender equality and women empowerment. The goal of UN Women is to enhance, not replace, the efforts by other parts of the UN system such as UNICEF, UNDP, and UNFPA, all of which will continue to work for gender equality and women's empowerment in their areas of expertise."

In accordance with the provisions of resolution 64/289, UN Women will work within the framework of the Charter of the United Nations, the Beijing Declaration and Platform for Action – including its twelve critical areas of concern and the outcome of the twenty-third special session of the General Assembly –as well as other applicable United Nations instruments, standards and resolutions that address gender equality and the empowerment and advancement of women.

Goals

UN Women is empowered to:

- To support inter-governmental bodies, such as the Commission on the Status of Women, in their formulation of policies, global standards and norms.
- To help UN member states implement the above standards, standing ready to provide suitable technical and financial support to those countries that request it and to forge effective partnerships with civil society.
- To enable member states to hold the UN system accountable for its own commitments on gender equality, including regular monitoring of system-wide progress.

UN Women

In July 2010, the United Nations General Assembly created UN Women, the United Nations Entity for Gender Equality and the Empowerment of Women.

In doing so, UN Member States took a historic step in accelerating the Organisation's goals on gender equality and the empowerment of women.

The creation of UN Women came about as part of the UN reform agenda, bringing together resources and mandates for greater impact. It will merge and build on the important work of four previously distinct parts of the UN system which focus exclusively on gender equality and women's empowerment:

- Division for the Advancement of Women (DAW)
- International Research and Training Institute for the Advancement of Women (INSTRAW)
- Office of the Special Adviser on Gender Issues and Advancement of Women (OSAGI)
- United Nations Development Fund for Women (UNIFEM)

The main roles of UN Women are:

- To support inter-governmental bodies, such as the Commission on the Status of Women, in their formulation of policies, global standards and norms
- To help Member States to implement these standards, standing ready to provide suitable technical and financial support to those countries that request it and to forge effective partnerships with civil society.
- To hold the UN system accountable for its own commitments on gender equality, including regular monitoring of system-wide progress.

Meeting the Needs of the World's Women

Over many decades, the UN has made significant progress in advancing gender equality, including through landmark agreements such as the Beijing Declaration and Platform for Action and the Convention on the Elimination of All Forms of Discrimination Against Women (CEDAW).

Gender equality is not only a basic human right, but its achievement has enormous socio-economic ramifications. Empowering women fuels thriving economies, spurring productivity and growth.

Yet gender inequalities remain deeply entrenched in every society. Women lack access to decent work and face occupational segregation and gender wage gaps. They are too often denied access to basic education and health care. Women in all parts of the world suffer violence and discrimination. They are under-represented in political and economic decision-making processes.

For many years, the UN has faced serious challenges in its efforts to promote gender equality globally, including inadequate funding and no single recognised driver to direct UN activities on gender equality issues.

UN Women — which will be operational by January 2011 — has been created to address such challenges. It will be a dynamic and strong champion for women and girls, providing them with a powerful voice at the global, regional and local levels.

Grounded in the vision of equality enshrined in the UN Charter, UN Women will, among other issues, work for the:

- elimination of discrimination against women and girls
- empowerment of women
- achievement of equality between women and men as partners and beneficiaries of development, human rights, humanitarian action and peace and security.

United Nations Development Fund for Women

The United Nations Development Fund for Women, commonly known as UNIFEM (from the French "Fonds de développement des Nations unies pour la femme") was established in December 1976 originally as the Voluntary Fund for the United Nations Decade for Women in the International Women's Year. Its first director was Dr. Margaret Snyder, Ph.D. It provides financial and technical assistance to innovative programmes and strategies that promote women's human rights, political participation and economic security. Since 1976 it has supported women's empowerment and gender equality through its programme offices and links with women's organisations in the major regions of the world. Its work on gender responsive budgets began in 1996 in Southern Africa and has expanded to include East Africa, Southeast Asia, South Asia, Central America and the Andean region. It has worked to increase awareness throughout the UN system of gender responsive budgets as a tool to strengthen economic governance in all countries.

UNIFEM was part of the United Nations Development Group (UNDG). It's role in the UNDG is now taken over by its successor, UN Women.

HRH Princess Basma bin Talal of Jordan was appointed UNIFEM goodwill ambassador in 1996.

On January 26, 2006 UNIFEM nominated Nicole Kidman as its goodwill ambassador.

The current Executive Director of UNIFEM is Inés Alberdi.

In January 2011, Unifem was merged into UN Women, a composite entity of the UN, along with International Research and Training Institute for the Advancement of Women (INSTRAW), Office of the Special Adviser on Gender Issues (OSAGI), and Division for the Advancement of Women (DAW).

References

1. "Frequently Asked Questions". UN Women. 2010-09-14. http://www.unwomen.org/faq/. Retrieved 2011-03-11.
2. UNDG Members
3. "Resolution on 6/311 on system-wide coherence". United Nations General Assembly. 2010-11-09. http://www.un.org/ga/search/view_doc.asp?symbol=A/RES/63/311. Retrieved 2011-03-13.
4. "Report on the Secretary General: Comprehensive proposal for the composite entity for gender equality and the empowerment of women". United Nations. 2010-01-06. http://www.un.org/ga/search/view_doc.asp?symbol=A/64/588. Retrieved 2011-03-13.
5. "Welcome to UN Women ? UN Women". Unwomen.org. 2010-07-02. http://www.unwomen.org/. Retrieved 2010-09-15.
6. "Michelle Bachelet's Appointment to Head UN Women Widely Applauded", Inter Press Service.
7. "General Debate: 65th Session". Gadebate.un.org. 2010-09-29. http://www.un.org/en/ga/65/meetings/generaldebate/View/Sept24.aspx. Retrieved 2011-03-11.
8. The various speeches from all the world leader from 23-25 & 27-30 September 2010 are listed at http://gadebate.un.org/
9. "Resolution on 64/289 on system-wide coherence.". United Nations General Assembly. 22010-07-21. http://www.un.org/ga/search/view_doc.asp?symbol=A/RES/64/289. Retrieved 2011-03-13.
10. "Executive Board". UN Women. 2010-11-10. http://www.unwomen.org/about-us/governance/executive-board/. Retrieved 2011-03-13.
11. United Nations General Assembly Resolution 133 session 31 on 16 December 1976 (retrieved 2008-04-18) http://www.undg.org/

index.cfm?P=13 BBC (2006-01-26). "Kidman becomes ambassador for UN". BBC. http://news.bbc.co.uk/2/hi/entertainment/4649476.stm. Retrieved 2009-02-02.

12. UNIFEM (2008). "Inés Alberdi Appointed as UNIFEM Executive Director". http://www.unifem.org/news_events/story_detail.php?StoryID=668.

8

India's "National Commission for Women" and Other Initiatives Regarding Women's Rights

The National Commission for Women was set up as statutory body in January 1992 under the National Commission for Women Act, 1990 (Act No. 20 of 1990 of Govt.of India) to :

- review the Constitutional and Legal safeguards for women ;
- recommend remedial legislative measures ;
- facilitate redressal of grievances and
- advise the Government on all policy matters affecting women.

In keeping with its mandate, the Commission initiated various steps to improve the status of women and worked for their economic empowerment during the year under report. The Commission completed its visits to all the States/UTs except Lakshadweep and prepared Gender Profiles to assess the status of women and their empowerment. It received a large number of complaints and acted suo-moto in several cases to provide speedy justice. It took up the issue of child marriage, sponsored legal awareness programmes, Parivarik Mahila Lok Adalats and reviewed laws such as Dowry Prohibition Act, 1961, PNDT Act 1994, Indian Penal Code 1860 and the National Commission for Women Act, 1990 to make them more stringent and effective. It organised workshops/consultations, constituted expert committees on economic empowerment of women, conducted workshops/seminars for gender awareness and took up publicity campaigns against female foeticide, violence against women, etc. in order to generate awareness in the society against these social evils.

A Brief History

The National Commission for Women was set up as statutory body in January 1992 under the National Commission for Women Act, 1990 (Act No. 20 of 1990 of Govt.of India) to review the Constitutional and legal safeguards for women; recommend remedial legislative measures, facilitate redressal of grievances and advise the Government on all policy matters affecting women.

The Committee on the Status of Women in India (CSWI) recommended nearly two decades ago, the setting up of a National Commission for women to fulfill the surveillance functions to facilitate redressal of grievances and to accelerate the socio-economic development of women.

- Successive Committees / Commissions / Plans including the National Perspective Plan for Women (1988-2000) recommended the constitution of an apex body for women.
- During 1990, the central government held consultations with NGOs, social workers and experts, regarding the structure, functions, powers, etc. of the Commission proposed to be set up.
- In May 1990, the Bill was introduced in the Lok Sabha.
- In July 1990, the HRD Ministry organised a National Level Conference to elicit suggestions regarding the Bill. In August 1990 the government moved several amendments and introduced new provisions to vest the commission with the power of a civil court.
- The Bill was passed and received accent of the President on 30th August 1990.
- The First Commission was constituted on 31st January 1992 with Mrs. Jayanti Patnaik as the Chairperson. The Second Commission was constituted on July 1995 with Dr. (Mrs.) Mohini Giri as the Chairperson. The Third Commission was constituted on January 1999 with Mrs. Vibha Parthasarathy as the Chairperson. The Fourth Commission was constituted on January 2002 and the government had nominated Dr. Poornima Advani as the Chairperson. The Fifth Commission has been constituted on February 2005 and the government has nominated Dr. Girija Vyas as the Chairperson.

Constitution

Constitution of the Commission

Section 3

National Commission for Women Act, 1990

(Act No. 20 of 1990 of Govt. of India)

The Central Government shall constitute a body to be known as the National Commission for Women to exercise the powers conferred on and to perform the functions assigned to, it under this Act.

The Commission shall consist of :-

(a) A Chairperson, committed to the cause of women, to be nominated by the Central Government.

(b) five Members to be nominated by the Central Government from amongst persons of ability, integrity and standing who have had experience in law or legislation, trade unionism, management of an industry potential of women, womenâ€™s voluntary organisations (including women activist), administration, economic development, health, education or social welfare;

Provided that at least one Member each shall be from amongst persons belonging to the Scheduled Castes and Scheduled Tribes respectively;

(c) a Member-Secretary to be nominated by the Central Government who shall be :-

   (i) an expert in the field of management, organisational structure or sociological movement, or

   (ii) an officer who is a member of a civil service of the Union or of an all-India service or holds a civil post under the Union with appropriate experience

Mandate

The Mandate of the Commission

Section 10

National Commission for Women Act, 1990

(Act No. 20 of 1990 of Govt. of India)

1. The commission shall perform all or any of the following functions, namely :

   - Investigate and examine all matters relating to the

safeguards provided for women under the Constitution and other laws;

- present to the Central Government, annually and at such other times as the Commission may deem fit, reports upon the working of those safeguard;
- make in such reports recommendations for the effective implementation of those safeguards for improving the conditions of women by the Union or any state;
- review, from time to time, the exiting provisions of the Constitution and other laws affecting women and recommend amendments thereto so as to suggest remedial legislative measures to meet any lacunae, inadequacies or shortcomings in such legislations;
- take up cases of violation of the provisions of the Constitution and of other laws relating to women with the appropriate authorities;
- look into complaints and take suo moto notice of matters relating to:
  - (i) deprivation of women's rights;
  - (ii) non-implementation of laws enacted to provide protection to women and also to achieve the objective of equality and development;
  - (iii) non-compliance of policy decisions,guidelines or instructions aimed at mitigating hardships and ensuring welfare and providing relief to women, and take up the issues arising out of such matters with appropriate authorities;
- call for special studies or investigations into specific problems or situations arising out of discrimination and atrocities against women and identify the constraints so as to recommend strategies for their removal;
- undertake promotional and educational research so as to suggest ways of ensuring due representation of women in all spheres and identify factors responsible for impeding their advancement, such as, lack of access to housing and basic services, inadequate support services and technologies for reducing drudgery and occupational health hazards and for increasing their productivity;
- participate and advice on the planning process of socio-economic development of women;

- evaluate the progress of the development of women under the Union and any State;
- inspect or cause to inspected a jail, remand home,women's institution or other place of custody where women are kept as prisoners or otherwise and take up with the concerned authorities for remedial action, if found necessary;
- fund litigation involving issues affecting a large body of women;
- make periodical reports to the Government on any matter pertaining to women and in particular various difficulties under which women toil;
- any other matter which may be referred to it by Central Government.

2. The Central Government shall cause all the reports referred to in clause (b) of sub-section (1) to be laid before each House of Parliament along with memorandum explaining the action taken or proposed to be taken on the recommendations relating to the Union and the reasons for the non-acceptance, if any, of any such recommendations.
3. Where any such report or any part thereof relates to any matter with which any State Government is concerned, the Commission shall forward a copy of such report or part to such State Government who shall cause it to be laid before the Legislature of the State along with a memorandum explaining the action taken or proposed to be taken on the recommendations relating to the State and the reasons for the non-acceptance, if any, of any such recommendations.
4. The Commission shall, while investigating any matter referred to in clause (a) or sub-clause (i) of clause (f) of sub-section (1), have all the powers of a civil court trying a suit and, in particular in respect of the following matters, namely:
   (a) summoning and enforcing the attendance of any person from any part of India and examining him on oath;
   (b) requiring the discovery and production of any document;
   (c) receiving evidence on affidavits;
   (d) requisitioning any public record or copy thereof from any court or office;
   (e) issuing commissions for the examination of witnesses and documents; and
   (f) any other matter which may be prescribed.

National Commission for Women Act, 1990 (No. 20 of 1990)[1]

An Act to constitute a National Commission for Women and to provide for matters connected therewith or incidental thereto.

Be it enacted by Parliament in the Forty-first Year of the Republic of India as follows:-

CHAPTER I
PRELIMINARY

1. Short title, extent and commencement:

(1) This Act may be called the National Commission for Women Act, 1990.

(2) It extends to the whole of India except the State of Jammu and Kashmir.

(3) It shall come into force on such date as the Central Government may by notification in the Official Gazette, appoint.

2. Definitions[2]

In this Act, unless the context otherwise requires,-

(a) "Commission" means the National Commission for Women constituted under Section 3;

(b) "Member" means a Member of the Commission and includes the Member-Secretary;

(c) "prescribed" means prescribed by rules made under this Act.

CHAPTER II
THE NATIONAL COMMISSION FOR WOMEN[3]

3. Constitution of the National Commission for Women:

(1) The Central Government shall constitute a body to be known as the National Commission for Women to exercise the powers conferred on, and to perform the functions, assigned to it under this Act.

(2) The Commission shall consist of-

(a) a Chairperson, committed to the cause of women, to be nominated by the Central Government;

---

1. The Act received the assent of the President on 30.8.1990.
2. The Act came into force on 31.1.1992, vide Notification No. S.O. 99(E) dated 31.1.1992.
3. The National Commission for Women was constituted on 31.1.1992. vide Notification No. S.O. 100(E), dated 31.1.1992.

(b) five Members to be nominated by the Central Government from amongst persons of ability, integrity and standing who have had experience in law or legislation, trade unionism, management of an industry or organisation committed to increasing the employment potential of women, women's voluntary organisations (including women activists), administration, economic development, health, education or social welfare:

Provided that at least one Member each shall be from amongst persons belonging to the Scheduled Castes and Scheduled Tribes respectively;

(c) a Member-Secretary to be nominated by the Central Government, who shall be-

(i) an expert in the field of management, organisational structure or sociological movement, or

(ii) an officer who is member of a civil service of the Union or of an all-India service or holds a civil post under the Union with appropriate experience.

4. Term of office and conditions of service of Chairperson and members:

(1) The Chairperson and every Member shall hold office for such period, not exceeding three years, as may be specified by the Central Government in this behalf.

(2) The Chairperson or a Member (other than the Member-Secretary who is a member of a civil service of the Union or of an all-India service or holds a civil port under the Union) may, by writing and addressed to the Central Government, resign from the office of Chairperson or, as the case may be, of the Member at any time.

(3) The Central Government shall remove a person from the office of Chairperson or Member referred to in sub-section (2) if that person-

(a) becomes an undischarged insolvent;

(b) gets convicted and sentenced to imprisonment for an offence which in the opinion of the Central Government involves moral turpitude;

(c) becomes of unsound mind and stands so declared by a competent court;

(d) refuses to act or becomes incapable of acting;

(e) is, without obtaining leave of absence from the Commission, absent from three consecutive meetings of the Commission; or

(f) in the opinion of the Central Government has so abused the position of Chairperson or Member as to render that person's continuance in office detrimental to the public interest:

Provided that no person shall be removed under this clause until that person has been given a reasonable opportunity of being heard in the matter.

(4) A vacancy caused under sub-section (2) or otherwise shall be filled by fresh nomination.

(5) The salaries and allowances payable to, and the other terms and conditions of service of, the Chairperson and Members shall be such as may be prescribed.[4]

5. Officers and other employees of the Commission:

(1) The Central Government shall provide the Commission with such officers and employees as may be necessary for the efficient performance of the functions of the Commission under this Act.

(2) The salaries and allowances payable to, and the other terms and conditions of service of, the officers and other employees appointed for the purpose of the Commission shall be such as may be prescribed.

6. Salaries and allowances to be paid out of Grants: The salaries and allowances payable to the Chairperson and Members and the administrative expenses, including salaries, allowances and pensions payable to the officers and other employees referred to in Section 5, shall be paid out of the grants referred to in sub-section (1) of Section 11.

7. Vacancies, not to invalidate proceeding of the Commission: No act or proceeding of the Commission shall be questioned or shall be invalid on the ground merely of the existence of any vacancy of defect in the constitution of the Commission.

4. The National Commission for Women (Salaries and Allowances of Chairperson and Members) Rules 1992 [G.S.R. 74(E), dated 31.1.1992]

8. Committees of the Commission

(1) The Commission may appoint such committees as may be necessary for dealing with such special issues as may be taken up by the Commission from time to time.

(2) The Commission shall have the power to co-opt as members of any committee appointed under sub-section (1) such number of persons, who are not Members of the Commission, as it may think fit and the persons so co-opted shall have the right to attend the meetings of the committee and take part in its proceedings but shall not have the right to vote.

(3) The person so co-opted shall be entitled to receive such allowances for attending the me mugs of the Committee as may be prescribed.[5]

9. Procedure to be Regulated by the Commission:

(1) The Commission or a committee thereof shall meet as and when necessary and shall meet at such time and place as the Chairperson may think fit.

(2) The Commission shall regulate its own procedure of the committees thereof.

(3) All orders and decisions of the Commission shall be authenticated by the Member Secretary or any other officer of the Commission duly authorised by the Member-Secretary in this behalf.

CHAPTER III

10. Functions of the Commission:

(1) The Commission shall perform all or any of the following functions, namely:-

(a) investigate and examine all matters relating to the safeguards provided for women under the Constitution and other laws;

(b) present to the Central Government, annually and at such other time as the Commission may deem fit, reports upon the working of those safeguards;

(c) make in such reports recommendations for the effective implementation of those safeguards for

5. The National Commission for Women (Allowances Payable to Co-opted Members) Rules 1992 [G.S.R. 118(E), dated 21.2.1992]

improving the conditions of women by the Union or any State;

(d) review, from time to time, the existing provisions of the Constitution and other laws affecting women and recommend amendments thereto so as to suggest remedial legislating measures to meet any lacunae, inadequacies or shortcomings in such legislations;

(e) take up the cases of violation of the provisions or the Constitution and of other laws relating to women with the appropriate authorities;

(f) look into complaints and take suo motu notice of matters relating to-

(i) deprivation of women's rights;

(ii) non-implementation of laws enacted to provide protection to women and also to achieve the objective of equality and development.

(iii) non-compliance of policy decisions, guidelines or instructions aimed at mitigating hardships and ensuring welfare and providing relief to women, and take up the issues arising out of such matters with appropriate authorities;

(g) call for special studies or investigations into specific problems or situations arising out of discrimination and atrocities against women and identify the constraints so as to recommend strategies for their removal;

(h) undertake promotional and educational research so as to suggest ways of ensuring due representation of women in all spheres and identify factors responsible for impeding their advancement, such as, lack of access to housing and basic services, inadequate support services and technologies for reducing drudgery and occupational health hazards and for increasing their productivity;

(i) participate and advise on the planning process of socio-economic development of women;

(j) evaluate the progress of the development of women under the Union and any State;

(k) inspect or cause to be inspected a jail, remand home, women's institution or other place of custody where women are kept as prisoners or otherwise, and take up with the concerned authorities for remedial action, if found necessary;

(l) fund litigation involving issues affecting a large body of women;

(m) make periodical reports to the Government on any matter pertaining to women and in particular various difficulties under which women toil;

(n) any other matter which may be referred to it by the Central Government.

(2) The Central Government shall cause all the reports referred to in clause (b) of sub-section (1) to be laid before each House of Parliament along with a memorandum explaining the action taken or proposed to be taken on the recommendations relating to the Union and the reasons for the non-acceptance, if any, of any of such recommendations.

(3) Where any such report or any part thereof relates to any matter with which any State Government is concerned, the Commission shall forward a copy of such report or part of such State Government who shall cause it to be laid before the Legislature of the State along with a memorandum explaining the action taken or proposed to be taken on the recommendations relating to the State and the reasons for the non-acceptance, if any, of any of such recommendations.

(4) The Commission shall, while investigating any matter referred to in clause (a) or sub-clause (i) of clause (f) of sub-section (1), have all the powers of a civil court trying a suit and, in particular, in respect of the following matters, namely:-

(a) summoning and enforcing the attendance of any person from any part of India and examining him on oath;

(b) requiring the discovery and production of any document;

(c) receiving evidence on affidavits;

(d) requisitioning any public record or copy thereof from any Court or office;

(e) issuing commissions for the examination of witnesses and documents; and

(f) any other matter which may be prescribed.

CHAPTER IV
FINANCE, ACCOUNTS AND AUDIT

11. Grants by the Central Government:

(1) The Central Government shall, after due appropriation made by Parliament by law in his behalf, pay to the Commission by way of grants such sums of money as the Central Government may think fit for being utilised for the purposes of this Act.

(2) The Commission may spend such sums as it thinks fit for performing thre functions under this Act, and such sums shall be treated as expenditure payable out of the grants referred to in sub-section (1).

12. Accounts and Audit:

(1) The Commission shall maintain proper accounts and other relevant records and prepare an annual statement of accounts in such form as may be prescribed by the Central Government in consultation with the Comptroller and Auditor-General of India.

(2) The accounts of the Commission shall be audited by the Comptroller and Auditor-General at such intervals as may be specified by him and any expenditure incurred in connection with such audit shall be payable by the Commission to the Comptroller and Auditor-General.

(3) The Comptroller and Auditor-General and any person appointed by him in connection with the audit of the accounts of the Commission under this Act shall have the same rights and privileges and the authority in connection with such audit as the Comptroller and Auditor-General generally has in connection with the audit of Government accounts and, in particular, shall have the right to demand the production of books, accounts, connected vouchers and other documents and papers and to inspect any of the offices of the Commission.

13. Annual Report: The Commission shall prepare, in such form and at such time, for each financial year, as may be prescribed, its annual report, giving a full account of its activities during the previous financial year and forward a copy thereof to the Central Government.

14. Annual report and Audit report to be laid before Parliament: The Central Government shall cause the annual report together with a memorandum of action taken on the recommendations contained therein, in so far as they relate to the Central Government, and the reasons for the non-acceptance, if any, of any of such recommendations and the audit report to be laid as soon as may be after the reports are received, before each House of Parliament.

CHAPTER V
MISCELLANEOUS

15. **Chairperson, Members and staff of the Commission to be public servants:** The Chairperson, the Members, officers and other employees of the Commission shall be deemed to be public servants within the meaning of Section 21 of Indian Penal Code (45 of 1860).

16. **Central Government to consult Commission:** The Central Government shall consult the Commission in all major policy matters affecting women.

17. **Power to make rules:**

(1) The Central Government may, by notification in the Official Gazette, make rules for carrying out the provisions of this Act.

(2) In particular, and without prejudice to the generality of the foregoing power, such rules may provide for all or any of the following matters, namely:-

(a)salaries and allowances payable to, and the other terms and conditions of service of, the Chairperson and Members under sub-section (5) of Section 4 and of officers and other employees under sub-section (2) of Section 5;

(b) allowances for attending the meetings of the committee by the co-opted persons under sub-section (3) of Section 8;

(c) other matters under clause (f) of sub-section (4) of Section 10;

(d) the form in which the annual statement of accounts shall be maintained under sub-section (1) of Section 12;

(e) the form in, and the time at, which the annual report shall be prepared under Section 13;

(f) any other matter which is required to be, or may be, prescribed.

(3) Every rule made under this Act shall be laid, as soon as may be after it is made, before each House of Parliament, while it is in session, for a total period of thirty days which may be comprised in one session or in two or more successive sessions, and if, before the expiry of the session immediately following the session or the successive sessions aforesaid, both Houses agree in making any modification in the rule or both Houses agree that the rule should not be made, the rule shall thereafter have effect only in such modified form or be of no effect, as the case may be; so, however, that any such modification or annulment shall be without prejudice to the validity of anything previously done under that rule.

Women's Reservation Bill in India

Women's Reservation Bill or the The Constitution (108th Amendment) Bill, is a pending bill in India which proposes to provide thirty three per cent of all seats in the Lower house of Parliament of India the Lok Sabha and state legislative assemblies shall be reserved for women. The Upper House Rajya Sabha passed it on 9 Mar 2010[1].

The seats to be reserved in rotation will be determined by draw of lots in such a way that a seat shall be reserved only once in three consecutive general elections.

Women's Reservations

Women get 33 percent reservation in gram panchayat (meaning village assembly, which is a form of local village government) and municipal elections. There is a long-term plan to extend this reservation to parliament and legislative assemblies. In addition, women in India get reservation or preferential treatments in education and jobs. Men consider this preferential treatment of women in India as discrimination against them in admissions to schools, colleges, and universities. For instance, several law schools in India have a 30% reservation for females. Progressive political opinion in India is strongly in favour of providing preferential treatment to women in order to create a level playing field for all of its citizens.

Since,

- More women participate in politics and society.
- Social norms in India strongly favour men, therefore,

reservation for women is expected to create equal opportunity for men and women.

- Due to female foeticide, infantacide and issues related to women's health, sex ratio in India is alarming at 1.06 males per female. It is expected this will change the society to give equal status to women.
- Women are supposedly more resistant to corruption. Therefore, this bill might prove to be a factor restraining the growth of corruption.
- Women will get 33% reservation after this bill is passed and condition of women will improve.

All India Democratic Women's Association

In spite of equality guaranteed by the constitution, gender-just laws are still to be realised. Even within the existing laws, on issues directly linked to women's rights, the courts have been generally conservative. A series of judicial pronouncements by the Supreme Court and some High Courts have been particularly biased against the poor, as well as women. These objectionable and sweeping judgments have eroded the democratic rights of the people while negating previous progressive Acts such as the Prohibition of Child Marriage or Sati Prohibition Act. The bias is also evident in the highly patriarchal and insensitive comments against working women or the Uniform Civil Code.

Along with legal reforms what is required is the reform in the mentality of many of those sitting as dispensers of justice in the courts of justice. The law must be made gender-just along with being enforceable and the courts more accessible.

Memorandum on Proposed Amendments to Maternity Benefit Act

3 July 2007

To

The Chairperson,
and the Hon'ble Members,
Parliamentary Standing Committee on Labour,
New Delhi.

Subject: Submission on the proposed amendments to the Maternity Benefit Act by AIDWA

Dear Chairperson and members of the Committee,

This presentation regarding the proposed Amendment to the

Maternity Benefit Act (1961) is being submitted by the All India Democratic Women's Association (AIDWA). AIDWA is a national women's organisation with a membership of more than one crore women, of whom an overwhelming majority are working women, and a large number belong to the most oppressed, and deprived sections of society.

AIDWA believes that the issue of availability of maternity entitlements for women in India is a matter of deep concern, in a situation where most working women are not able to access what is their basic right. The huge majority of working women fall within the unorganised sector, and though the Act itself states that they too are entitled to maternity benefits, the reality is that most of these women are denied their rights. Indeed, in many cases, pregnancy (or even marriage in some cases) is a reason for depriving the poor woman of her job. Ironically, the situation gets aggravated by the presence of this protective legislation, which often serves to make women more vulnerable in the job market.

Hence one of the most important tasks of the Labour Ministry would be to make sure that the maternity entitlements of women reach them when they are most needed. Enhancing the entitlements should also be accompanied by measures to ensure that women don't become victims of this unjust practice of reducing women's employment which is engaged in by many employers to avoid their commitment on maternity benefits. Unfortunately, the legal provision for penalising the employers who resort to such tactics is observed more in the breach. This lacuna will have to be dealt with seriously.

In this context, an Amendment has been proposed by the Ministry of Labour regarding upgradation of the bonus amount payable by the employer, if no prenatal and post confinement care is provided to the working mother. This is welcome even if there is limited intervention on this issue. However, considering the escalation in the prices of all essentials in the past 50 years, the amount of increase envisaged is very meagre. AIDWA suggests that the amount should be increased to Rs. 5000/-, to provide some relief for the pregnant woman and the lactating mother. The payment of the amount should be done in 3 instalments – twice in the prenatal stage, and once in the post natal stage. This also assumes that the Janani Suraksha Yojana will be available at least at the time of delivery.

Secondly, the amendment has suggested that the amount of maternity bonus should be enhanceable by notification, as and when the need arises. This is acceptable. However, there is no need to prescribe an upper limit on the amount that would be payable as medical bonus.

Over and above these aspects, AIDWA would like to bring to the attention of the members the urgent need to expand the scope of maternity entitlements and improve their implementation. The Hon'ble members are no doubt aware that the recent National Family Health Survey outcomes show an unacceptable degree of malnutrition prevalent amongst women, and a very high MMR. One third of all women in this country are malnourished and over half of the women are anaemic. The corresponding figure for men is 28% indicating that even within poverty there is a definite female preponderance. Anaemia, a good index of the quality of nutrition in relation to women's nutritional needs is at 56.2%- over twice the corresponding level for men (24.3%). Children who are more vulnerable are much more affected. Over 45.9% of children are underweight and 79.2% are anaemic. And of these underweight children almost 38.4% are stunted – their growths affected by lack of nutrition – while 19.1% are wasted – literally starving. The MMR at 301 per lakh live births is also a damning indicator of the vulnerability of mothers.

Thus, it is a matter of concern that even the minimum provisions made by the State to protect working women during the time of pregnancy and child birth do not reach them.

The important issues that have to be addressed include

1. Safeguarding the job of working women while enhancing the maternity entitlement to an acceptable level.
2. Registration of women in the unorganised sector and creating a monitoring structure for maternity entitlements.
3. Extensive provision of crèche facilities for working women, and facilities for breastfeeding the child at the work site.
4. Providing adequate maternity leave with pay.

In marginal industries, and in the unorganised sector, the state can create a mechanism by which it can contribute to the provision of the above minimum set of maternity entitlements. At the same time, employers must not be allowed to abdicate from their primary responsibility on this score.

Hence, along with the present amendments that have been suggested to the Act, we request this Committee to undertake a larger review of maternity entitlements, addressing issues like broadening the scope of the Act, and improving access and implementation of this important legislation, so that many more working women can be benefited and the health rights of mother and child can be legally safeguarded.

Thanking You,

Yours faithfully,

Sudha Sundararaman
General Secretary

References

1. "Rajya Sabha passes Women's Reservation Bill". *The Times of India*. 9 March 2010. http://timesofindia.indiatimes.com/india/Rajya-Sabha-votes-on-Womens-Reservation-Bill/articleshow/5663003.cms.
2. Women are seeking 33% reservation in jobs, promotions.
3. Women's Bill: What's the fuss about? Rediff 24 August 2005.
4. The reservations business *Indian Express*, 11 August 1998.
5. Law schools set aside 30% quota for girls *Times of India*.

9

Women Against Sexual Harassment

PROTECTION OF WOMEN AGAINST SEXUAL HARASSMENT AT WORK PLACE BILL, 2010

The Bill lays down the definition of sexual harassment and seeks to provide a mechanism for redressing complaints. It provides for the constitution of an 'Internal Complaints Committee' at the work place and a 'Local Complaints Committee' at the district and block levels. A District Officer (District Collector or Deputy Collector), shall be responsible for facilitating and monitoring the activities under the Act.

Highlights of the Bill

- The Bill defines sexual harassment at the work place and creates a mechanism for redressal of complaints. It also provides safeguards against false or malicious charges.
- Every employer is required to constitute an Internal Complaints Committee at each office or branch with 10 or more employees. The District Officer is required to constitute a Local Complaints Committee at each district, and if required at the block level.
- The Complaints Committees have the powers of civil courts for gathering evidence.
- The Complaints Committees are required to provide for conciliation before initiating an inquiry, if requested by the complainant.
- Penalties have been prescribed for employers. Non-compliance with the provisions of the Act shall be punishable with a fine

of up to Rs 50,000. Repeated violations may lead to higher penalties and cancellation of licence or registration to conduct business.

Key Issues and Analysis

- There could be feasibility issues in establishing an Internal Complaints Committee at every branch or office with 10 or more employees.
- The Internal Complaints Committee has been given the powers of a civil court. However, it does not require members with a legal background nor are there any provisions for legal training.
- The Bill provides for action against the complainant in case of a false or malicious complaint. This could deter victims from filing complaints.
- Two different bodies are called 'Local Complaints Committee'. The Bill does not clearly demarcate the jurisdiction, composition and functions of these Committees.
- Cases of sexual harassment of domestic workers have been specifically excluded from the purview of the Bill.
- Unlike sexual harassment legislation in many other countries, this Bill does not provide protection to men.

THE PROTECTION OF WOMEN AGAINST SEXUAL HARASSMENT AT WORK PLACE BILL, 2010

Bill No. 144 of 2010

ARRANGEMENT OF CLAUSES

CHAPTER I

PRELIMINARY

CLAUSES

1. Short title, extent and commencement.
2. Definitions.
3. Prevention of sexual harassment.

CHAPTER II

CONSTITUTION OF INTERNAL COMPLAINTS COMMITTEE

4. Constitution of Internal Complaints Committee.

CHAPTER III
CONSTITUTION OF LOCAL COMPLAINTS COMMITTEE

5. Notification of District Officer.
6. Constitution and Jurisdiction of Local Complaints Committee.
7. Composition, tenure and other terms and conditions of Local Complaints Committee.
8. Grants and audit.

CHAPTER IV
COMPLAINT

9. Complaint of sexual harassment.
10. Conciliation.
11. Inquiry into complaint.

CHAPTER V
ENQUIRY INTO COMPLAINT

12. Action during pendency of inquiry.
13. Inquiry report.
14. Punishment for false or malicious complaint and false evidence.
15. Determination of compensation.
16. Prohibition of publication or making known contents of complaint and inquiry proceedings.
17. Penalty for publication or making known contents of complaint and inquiry proceedings.
18. Appeal.

CHAPTER VI
DUTIES OF EMPLOYER

CLAUSES

19. Duties of employer.

CHAPTER VII
DUTIES AND POWERS OF DISTRICT OFFICER

20. Duties and powers of District Officer.

CHAPTER VIII
MISCELLANEOUS

21. Committee to submit annual report.

THE PROTECTION OF WOMEN AGAINST SEXUAL HARASSMENT AT WORKPLACE BILL, 2010

A BILL

to provide protection against sexual harassment of women at workplace and for the prevention and redressal of complaints of sexual harassment and for matters connected therewith or incidental thereto.

WHEREAS sexual harassment results in violation of the fundamental rights of a woman to equality under articles 14 and 15 of the Constitution of India and her right to life and to live with dignity under article 21 of the Constitution and right to practice any profession or to carry on any occupation, trade or business which includes a right to a safe environment free from sexual harassment;

AND WHEREAS the protection against sexual harassment and the right to work with dignity are universally recognised human rights by international conventions and instruments such as Convention on the Elimination of all Forms of Discrimination against Women, which has been ratified on the 25th June, 1993 by the Government of India;

AND WHEREAS it is expedient to make provisions for giving effect to the said Convention for protection of women against sexual harassment at workplace;

TO BE INTRODUCED IN LOK SABHA

BE it enacted by Parliament in the Sixty-first Year of the Republic of India as follows:—

CHAPTER I

PRELIMINARY

Short title, extent and commencement.

1. (1) This Act may be called the Protection of Women against Sexual Harassment at Workplace Act, 2010.

   (2) It extends to the whole of India.

   (3) It shall come into force on such date as the Central Government may, by notification in the Official Gazette, appoint.

Definition

2. In this Act, unless the context otherwise requires,—

   (a) "aggrieved woman" in relation to a workplace means a woman, of any age, who alleges to have been subjected to any act of sexual harassment by the respondent and includes a woman whether employed or not;

   (b) "appropriate Government" means—

      (i) in relation to a workplace which is established, owned, controlled or wholly or substantially financed by funds provided directly or indirectly—

         (A) by the Central Government or the Union territory administration, the Central Government;

         (B) by the State Government

      (ii) in relation to any workplace not covered under sub-clause (i) and falling within its territory, the State Government;

   (c) "Chairperson" means the Chairperson of the Local Complaints Committee nominated under sub-section (1) of section 7;

   (d) "District Officer" means an officer notified under section 5;

   (e) "employee" means a person employed at a workplace for any work on regular, temporary, ad hoc or daily wage basis, either directly or through an agent, including a contractor, with or without the knowledge of the principal employer, whether for remuneration or not, or working on a voluntary basis or otherwise, whether the terms of employment are express or implied and includes a co-worker, a contract worker, probationer, trainee, apprentice or called by any other such name; but does not include domestic worker working at home;

(f) "employer" means—

(i) in relation to any department, organisation, undertaking, establishment, enterprise, institution, office, branch or unit of the appropriate Government or a local authority, the head of that department, organisation, undertaking, establishment, enterprise, institution, office, branch or unit or such other officer as the appropriate Government or the local authority, as the case may be, may by an order specify in this behalf;

(ii) in any workplace not covered under sub-clause (i), any person responsible for the management, supervision and control of the workplace;

(g) "Internal Committee" means an Internal Complaints Committee constituted under section 4;

(h) "Local Committee" means the Local Complaints Committee constituted under section 6;

(i) "Member" means a Member of the Internal Committee or the Local Committee, as the case may be;

(j) "prescribed" means prescribed by rules made under this Act;

(k) "Presiding Officer" means the Presiding Officer of the Internal Complaints Committee nominated under sub-section (2) of section 4;

(l) "respondent" means a person against whom the aggrieved woman has made a complaint under section 9;

(m) "sexual harassment" includes such unwelcome sexually determined behaviour (whether directly or by implication) as—

(i) physical contact and advances; or

(ii) a demand or request for sexual favours; or

(iii) sexually coloured remarks; or

(iv) showing pornography; or

(v) any other unwelcome physical, verbal or non-verbal

conduct of sexual nature;

(n) "workplace" includes—

(i) any department, organisation, undertaking, establishment, enterprise, institution, office, branch or unit which is established, owned, controlled or wholly or substantially financed by funds provided directly or indirectly by the appropriate Government or the local authority or a Government company or a corporation or a co-operative society;

(ii) any private sector organisation or a private venture, undertaking, enterprise, institution, establishment, society, trust, non-governmental organisation, unit or service provider carrying on commercial, professional, vocational, educational, entertainment, industrial, health services or financial activities including production, supply, sale, distribution or service;

(iii) hospitals or nursing homes;

(iv) any place visited either by air, land, rail or sea by the employee arising out of, or during and in the course of employment;

(o) "unorganised sector" in relation to a workplace means an enterprise owned by individuals or self employed workers and engaged in the production or sale of goods or providing service of any kind whatsoever, and where the enterprise employs workers, the number of such workers is less than ten.

Prevention of sexual harassment.

3. No woman shall be subjected to sexual harassment at any workplace which may include, but is not limited to—

(i) implied or overt promise of preferential treatment in her employment; or

(ii) implied or overt threat of detrimental treatment in her employment; or

(iii) implied or overt threat about her present or future employment status; or

(iv) conduct of any person which interferes with her work or creates an intimidating or offensive or hostile work environment for her; or

(v) humiliating conduct constituting health and safety problems for her.

CHAPTER II
CONSTITUTION OF INTERNAL COMPLAINTS COMMITTEE

Constitution of Internal Complaints Committee.

4. (1) Every employer of a work place shall, by an order in writing, constitute a Committee to be known as the "Internal Complaints Committee":

Provided that where the offices or administrative units of the workplace are located at different places or divisional or sub-divisional level, the Internal Committee shall be constituted at all administrative units or offices.

(2) The Internal Committee shall consist of the following members to be nominated by the employer, namely:—

(a) a Presiding Oficer who shall be woman employed at a senior level at workplace from amongst the employees:

Provided that in case a senior level woman employee is not available, the Presiding Officer shall be nominated from other offices or administrative units of the workplace referred to in sub-section (1):

Provided further that in case the other offices or administrative units of the workplace do not have a senior level woman employee, the District Officer notified under section 5 may nominate a member of the Local Complaints Committee in that area to act as the Presiding Officer;

(b) not less than two Members from amongst employees preferably committed to the cause of women or who have had experience in social work or have legal knowledge;

(c) one member from amongst non-governmental organisations or associations committed to the cause of women:

Provided that at least one-half of the total Members so nominated shall be women.

(3) The Presiding Officer and every Member of the Internal

Committee shall hold office for such period, not exceeding three years, from the date of their nomination as may be specified by the employer.

(4) The Presiding Officer and Members of the Committee shall be paid such fees or allowances for holding the proceedings of the Internal Committee by the employer as may be prescribed.

(5) Where the Presiding Officer or any Member of the Internal Committee,—

(a) contravenes the provisions of Section 16; or

(b) is adjudged an insolvent; or

(c) engages during his term of office in any paid employment outside the duties of his office; or

(d) is unfit to continue in office by reason of infirmity of mind or body; or

(e) is of unsound mind and stands so declared by a competent court; or

(f) is convicted and sentenced to imprisonment for an offence which in the opinion of the Central Government involves moral turpitude; or

(g) has so abused his position as to render his continuance in office prejudicial to the public interest, such Presiding Officer or Member, as the case may be, shall be removed from the Committee and the vacancy so created or any casual vacancy shall be filled by fresh nomination in accordance with the provisions of this section.

CHAPTER III

CONSTITUTION OF LOCAL COMPLAINTS COMMITTEE

Notification of District Officer.

5. The appropriate Government may notify a District Magistrate or Additional District Magistrate or the Collector or Deputy Collector as a District Officer for every District to exercise powers or discharge functions under this Act.

Constitution and jurisdiction of Local Complaints Committee.

6. (1) Every District Officer shall constitute in the district concerned, a committee to be known as the "Local Complaints Committee".

(2) Where constitution of the Internal Committee at a

workplace is not feasible on account of less than ten persons being employed at such workplace or where the complaint is against the employer himself, the District Officer shall, constitute at every concerned block, taluka or tehsil in rural or tribal area and ward or municipality in urban area, additional Local Committee also to be known as the "Local Complaints Committee" for that area concerned.

(3) The jurisdiction of the Local Committee shall extend to the area within the district, or block, taluka or tehsil or ward or municipality level where it is constituted.

Composition, Tenure and Other Terms and Conditions of Local Complaints Committee

7. (1) The Local Complaints Committee shall consist of the following members to be nominated by the District Officer, namely:—

(a) a Chairperson to be nominated from amongst the eminent women in the field of social work and committed to the cause of women;

(b) one Member to be nominated from amongst the women working in block, taluka or tehsil or ward or municipality in the district;

(c) two Members, of whom at least one shall be a woman, to be nominated from amongst such non-governmental organisations or associations committed to the cause of women, which may be prescribed:

Provided that at least one of the nominees should, preferably, have a background in law or legal knowledge;

(d) the Protection Officer appointed under sub-section (1) of section 8 of the Protection of Women from Domestic Violence Act, 2005 in the District, in which block, taluka or tehsil in rural or tribal area or ward or municipality in urban area, the Local Committee is constituted:

Provided that at least one-half of the total Members so nominated shall be women.

(2) The Chairperson and every Member of the Local Committee shall hold office for such period, not

exceeding three years, from the date of their appointment as may be prescribed.

(3) Where the Chairperson or any Member of the Local Committee contravenes the provisions of Section 16, such Chairperson or Member, as the case may be, shall be removed from the Local Committee and the vacancy so created or any casual vacancy shall be filled by fresh nomination in accordance with the provisions of this section.

(4) The Chairperson and Members of the Local Committee shall be entitled to such fees or allowances for holding the proceedings of the Local Committee as may be prescribed.

Grants and Audit

8. (1) The Central Government may, after due appropriation made by Parliament by law in this behalf, make to the State Government grants of such sums of money as the Central Government may think fit, for being utilised for the payment of fees or allowances referred to in sub-section (4) of section 7.

(2) The State Government may set up an agency and transfer the grants made under sub-section (1) to that agency.

(3) The agency shall pay to the District Officer, such sums as may be required for the payment of fees or allowances referred to in sub-section (4) of section 7.

(4) The accounts of the agency referred to in sub-section (2) shall be maintained and audited in such manner as may, in consultation with the Accountant General of the State, be prescribed and the person holding the custody of the accounts of the agency shall furnish, to the State Government, before such date, as may be prescribed, its audited copy of accounts together with auditors' report thereon.

CHAPTER IV

COMPLAINT

Complaint of sexual harassment.

9. (1) Any aggrieved woman may make, in writing, a complaint of sexual harassment at workplace to the Internal Committee if so constituted, or the Local Committee, in case it is not so constituted:

Provided that where such complaint cannot be made in writing, the Presiding Officer or any Member of the Internal Committee or the Chairperson or any Member of the Local Committee, as the case may be, shall render all reasonable assistance to the woman for making the complaint in writing.

(2) Where the aggrieved woman is unable to make a complaint on account of her physical or mental incapacity or death or otherwise, her legal heir or such other person as may be prescribed may make a complaint under this section.

Conciliation.

10. (1) The Internal Committee or, as the case may be, the Local Committee, may, before initiating inquiry under Section 11 and at the request of the aggrieved woman take steps to settle the matter between her and the respondent through conciliation.

(2) Where a settlement has been arrived at under sub-section (1), the Internal Committee or the Local Committee, as the case may be, shall record the settlement so arrived and forward the same to the employer or the District Officer to take action as specified in the recommendation.

(3) The Internal Committee or the Local Committee, as the case may be, shall provide the copies of the settlement as recorded under sub-section (2) to the aggrieved woman and the respondent.

(4) Where a settlement is arrived at under sub-section (1), no further inquiry shall be conducted by the Internal Committee or the Local Committee, as the case may be.

Inquiry into complaint.

11. (1) Subject to the provisions of section 10 and section 16, the Internal Committee or the Local Committee, as the case may be, shall proceed to make inquiry into the complaint in such manner as may be prescribed:

Provided that where the aggrieved woman informs the Internal Committee or the Local Committee, as the case may be, that any term or condition of the settlement arrived at under sub-section (2) of section 10 has not been complied with by the respondent, the Internal Committee or the Local Committee shall proceed to make an inquiry into the complaint.

5 of 1908.

(2) For the purpose of making inquiry under sub-section (1), the Internal Committee or the Local Committee, as the case may be, shall have the same powers as are vested in a civil court under the Code of Civil Procedure, 1908 when trying a suit in respect of the following matters, namely:

(a) summoning and enforcing the attendance of any person and examining him on oath;

(b) requiring the discovery and production of documents; and

(c) any other matter which may be prescribed.

(3) The inquiry under sub-section (1) shall be completed within a period of ninety days.

CHAPTER V

INQUIRY INTO COMPLAINT

Action during pendency of inquiry.

12. (1) During the pendency of inquiry, on a written request made by the aggrieved woman, the Internal Committee or the Local Committee, as the case may be, may recommend to the employer to:

(a) transfer the aggrieved woman or the respondent to any other workplace; or

(b) grant leave to the aggrieved woman; or

(c) grant such other relief to the aggrieved woman as may be prescribed.

(2) The leave granted to the aggrieved woman under this section shall be in addition to the leave she would be entitled to otherwise if the case is proved.

(3) On the recommendation of the Internal Committee or the Local Committee, as the case may be, under sub-section (1), the employer shall implement the recommendations made under sub-section (1) and send the report of such implementation to the Internal Committee or the Local Committee, as the case may be.

Inquiry report.

13. (1) On the completion of an inquiry under this Act, the Internal Committee or the Local Committee, as the case may be, shall provide a report of its findings to the employer, or as the case may be, the District Officer and such report be made available to the concerned parties.

(2) Where the Internal Committee or the Local Committee, as the case may be, arrives at the conclusion that the allegation against the respondent has not been proved, it shall recommend to the employer and the District Officer that no action is required to be taken in the matter.

(3) Where the Internal Committee or the Local Committee, as the case may be, arrives at the conclusion that the allegation against the respondent has been proved, it shall recommend to the employer or the District Officer, as the case may be:

(i) to take action for sexual harassment as a misconduct in accordance with the provisions of the service rules applicable to the respondent or where no such service rules have been made, in such manner as may be prescribed;

(ii) to deduct, notwithstanding anything in the service rules applicable to the respondent, from the salary or wages of the respondent such sum of compensation to be paid to the aggrieved woman or to legal heirs, as it may determine, in accordance with the provisions of section 15:

Provided that in case the employer is unable to make such deduction from the salary of the respondent due to his being absent from duty or cessation of employment it may direct to the respondent to pay such compensation to the aggrieved woman.

(4) The employer or the District Officer shall act upon the recommendation within sixty days of its receipt by him.

Punishment for false or malicious complaint and false evidence.

14. (1) Where the Internal Committee or the Local Committee, as the case may be, arrives at a conclusion that the

allegation against the respondent is false or malicious or the aggrieved woman or any other person making the complaint has produced any forged or misleading document, it may recommend to the employer or the District Officer, as the case may be, to take action against the woman or the person who has made the complaint under sub-section (1) or sub-section (2) of section 9, as the case may be, in accordance with the provisions of the service rules applicable to her or him or where no such service rules exist, in such manner as may be prescribed:

Provided that a mere inability to substantiate a complaint or provide adequate proof need not attract action against the complainant under this section:

Provided further that the malicious intent or falsehood on part of the complainant shall be established after an inquiry in accordance with the procedure prescribed, before any action is recommended.

(2) Where the Internal Committee or the Local Committee, as the case may be, arrives at a conclusion that during the inquiry any witness has given false evidence or produced any forged or misleading document, it may recommend to the employer of the witness or the District Officer, as the case may be to take action in accordance with the provisions of the service rules applicable to the said witness or where no such service rules exist, in such manner as may be prescribed.

Determination of compensation.

15. For the purpose of determining the compensation to be paid to the aggrieved woman under clause (ii) of sub-section (3) of section 13, the Internal Committee or the Local Committee, as the case may be, shall have regard to:

(a) the mental trauma, pain, suffering and emotional distress caused to the aggrieved woman;

(b) the loss in the career opportunity due to the incident of sexual harassment;

(c) medical expenses incurred by the victim for physical or psychiatric treatment;

(d) the income and financial status of the respondent;

(e) feasibility of such payment in lump sum or in instalments.

Prohibition of publication or making known contents of complaint and inquiry proceedings.

22 of 2005.

16. Notwithstanding anything contained in the Right to Information Act, 2005, the contents of the complaint made under section 9, the identity and addresses of the aggrieved woman, respondent and witnesses, any information relating to conciliation and inquiry proceedings, recommendations of the Internal Committee or the Local Committee, as the case may be, and the action taken by the employer or the District Officer under the provisions of this Act shall not be published, communicated or made known to the public, press and media in any manner:

Provided that information may be disseminated regarding the justice secured to any victim of sexual harassment under this Act without disclosing the name, address, identity or any other particulars calculated to lead to the identification of the aggrieved woman and witnesses.

Penalty for publication or making known contents of complaint and inquiry proceedings.

17. Where any person entrusted with the duty to handle or deal with the complaint, inquiry or any recommendations or action to be taken under the provisions of this Act, contraveness the provisions of section 16, he shall be liable for penalty in accordance with the provisions of the service rules applicable to the said person or where no such service rules exist, in such manner as may be prescribed.

Appeal.

18. (1) Any person aggrieved from the recommendations made under sub-section (2) of section 13 or under clause (i) or clause (ii) of sub-section (3) of section 13 or subsection (1) or sub-section (2) of section 14 or section 17 or non-implementation of such recommendations may prefer an appeal to the court or tribunal in accordance with the provisions of the service rules applicable to the said person or where no such service rules exist then, without prejudice to provisions contained in any other law for the time being in force, the person aggrieved

may prefer an appeal in such manner as may be prescribed.

(2) The appeal under sub-section (1) shall be preferred within a period of thirty days of the recommendations.

CHAPTER VI
DUTIES OF EMPLOYER

Duties of employer.

19. Every employer shall—

(a) provide a safe working environment at the workplace which shall include safety from the persons coming into contact at the workplace;

(b) display at any conspicuous place in the workplace, the order constituting, the Internal Committee under sub-section (1) of section 4;

(c) undertake workshops and training programmes at regular intervals for sensitising the employees regarding the provisions of this Act;

(d) provide necessary facilities to the Internal Committee or the Local Committee, as the case may be, for dealing with the complaint and conducting inquiry;

(e) assist in securing the attendance of respondent and witnesses before the Internal Committee or the Local Committee, as the case may be;

(f) make available such information to the Internal Committee or the Local Committee, as the case may be, as it may require having regard to the complaint made under sub-section (1) of section 9;

(g) provide assistance to the woman if she so chooses to file a complaint in relation to the offence under the Indian Penal Code or any other law for the time being in force;

45 of 1860.

(h) initiate action, under the Indian Penal Code or any other law for the time being in force, against the perpetrator after the conclusion of the inquiry, or without waiting for the inquiry, where the perpetrator is not an employee in the workplace at which the incident of sexual harassment took place.

CHAPTER VII

DUTIES AND POWERS OF DISTRICT OFFICER

Duties and power of District Officer.

20. The District Officer shall,—

(a) monitor the timely submission of reports furnished by the Internal Committee or the Local Committee;

(b) take such measures as may be necessary for engaging non-governmental organisations for creation of awareness on sexual harassment and the rights of the women.

CHAPTER VIII

MISCELLANEOUS

Committee to submit annual report.

21. (1) The Internal Committee or the Local Committee, as the case may be, shall in each calendar year prepare, in such form and at such time as may be prescribed, an annual report and submit the same to the employer and the District Officer.

(2) The District Officer shall forward a brief report on the annual reports received under sub-section (1) to the State Government.

Employer to include information in annual report.

22. The employer shall include in its report the number of cases filed, if any, and their disposal under this Act in the annual report of his organisation or where no such report is required to be prepared, intimate such number of cases, if any, to the District Officer.

Appropriate Government to monitor implementation and maintain data.

23. The appropriate Government shall monitor the implementation of this Act and maintain data on the number of cases filed and disposed of in respect of all cases of sexual harassment at workplace.

Power to call for information and inspection of records.

24. (1) The appropriate Government, on being satisfied that it is necessary in the public interest or in the interest of women employees at a workplace to do so, by order in writing:

(a) call upon the employer or District Officer to furnish in writing such information relating to sexual harassment as it may require;

(b) authorise any officer to make inspection of the records and workplace in relation to sexual harassment, who shall submit a report of such inspection to it within such period as may be specified in the order.

(2) Every employer and District Officer shall produce on demand before the officer making the inspection all information, records and other documents in his custody having a bearing on the subject matter of such inspection.

4. (1) Every employer of a work place shall, by an order in writing, constitute a Committee to be known as the "Internal Complaints Committee":

Penalty for Noncompliance with Provisions of Act.

25. (1) Where the employer fails to—

(a) constitute an Internal Committee under sub-section (1) of section 4;

(b) take action under sections 13, 14 and 22; and

(c) contravenes or attempts to contravene or abets contravention of other provisions of this Act or any rules made thereunder, he shall be punishable with fine which may extend to fifty thousand rupees.

(2) If any employer, after having been previously convicted of an offence punishable under this Act subsequently commits and is convicted of the same offence, he shall be liable to:

(i) twice the punishment, which might have been imposed on a first conviction, subject to the punishment being maximum provided for the same offence:

Provided that in case a higher punishment is prescribed under any other law for the time being in force, for the offence for which the accused is being prosecuted, the court shall take due cognizance of the same while awarding the punishment.

(ii) cancellation, of his licence or withdrawal, or non-renewal, or approval, or cancellation of the registration, as the case may be, by the Government or local authority required for carrying on his business or activity.

Cognizance of offence by courts.

26. (1) No court shall take cognizance of any offence punishable under this Act or any rules made thereunder, save on a complaint made by the aggrieved woman or any person authorised by the Internal Committee or Local Committee in this behalf.

(2) No court inferior to that of a Metropolitan Magistrate or a Judicial Magistrate of the first class shall try any offence punishable under this Act.

(3) Every offence under this Act shall be non-cognizable.

Act not in derogation of any other law.

27. The provisions of this Act shall be in addition to and not in derogation of the provisions of any other law for the time being in force.

Power of the appropriate Government to make rules.

28. (1) The Central Government may, by notification in the Official Gazette, make rules for carrying out the provisions of this Act.

(2) In particular and without prejudice to the generality of the foregoing power, such rules may provide for all or any of the following matters, namely:

(a) the fees or allowances to be paid to the Presiding Officer and Members under sub-section (4) of section 4;

(b) the fees or allowances to be paid to the Chairperson, and Members under sub-section (4) of section 7;

(c) the person who may make complaint under sub-section (2) of section 9;

(d) the manner of inquiry under sub-section (1) of section 11;

(e) the powers for making inquiry under clause (c) of sub-section (2) of section 11;

(f) the relief to be recommended under clause (c) of sub-section (1) of section 12;

(g) the manner of action to be taken under clause (i) of sub-section (3) of section 13;

(h) the manner of action to be taken under sub-sections (1) and (2) of section 14;

(i) the manner of action to be taken under section 17;

(j) the manner of appeal under sub-section (1) of section 18; and

(k) the form and time for preparation of annual report by Internal Committee and the Local Committee under sub-section (1) of section 21.

(3) Every rule made by the Central Government under this Act shall be laid as soon as may be after it is made, before each House of Parliament, while it is in session, for a total period of thirty days which may be comprised in one session or in two or more successive sessions, and if, before the expiry of the session immediately following the session or the successive sessions aforesaid, both Houses agree in making any modification in the rule or both Houses agree that the rule should not be made, the rule shall thereafter have effect only in such modified form or be of no effect, as the case may be; so, however, that any such modification or annulment shall be without prejudice to the validity of anything previously done under that rule.

(4) Any rule made under sub-section (4) of section 8 by the State Government shall be laid, as soon as may be after it is made, before each House of the State Legislature where it consists of two Houses, or where such Legislature consists of one House, before that House.

Power to remove difficulties.

29. (1) If any difficulty arises in giving effect to the provisions of this Act, the Central Government may, by order published in the Official Gazette, make such provisions, not inconsistent with the provisions of this Act, as may appear to it to be necessary for removing the difficulty:

Provided that no such order shall be made under this section after the expiry of a period of two years from the commencement of this Act.

(2) Every order made under this section shall be laid, as soon as may be after it is made, before each House of Parliament.

STATEMENT OF OBJECTS AND REASONS

1. Sexual harassment at a workplace is considered violation of women's right to equality, life and liberty. It creates an insecure and hostile work environment, which discourages women's participation in work, thereby adversely affecting their social and economic empowerment and the goal of inclusive growth.

2. The Constitution of India embodies the concept of equality under articles 14 and 15 and prohibits discrimination on grounds of religion, race, caste, sex or place of birth or any of them. Article 19(1)(g) gives the fundamental right to all citizens to practise any profession, or to carry on any occupation, trade or business. This right pre-supposes the availability of an enabling environment for women, which is equitous, safe and secure in every aspect. Article 21, which relates to the right to life and personal liberty, includes the right to live with dignity, and in the case of women, it means that they must be treated with due respect, decency and dignity at the workplace.

3. Article 11 of the Convention on Elimination of All Forms of Discrimination (CEDAW), to which India is a party, requires State parties to take all appropriate measures to eliminate discrimination against women in the field of employment. In its General Recommendation No. 19 (1992), the United Nations Committee on CEDAW further clarified that equality in employment can be seriously impaired when women are subjected to gender-specific violence, such as sexual harassment at the workplace. India's commitment to protection and promotion of women's constitutional rights as well as respect for its obligations under various international treaties is unequivocal.

4. With more and more women joining the workforce, both in organised and unorganised sectors, ensuring an enabling working environment for women through legislation is felt imperative by the Government. The proposed legislation contains provisions to protect every woman from any act of sexual harassment irrespective of whether such woman is employed or not.

5. The Supreme Court of India in the case of Vishaka & Ors. v. State of Rajasthan & Ors. [1997 (7) SCC 323], also reaffirmed that sexual harassment at workplace is a form of

discrimination against women and recognised that it violates the constitutional right to equality and provided guidelines to address this issue pending the enactment of a suitable legislation.

6. It is, thus, proposed to enact a comprehensive legislation to provide for safe, secure and enabling environment to every woman, irrespective of her age or employment status (other than domestic worker working at home), free from all forms of sexual harassment by fixing the responsibility on the employer as well as the District Magistrate or Additional District Magistrate or the Collector or Deputy Collector of every District in the State as a District Officer and laying down a statutory redressal mechanism.
7. The notes on clauses explain in detail the various provisions contained in the Bill.
8. The Bill seeks to achieve the above objectives.

NEW DELHI; KRISHNA TIRATH
The 18th November, 2010.

PRESIDENT'S RECOMMENDATION UNDER ARTICLE 117 OF THE CONSTITUTION OF INDIA

[Copy of letter dated 24 November, 2010 from Smt. Krishna Tirath, Minister of State for Women and Child Devclopment to the Secretary-General, Lok Sabha] The President, having been informed of the subject matter of the Protection of Women against Sexual Harassment at Workplace Bill, 2010, recommends the introduction and consideration of the Bill in Lok Sabha under article 117(1) and (3) of the Constitution.

Notes on Clauses

Clause 2 : This clause provides for definitions. It defines the various expressions used in the proposed legislation which, inter alia, include the expressions "aggrieved woman", "appropriate Government", "Chairperson", "District Officer", "employee", "employer", "Internal Committee", "Local Committee", "respondent", "sexual harassment", "workplace" and "unorganised sector."

Clause 3 : This clause makes provision for prevention of sexual harassment. It provides that no woman shall be subjected to sexual harassment at any workplace. The harassment may include, but is not limited to—(i) implied or overt promise of preferential treatment in her employment; or (ii) implied or overt threat of detrimental treatment in her employment; or (iii) implied or overt threat about her present or future employment status; (iv) conduct of any person which interferes with her work or creates an intimidating or offensive or hostile work environment for her; or (v) humiliating conduct constituting health and safety problems for her.

Clause 4 : This clause provides for the constitution of Internal Complaints Committee. It provides that every employer of a workplace shall constitute, by an order in writing, a Committee to be known as the "Internal Complaints Committee". It further provides that where the offices or administrative units of the workplace are located at different places or divisional or sub-divisional level, the Internal Committee shall be constituted at all administrative units or offices.

It also provides that employer shall nominate members of the Internal Committee which shall consist of—(a) a Presiding Officer who shall be a woman employed at a senior level at workplace from amongst the employees; (b) not less than two Members from amongst employees preferably committed to the cause of women or who have had experience in social work or have legal knowledge and (c) one member from amongst non-governmental organisations or associations committed to the cause of women. Out of these members at least one-half shall be nominated from amongst women.

It also provides that the term of the Presiding Officer and every Member of the Internal Committee shall be specified by the employer which shall not exceed three years from the date of their nomination and their fees or allowances for holding the proceedings of the Internal Committee, as may be prescribed by rules made in this behalf, shall be paid by the employer.

It also provides that in case a senior level woman employee is not available at a work place, the Presiding Officer shall be nominated from other offices or administrative units of the workplace. It further Provides that in case the other offices or administrative units of the workplace do not have a senior level woman employee, the District Officer may nominate a member of the Local Complaints Committee in that area to act as the Presiding Officer.

It also provides that the Presiding Officer or any Member of the Internal Committee shall be removed from the Committee, if he—(a) contravenes the provisions of section 16 relating to prohibition of publication or making known contents of complaint and enquiry proceedings; or (b) is adjudged an insolvent; or (c) engages during his term of office in any paid employment outside the duties of his office; or (d) is unfit to continue in office by reason of infirmity of mind or body; or (e) is of unsound mind and stands so declared by a competent court; or (f) is convicted and sentenced to imprisonment for an offence which in the opinion of the Central Government involves moral turpitude; or (g) has so abused his position as to render his continuance in office prejudicial to the public interest, and the vacancy so created or any casual vacancy shall be filled by fresh nomination in accordance with the provisions of this clause.

Clause 5 : This clause provides for notification of the District Officer. It provides that the appropriate Government may notify a District Magistrate or Additional District Magistrate or the Collector or Deputy Collector as a District Officer for every District to exercise powers or discharge functions under the proposed legislation.

Clause 6 : This clause provides for constitution and jurisdiction of the Local Complaints Committee. It provides that every District Officer shall constitute in the district concerned, a committee to be known as the "Local Complaints Committee".

It further provides that where constitution of the Internal Committee at a workplace is not feasible on account of less than ten persons being employed at such work place or where the complaint is against the employer himself, the District Officer shall, constitute at every concerned block, taluka or tehsil in rural or tribal area and ward or municipality in urban area, additional Local Committee which shall also be known as the "Local Complaints Committee" for that area concerned.

It also provides that the jurisdiction of the Local Committee shall extend to the area within the district, or block, taluka or tehsil or ward or municipality level where it is constituted.

Clause 7 : This clause provides for composition, tenure and other terms and conditions of Local Complaints Committee. It provides that the members of Local Complaints Committee shall be nominated by the District Officer which shall consist of —(a) a Chairperson to be nominated from amongst the eminent women in the field of social work and committed to the cause of women; (b) one Member to be nominated from amongst the women working in block, taluka or tehsil or ward or municipality in the district;

(c) two Members, of whom at least one shall be a woman, to be nominated from amongst such non-governmental organisations or associations committed to the cause of women, which may be prescribed provided that one of the nominees should, preferably, have background in law or legal knowledge; and (d) the Protection Officer appointed under sub-section (1) of section 8 of the Protection of Women from Domestic Violence Act, 2005 in the District, in which block, taluka or tehsil in rural or tribal area or ward or municipality in urban area, the Local Committee is constituted. At least one-half of the total Members so nominated shall be women.

It further provides that the Chairperson and every Member of the Local Committee shall hold office for such period as may be specified by rules which shall not exceed three years from the date of their appointment.

It also provides that the Chairperson or any Member of the Local Committee shall be removed from the Local Committee if he contravenes the provisions of clause 16 relating to prohibition of publication or making known contents of complaint and enquiry proceedings and the vacancy so created or any casual vacancy shall be filled by fresh nomination in accordance with the provisions of this clause. The Chairperson and Members of the Local Committee shall be entitled to such fees or allowances for holding the proceeding of the Local Committee as may be prescribed by rules.

Clause 8 : This clause provides for grants and audit. It provides that the Central Government may, after due appropriation made by Parliament by law in this behalf, make to the State Government grants of such sums of money as the Central Government may think fit, for being utilised for the payment of fees or allowances of the Chairperson and Members of the Local Committee.

It also empowers the State Government to set up an agency and transfer the grants made under sub-clause (1) to that agency and the agency shall pay to the District Officer, such sums as may be required for the payment of fees or allowances of the Chairperson and Members of the Local Committee.

It also provides that the accounts of the agency shall be maintained and audited in such manner as may be prescribed by rules in consultation with the Accountant General of the State and the person holding the custody of the accounts of the agency shall furnish its audited copy of accounts together with auditors report thereon to the State Government before such date as may be specified by rules.

Clause 9 : This clause provides for making of complaint of sexual harassment. It provides that any aggrieved woman may, at her option, make in writing a complaint of sexual harassment at workplace to the Internal Committee if so constituted, or the Local Committee if an internal committee is not constituted or if the complaint is against the employer himself. It further provides that in a case where such complaint cannot be made in writing, the Presiding Officer or any Member of the Internal Committee or the Chairperson or any Member of the Local Committee, as the case may be, shall provide all reasonable assistance to the woman for making the complaint in writing.

It also provides that in a case where the aggrieved woman is unable to make a complaint on account of her physical or mental incapacity or death or otherwise, her legal heir or such other person as may be prescribed may make a complaint under this clause.

Clause 10 : This clause makes provision for conciliation. It provides that before initiating enquiry under clause 11 and at the request of the aggrieved woman, the Internal Committee and the Local Committee may take steps to settle the matter between her and the respondent through conciliation and where a settlement has been arrived, the Internal Committee or the Local Committee shall record the settlement so arrived and forward the same to the employer or the District Officer to take action as specified in the recommendation.

It further provides that the Internal Committee or the Local Committee shall provide the copies of the recorded settlement to the aggrieved woman and the respondent and no further enquiry shall be conducted by the Internal Committee or the Local Committee.

Clause 11 : This clause makes provision for inquiry into complaint. It provides that subject to the provisions of clause 10 and clause 16, the Internal Committee or the Local Committee shall proceed to make enquiry into the complaint in such manner as may be prescribed by rules.

It further provides that if the aggrieved woman informs that any term or condition of the settlement arrived at under sub-clause (2) of clause 10 has not been complied with by the respondent, then the Internal Committee or the Local Committee shall proceed to make an enquiry into the complaint.

It also provides that for the purpose of making enquiry, the Internal Committee or the Local Committee shall have the same powers as are vested in a civil court under the Code of Civil Procedure, 1908 when trying a suit in respect of the matters relating to: (a) summoning and enforcing the attendance of any person and examining him on oath; (b) requiring the discovery and production of documents; and (c) any other matter which may be prescribed by rules. The enquiry under this clause shall be completed within a period of ninety days.

Clause 12 : This clause provides for action during pendency of enquiry. It provides that during the pendency of enquiry, on a written request made by the aggrieved woman, the Internal Committee or the Local Committee may recommend to the employer to: (a) transfer the aggrieved woman or the respondent to any other workplace; or (b) grant leave to the aggrieved woman; or (c) grant such other relief to the aggrieved woman as may be prescribed by rules.

It further makes it clear that the leave granted to the aggrieved woman under this clause shall be in addition to the leave she would be entitled to otherwise if the case is proved.

It also casts a duty on employer to implement the recommendations of the Internal Committee or the Local Committee and send the report of such implementation to the Internal Committee or the Local Committee.

Clause 13 : This clause provides for enquiry report. It provides that on the completion of an enquiry under the proposed legislation, the Internal Committee or the Local Committee shall provide a report of its findings to the employer or to the District Officer, as the case may be, and such report shall be made available to the concerned parties.

It further provides that in case the Internal Committee or the Local Committee arrives at the conclusion that the allegation against the respondent has not been proved, it shall recommend to the employer or to the District Officer, as the case may be, that no action is required to be taken in the matter.

It also provides that in case it arrives at the conclusion that the allegation against the respondent has been proved, then, it shall recommend to the employer or the District Officer– (i) to take action for sexual harassment as a misconduct in accordance with the provisions of the service rules applicable to the respondent or where no such service rules have been made, in such manner as may be prescribed by rules; and (ii) notwithstanding any thing contained in the service rules applicable to the respondent, to deduct from the salary or wages of the respondent such sum of compensation to be paid to the aggrieved woman or to her legal heirs, as it may determine, in accordance with the provisions of clause 15 and in case the employer is unable to make such deduction from the salary of the respondent due to his being absent from duty or cessation of employment it may direct to the respondent to pay such compensation to the aggrieved woman.

It also provides that the employer and the District Officer shall act upon the recommendation within sixty days of its receipt by him.

Clause 14 : This clause provides for punishment for false or malicious complaint and false evidence. It provides that where the Internal Committee or the Local Committee arrives at a conclusion that the allegation against the respondent is false or malicious or the aggrieved woman or any other person making the complaint has produced any forged or misleading document, then, it may recommend to the employer or the District Officer to take action against the woman or the person who has made the complaint in accordance with the provisions of the service rules applicable to her or him or where no such service rules exist, in such manner as may be prescribed by rules.

It further provides that a mere inability to substantiate a complaint or provide adequate proof need not attract action against the complainant under this clause and the malicious intent or falsehood on part of the complainant shall be established after an enquiry in accordance with the procedure prescribed by rule before any action is recommended.

It also provides that where the Internal Committee or the Local Committee arrives at a conclusion that during the enquiry any witness has given false evidence or produced any forged or misleading document, then, it may recommend to the employer of the witness or the District Officer to take action in accordance with the provisions of the service rules applicable to the said witness or where no such service rules exist, in such manner as may be prescribed by rules.

Clause 15 : This clause provides for determination of compensation. It provides that for the purpose of determining the compensation to be paid to the aggrieved woman, the Internal Committee or the Local Committee shall have regard to— (a) the mental trauma, pain, suffering and emotional distress caused to the aggrieved woman; (b) the loss in the career opportunity due to the incident of sexual harassment; (c) medical expenses incurred by the victim for physical or psychiatric treatment; (d) the income and financial status of the respondent; and (e) feasibility of such payment in lump sum or in instalments.

Clause 16 : This clause provides for prohibition of publication or making known contents of complaint and enquiry proceedings. It provides that notwithstanding anything contained in the Right to Information Act, 2005, the contents of the complaint made under clause 9, the identity and addresses of the aggrieved woman, respondent and witnesses, any information relating to conciliation and enquiry proceedings, recommendations of the Internal Committee or the Local Committee, and the action taken by the employer or the District Officer under the provisions of the proposed legislation shall not be published, communicated or made known to the public, press and media in any manner.

It further provides that information may be disseminated regarding the justice secured to any victim of sexual harassment under the proposed legislation without disclosing the name, address, identity or any other particulars calculated to lead to the identification of the aggrieved woman and witnesses.

Clause 17 : This clause provides for penalty for publication or making known contents of complaint and enquiry proceedings. It provides that where any person entrusted with the duty to handle or deal with the complaint, enquiry or any recommendations or action to be taken under the provisions of the proposed legislation contravenes the provisions of clause 16 relating to prohibition of publication or making known contents of complaint and enquiry proceedings, he shall be liable for penalty in accordance with the provisions of the service rules applicable to the said person or where no such service rules exist, in such manner as may be prescribed by rules.

Clause 18 : This clause provides for appeal. It provides that any person aggrieved by the recommendations made by the Internal Committee or the Local Committee or nonimplementation of such recommendations or by imposition or penalty under clause 17 may prefer an appeal to the court or tribunal in accordance with the provisions of the service rules applicable to the said person or where no such service rules exist then, without prejudice to provisions contained in any other law for the time being in force, the person aggrieved may prefer an appeal in such manner as may be prescribed by rules.

It further provides that the appeal under this clause shall be preferred within thirty days of the recommendations.

Clause 19 : This clause lays down duties of employer. It provides that every employer shall– (a) provide a safe working environment at the workplace which shall include safety from the persons coming into contact at the workplace; (b) display the order constituting the Internal Committee at any conspicuous place in the workplace; (c) undertake workshops and training programmes at regular intervals for sensitising the employees regarding the provisions of the proposed legislation; (d) provide necessary facilities to the Internal Committee or the Local Committee, as the case may be, for dealing with the complaint and conducting enquiry; (e) assist in securing the attendance of respondent and witnesses before the Internal Committee or the Local Committee, as the case may be; (f) make available such information to the Internal Committee or the Local Committee as it may require having regard to the complaint; (g) provide assistance to the woman if she so chooses to file a complaint in relation to the offence under the Indian Penal Code or any other law for the time being in force; and (h) initiate action, under the Indian Penal Code or any other law for the time being in force, against the perpetrator after the conclusion of the enquiry, or without waiting for the enquiry, where the perpetrator is not an employee in the workplace at which the incident of sexual harassment took place.

Clause 20 : This clause lays down duties and powers of District Officer. It provides that the District Officer shall monitor the timely submission of reports furnished by the Internal Committee or the Local Committee; and take such measures as may be necessary for engaging non-governmental organisations for creation of awareness on sexual harassment and the rights of the women.

Clause 21 : This clause provides submission of annual report by Committee. It provides that the Internal Committee and the Local Committee shall in each calendar year prepare an annual report in such form and at such time as may be prescribed by rules and submit the same to the employer and the District Officer. It further provides that the District Officer shall forward a brief report on the annual reports received under this clause to the State Government.

Clause 22 : This clause lays down information which the employer shall include in annual report. It provides that the employer shall include in its report the number of cases filed, if any, and their disposal under the proposed legislation in the annual report of his organisation or where no such report is required to be prepared, intimate such number of cases, if any, to the District Officer.

Clause 23 : This clause provides for monitoring, implementation and maintance of data by appropriate Government. It provides that the appropriate Government shall monitor the implementation of the proposed legislation and maintain data on the number of cases filed and disposed of in respect of all cases of sexual harassment at workplace.

Clause 24 : This clause empowers appropriate Government to call for information and inspection of records. It provides that the appropriate Government, on being satisfied that it is necessary in the public interest or in the interest of women employees at a workplace to do so, by order in writing call upon any employer or District Officer to furnish in writing such information relating to sexual harassment as it may require; and authorise any officer to make inspection of the records and workplace in relation to sexual harassment, who shall submit a report of such inspection to it within such period as may be specified in the order.

It further provides that every employer and District Officer shall produce on demand before the officer making the inspection of all information, records and other documents in his custody having a bearing on the subject matter of such inspection.

Clause 25 : This clause provides for penalty for non-compliance with provisions of the proposed legislation. It provides that where the employer fails to– (a) constitute a Internal Committee; (b) take action under clauses 13, 14 and 22; and (c) contravenes or attempts to contravene or abets contravention of other provisions of the proposed legislation or any rules made thereunder, then, he shall be punishable with fine which may extend to fifty thousand rupees.

It further provides that if any employer, after having been previously convicted of an offence punishable under the proposed legislation subsequently commits and is convicted of the same offence, then, he shall be liable to—(i) twice the punishment, which might have been imposed on a first conviction, subject to the punishment being maximum provided for the same offence. However, in case a higher punishment is prescribed under any other law for the time being in force, for the offence for which the accused is being prosecuted, the court shall take due cognizance of the same while awarding the punishment; and (ii) cancellation, of his licence or withdrawal, or non-renewal, or approval, or cancellation of the registration, as the case may be, by the Government or local authority, required for carrying on his business or activity.

Clause 26 : This clause provides for cognizance of offence by courts. It provides that no court shall take cognizance of any offence punishable under the proposed legislation or any rules made thereunder, save on a complaint made by the aggrieved women or any person authorised by the Internal Committee or Local Committee in this behalf.

It further provides that no court inferior to that of a Metropolitan Magistrate or a Judicial Magistrate of the first class shall try any offence punishable under the proposed legislation and every offence under the proposed legislation shall be non-cognizable.

Clause 27 : This clause provides that the provisions of the proposed legislation shall be in addition to and not in derogation of the provisions of any other law for the time being in force.

Clause 28 : This clause empowers the appropriate Government to make rules. It provides that the Central Government may, by notification in the Official Gazette, make rules for carrying out the provisions of the proposed legislation. It further specifies the matters for which such rules may be made.

It also provides that every rule made by the Central Government shall be laid before each House of Parliament and every rule made by the State Government shall be laid before each House of the State Legislature where it consists of two Houses, or where such Legislature consists of one House, before that House.

Clause 29 : This clause provides for power to remove difficulties. It provides that if any difficulty arises in giving effect to the provisions of the proposed legislation, the Central Government may, by order published in the Official Gazette, make such provisions, not inconsistent with the provisions of the proposed legislation, as may appear to it to be necessary for removing the difficulty.

It further provides that no such order shall be made under this clause after the expiry of a period of two years from the commencement of the proposed legislation. It also provides that every order made under this clause shall be laid, as soon as may be after it is made, before each House of Parliament.

FINANCIAL MEMORANDUM

Sub-clause (1) of clause 6 of the Bill empower every District Officer to constitute a Local Complaints Committee in the District concerned and sub-clause (2) provides for additional Local Complaints Committees at Block, Taluk or Tehsil in rural or tribal areas and ward or municipality in urban area, wherever required. Sub-clause (4) of clause 7 provides for payment of fees or allowances to the Chairperson and Members of the Local Complaints Committee for conducting the proceedings of the Committee.

2. Sub-clause (1) of clause 8 of the Bill provides that the Central Government may, after due appropriation made by Parliament, by law in this behalf, make to the State Government grant of such sum of money as the Central Government may think fit for being utilised for the payment of fees and allowances to the Chairperson and Members of the Local Complaints Committee.

3. The Central Government will meet the entire expenditure on fees and allowances payable to the Chairperson and Members of the Local Complaints Committee till the financial year 2012 (i.e. the end of the 11th Plan period). The annual expenditure of fees and allowances is estimated at Rs.13.38 crore. The Central Government will specify the sharing pattern between the Central Government and State Governments beyond 2012.

MEMORANDUM REGARDING DELEGATED LEGISLATION

Sub-clause (1) of clause 28 of the Bill provides that the Central Government may, by notification in the Official Gazette, make rules for carrying out the provisions of the proposed legislation.

Sub-clause (2) specifies the matters in respect of which such rules may be made. These matters, inter alia, include — (a) the fees or allowances to be paid to the Presiding Officer and Members under sub-clause (4) of clause 4; (b) the fees or allowances to be paid to the Chairperson, and Members under sub-clause (4) of clause 7; (c) the person who may make complaint under sub-clause (2) of clause 9; (d) the manner of enquiry under sub-clause (1) of clause 11; (e) the powers for making enquiry under item (c) of sub-clause (2) of clause 11; (f) the relief to be recommended under item (c) of sub-clause (1) of clause 12; (g) the manner of action to be taken under item (i) of sub-clause (3) of clause 13; (h) the manner of action to be taken under sub-clauses (1) and (2) of clause 14; (i) the manner of action to be taken under clause 17; (j) the manner of appeal under sub-clause (1) of clause 18; and (k) the form and time for preparation of annual report by Internal Committee and the Local Committee under sub-clause (1) of clause 21.

2. Sub-clause (3) of clause 28 provides that every rule made by the Central Government shall be laid, as soon as may be after it is made, before each House of Parliament.

Sub-clause (4) of that clause provides that any rule made by the State Government shall be laid before each House of the State Legislature where it consists of two Houses, or where such Legislature consists of one House, before that House. 3. The matters in respect of which the Central Government may make rules are matters of procedure and administrative detail and it is not practicable to provide for them in the Bill itself. The delegation of legislative power is, therefore, of a normal character.

the State government and the law before each. [illegible] of them [illegible] [illegible] [illegible] of two [illegible], or if there exists [illegible] legislative conduct at one, [illegible] and that [illegible]. The matters in respect of which the Central Government with the other [illegible] matters of procedure and administrative, would find it not immediately to provide for them in the Schedule. The delegation of legislative power is therefore, of a normal character.

10

Indian Law for Protection of Women from Domestic Violence

Protection of Women from Domestic Violence Act 2005

The Protection of Women from Domestic Violence Act 2005 was brought into force by the Indian government from October 26, 2006. The Act was passed by the Parliament in August 2005 and assented to by the President on 13 September 2005. As of November 2007, it has been ratified by four of twenty-eight state governments in India; namely Andhra Pradesh, Tamil Nadu, Uttar Pradesh and Orissa. Of about 8,000 criminal cases registered all over India under this act, Rajasthan had 3440 cases, Kerala had 1,028 cases, while Punjab had 172 cases registered.

Definition

Domestic Violence

(1) For the purposes of this Act, any conduct of the respondent shall constitute domestic violence if he: (a) habitually assaults or makes the life of the aggrieved person miserable by cruelty of conduct even if such conduct does not amount to physical ill-treatment; or (b) forces the aggrieved person to lead an immoral life; or (c) otherwise injures or harms the aggrieved person.

(2) Nothing contained in clause (c) of sub-section (1) shall amount to domestic violence if the pursuit of course of conduct by the respondent was reasonable for his own protection or for the protection of his or another's property.

Scope

Primarily meant to provide protection to the wife or female live-in partner from domestic violence at the hands of the husband or male live-in partner or his relatives, the law also extends its protection to women who are sisters, widows or mothers. Domestic violence under the act includes actual abuse or the threat of abuse whether physical, sexual, verbal, emotional or economic. Harassment by way of unlawful dowry demands to the woman or her relatives would also be covered under this definition.

The salient features of the Protection from Domestic Violence Act, 2005 are as follows:

- The Act seeks to cover those women who are or have been in a relationship with the abuser where both parties have lived together in a shared household and are related by consanguinity, marriage or a relationship in the nature of marriage, or adoption; in addition relationship with family members living together as a joint family are also included. Even those women who are sisters, widows, mothers, single women, or living with the abuser are entitled to get legal protection under the proposed Act.
- "Domestic violence" includes actual abuse or the threat of abuse that is physical, sexual, verbal, emotional and economic. Harassment by way of unlawful dowry demands to the woman or her relatives would also be covered under this definition.
- One of the most important features of the Act is the woman's right to secure housing. The Act provides for the woman's right to reside in the matrimonial or shared household, whether or not she has any title or rights in the household. This right is secured by a residence order, which is passed by a court. These residence orders cannot be passed against anyone who is a woman.
- The other relief envisaged under the Act is that of the power of the court to pass protection orders that prevent the abuser from aiding or committing an act of domestic violence or any other specified act, entering a workplace or any other place frequented by the abused, attempting to communicate with the abused, isolating any assets used by both the parties and causing violence to the abused, her relatives and others who provide her assistance from the domestic violence.
- The draft Act provides for appointment of Protection Officers and NGOs to provide assistance to the woman w.r.t medical examination, legal aid, safe shelter, etc.

- The Act provides for breach of protection order or interim protection order by the respondent as a cognizable and non-bailable offence punishable with imprisonment for a term which may extend to one year or with fine which may extend to twenty thousand rupees or with both. Similarly, non-compliance or discharge of duties by the Protection Officer is also sought to be made an offence under the Act with similar punishment.

While "economic abuse" includes deprivation of all or any economic or financial resources to which the victim is entitled under any law or custom whether payable under an order of a Court or otherwise or which the victim requires out of necessity including, but not limited to, household necessities for the aggrieved person and her children, if any, stridhan, property, jointly or separately owned by her, payment of rental related to the shared household and maintenance and disposal of household effects, any alienation of assets whether movable or immovable, valuables, shares, securities, bonds and the like or other property in which the victim has an interest or is entitled to use by virtue of the domestic relationship or which may be reasonably required by the victim or her children or her stridhan or any other property jointly or separately held by the victim and prohibition or restriction to continued access to resources or facilities which the victim is entitled to use or enjoy by virtue of the domestic relationship including access to the shared household, "physical abuse" means any act or conduct which is of such a nature as to cause bodily pain, harm or danger to life, limb, or health or impair the health or development of the victim and includes assault, criminal intimidation and criminal force.

Criticism

Men's organisations such as Save Indian Family and Save Family Foundation have criticised the law since it is not gender neutral and abused men are not covered. Moreover, it might be abused by women and their families during family disputes. Renuka Chowdhury, the Indian Minister for Women and Child Development, agreed in a *Hindustan Times* article that "an equal gender law would be ideal. But there is simply too much physical evidence to prove that it is mainly the woman who suffers at the hands of man". In a CNN-IBN Interview, she commented that "this act won't hit good hubbies". The former Attorney General of India Soli Sorabjee has also criticised the broad definition of verbal abuse in the act. According to President of India in one of her speech, she said : " Another disquieting trend has been that women themselves have not been innocent of abusing women. At times women have played an unsavory, catalytic role in perpetrating violence whether against the daughter-in-law, the mother-in-law or female domestic helps. Instances exist whereby protective legal provisions for the benefit of women have been subjected to distortion and misuse to wreak petty vengeance and to settle scores. Some surveys have concluded that around 80 percent of dowry complaints are false and were registered primarily to settle scores. It is unfortunate if laws meant to protect women get abused as instruments of oppression.

Conclusion

The Protection of Women from Domestic Violence Act 2005 has come into effect from today. Ministry of Women and Child Development has issued notification for enactment of the Act and laying down the rules framed for the implementation of the Act.

Primarily meant to provide protection to the wife or female live-in partner from violence at the hands of the husband or male live-in partner or his relatives, the law also extends its protection to women who are sisters, widows or mothers. Domestic violence under the act includes actual abuse or the threat of abuse whether physical, sexual, verbal, emotional or economic. Harassment by way of unlawful dowry demands to the woman or her relatives would also be covered under this definition.

Ministry of Women and Child Development had issued a notification to bring it into force from 26th October, 2006. The Act was passed by the Parliament in August last year and assented to by the President on 13th September, 2005. But implementation was pending as detailed consultations were required with the State and other agencies for framing the rules.The Ministry has simultaneously issued another notification laying down the rules framed for the implementation of the Act. These rules provide for, among other things, appointment of protection officers, service providers and counselors. Action to be taken in the event of the respondent breaching the protection order passed by the Magistrate in favour of the aggrieved woman is also prescribed in these rules.

The Act will go a long way to provide relief to the women from domestic violence and get their due. The Ministry has requested all State Governments and Union Territories to ensure that the necessary administrative arrangements are immediately put in place for the commencement of the Act.

The salient features of the Protection from Domestic Violence Act, 2005 are as follows:

The Act seeks to cover those women who are or have been in a relationship with the abuser where both parties have lived together in a shared household and are related by consanguinity, marriage or a relationship in the nature of marriage, or adoption; in addition relationship with family members living together as a joint family are also included. Even those women who are sisters, widows, mothers, single women, or living with the abuser are entitled to get legal protection under the proposed Act.

Physical abuse - Beating, pushing, shoving

Sexual abuse - Forcing to have intercourse or look at pornography

Verbal abuse - Insulting

Economic abuse - Not providing for wife and children

'Domestic violence' includes actual abuse or the threat of abuse that is physical, sexual, verbal, emotional and economic. Harassment by way of unlawful dowry demands to the woman or her relatives would also be covered under this definition.

Right to Secure Housing

One of the most important features of the Act is the woman's right to secure housing. The Act provides for the woman's right to reside in the matrimonial or shared household, whether or not she has any title or rights in the household. This right is secured by a residence order, which is passed by a court. These residence orders cannot be passed against anyone who is a woman.

Preventive Order

The other relief envisaged under the Act is that of the power of the court to pass protection orders that prevent the abuser from aiding or committing an act of domestic violence or any other specified act, entering a workplace or any other place frequented by the abused, attempting to communicate with the abused, isolating any assets used by both the parties and causing violence to the abused, her relatives and others who provide her assistance from the domestic violence.

The Act provides for appointment of Protection Officers and NGOs to provide assistance to the woman w.r.t medical examination, legal aid, safe shelter, etc.

Non-bailable Offence

The Act provides for breach of protection order or interim protection order by the respondent as a cognizable and non-bailable offence punishable with imprisonment for a term which may extend to one year or with fine which may extend to twenty thousand rupees or with both. Similarly, non-compliance or discharge of duties by the Protection Officer is also sought to be made an offence under the Act with similar punishment.

Covering Legal Loophole

Presently, where a woman is subjected to cruelty by her husband or his relatives, it is an offence under section 498A of the Indian Penal Code. The civil law does not, however, address this phenomenon in its entirety. Therefore, it was necessary to enact a law, keeping in view the rights guaranteed under articles 14, 15 and 21 of the Constitution to provide for a remedy under the civil law, which is intended to protect the woman from being victims of domestic violence and to prevent the occurrence of domestic violence in the society. The new Act is an important step in that direction.

In sum, the Protection of Women from Domestic Violence Act, India 2005 has come into force from 26.10.2006. The Act is aimed at providing protection to wife or female live-in partner from violence at the hands of the husband or male live-in partner or his relatives. The Law extends protection to women who are sisters including adopted sisters and mothers. Domestic violence under the Act includes actual abuse or threat of abuse, whether physical, sexual, verbal, emotional, or economic. Harassment by way of unlawful dowry demands to the women victim or her relatives would also be covered under the definition of Domestic violence. The Department of Social Welfare, Government of Delhi is the Nodal Department for the implementation of provisions under the Act. For effective implementation, the Rules provide for:

- Appointment of Protection Officers in each district as per section 8 of the Act and provide them with necessary infrastructure to enable them to start functioning.
- Invite applications from service providers as per Rule 11 and register them after due verification as regards their suitability.
- Publish the names and addresses with telephone number of the Protection Officers and the service providers.
- Wide publicity to the provisions of the Act.

The Department of Social Welfare has taken decision to appoint 18 Protection Officers on contract basis for which advertisements in *Times of India* also appeared on 11.12.06. Meanwhile, the Department has designated 9 Welfare Officers as Protection Officers who are currently functioning from their present place of posting in various offices of Deptt. of Social Welfare. The Protection Officers shall be under the control and supervision of the Magistrates and shall perform the duties imposed by the Magistrates {as per Section 9(2)}.

The Rules provide for duties and functions of the Protection Officers which shall be as under:

- to assist the aggrieved person in making a complaint under the Act. If the aggrieved person so desires;
- to provide her information on the rights of aggrieved persons under the Act.
- to assist the person in making any application under section 12, or sub-section (2) of section 23 or any other provision of the Act.
- to prepare a "Safety Plan" including measures to prevent further domestic violence to the aggrieved person after making an assessment of the dangers involved in the situation and on an application being moved under section 12;
- to provide legal aid to the aggrieved person, through the State Legal Aid Services Authority;
- to assist the aggrieved person and any child in obtaining medical aid at a medical facility including providing transportation to get the medical facility;
- to assist in obtaining transportation for the aggrieved person and any child to the shelter;
- to inform the service providers registered under the Act that their services may be required in the proceedings under the Act and to invite applications from service providers seeking particulars of their members to be appointed as counsellors in proceedings under the Act under sub-section (1) of section 14 or Welfare Experts under Section 15;
- to scrutinise the applications for appointment as Counsellors and forward a list of available Counsellors to the Magistrate;
- to revise once in three years the list of available counselors by inviting fresh application and forward a revised list of Counsellors on the basis thereof to the concerned Magistrate;

- to maintain a record and copies of the report and documents forwarded under section 9, 12, 20, 21, 22, 23 or any other provisions of the Act of these rules;
- to provide all possible assistance to the aggrieved person and the children to ensure that the aggrieved person is not victimised or pressurised as a consequence of reporting the incidence of domestic violence;
- to liaise between the aggrieved person or persons, police and service provider kin the manner provided under the Act and these rules;
- to maintain proper records of the service providers, medical facility and shelter home in the area of his jurisdiction.

Similarly, the Service Provider is entrusted with the responsibility to record domestic incident report and get aggrieved person medical aid, legal aid and shelter. The Service Provider should be a registered organisation as per Section 10(1) of the Act.

The Protections Officers are to be attached with the Magistrates of the courts for the area notified for each protection officer. Therefore, the Protection Officers are required to function from all the district Courts and needs a premises within the court. For effective implementation, they need to be provided with vehicles for spot visits and making reports, staff to assist in maintaining records and corresponding with the aggrieved person, furniture and fixtures for establishing the office. The implementation of the Act provides for effective coordination and correspondence between Protection Officers, Police aggrieved persons and her family/ relatives, district court, there is likely to be a number of cases being registered under the Act. This also requires a great coordination and monitoring among all these stakeholders as all the actions have to be reported within the specified time . Although the rules of the Act provide for appointment of Protection Officers only, there is requirement of a monitoring authority/officer in view of the volume of work in each case, and the number of cases likely to be registered under the Act. Accordingly, it is proposed that a Chief Protection Officer may also be appointed for addressing all the requirements under the scheme for implementation of Protection of Women from Domestic Violence Act 2005. The Chief Protection Officer can function from office in Head Quarters of Department of Social Welfare.

Implementation of Protection of Women From Domestic Violence Act 2005

Protection of Women from Domestic Violence (PWDV) Act 2005 is a central Act which has come into force from 26.10.2006. This Act is aimed at providing protection to wife or female live-in partner from violence at the hands of the husband or male live-in partner or his relatives. The law extends protection to women who are sisters including adopted sisters and mothers. Domestic violence under the Act includes actual abuse or threat of abuse, whether physical, sexual, verbal, emotional, or economic. Harassment by way of unlawful dowry demands to women victims or her relatives would also be covered under the definition of Domestic violence.

As per the provisions of the Act, Protection Officer is the key officer working under Magistrate, who would be providing various relieves to aggrieved women in terms of monetary relief, counseling, legal aid, protection from the accused, social and economic security after investigating into the cases and preparing safety plan. Based on these Domestic Incident Reports, the protection orders are obtained from the Magistrates to provide relief to aggrieved women.

The Department of Women & Child Development, GNCT of Delhi has appointed 18 Protection Officers in all the Districts of Delhi. The Service Providers as per the Act have been identified to provide various services to aggrieved women like counseling, legal aid, shelter and health checkup. Workshops and trainings programmes have been organised for the functionaries as stakeholders in the implementation of PWDV Act.

Publicity is given through print media for provisions under this Act.

Total 5355 complaints were received by Protection Officers till June 2009 under PWDV Act, 2005.

THE PROTECTION OF WOMEN FROM DOMESTIC VIOLENCE ACT, 2005

NO. 43 OF 2005

[13th September, 2005.]

An Act to provide for more effective protection of the rights of women guaranteed under the Constitution who are victims of violence of any kind occurring within the family and for matters connected therewith or incidental thereto.

BE it enacted by Parliament in the Fifty-sixth Year of the Republic of India as follows:-

CHAPTER I
PRELIMINARY

1. Short title, extent and commencement.

(1) This Act may be called the Protection of Women from Domestic Violence Act, 2005.

(2) It extends to the whole of India except the State of Jammu and Kashmir.

(3) It shall come into force on such date as the Central Government may, by notification in the Official Gazette, appoint.

2. Definitions.

In this Act, unless the context otherwise requires,-

(a) "aggrieved person" means any woman who is, or has been, in a domestic relationship with the respondent and who alleges to have been subjected to any act of domestic violence by the respondent;

(b) "child" means any person below the age of eighteen years and includes any adopted, step or foster child;

(c) "compensation order" means an order granted in terms of section 22;

(d) "custody order" means an order granted in terms of section 21;

(e) "domestic incident report" means a report made in the prescribed form on receipt of a complaint of domestic violence from an aggrieved person;

(f) "domestic relationship" means a relationship between two persons who live or have, at any point of time, lived together in a shared household, when they are related by consanguinity, marriage, or through a relationship in the nature of marriage, adoption or are family members living together as a joint family;

(g) "domestic violence" has the same meaning as assigned to it in section 3;

(h) "dowry" shall have the same meaning as assigned to it in section 2 of the Dowry Prohibition Act, 1961 (28 of 1961);

(i) "Magistrate" means the Judicial Magistrate of the first class, or as the case may be, the Metropolitan Magistrate, exercising jurisdiction under the Code of Criminal Procedure, 1973 (2 of 1974) in the area where the aggrieved person resides temporarily or otherwise or the respondent resides or the domestic violence is alleged to have taken place;

(j) "medical facility" means such facility as may be notified by the State Government to be a medical facility for the purposes of this Act;

(k) "monetary relief" means the compensation which the Magistrate may order the respondent to pay to the aggrieved person, at any stage during the hearing of an application seeking any relief under this Act, to meet the expenses incurred and the losses suffered by the aggrieved person as a result of the domestic violence;

(l) "notification" means a notification published in the Official Gazette and the expression "notified" shall be construed accordingly;

(m) "prescribed" means prescribed by rules made under this Act;

(n) "Protection Officer" means an officer appointed by the State Government under sub-section (1) of section 8;

(o) "protection order" means an order made in terms of section 18;

(p) "residence order" means an order granted in terms of sub-section (1) of section 19;

(q) "respondent" means any adult male person who is, or has been, in a domestic relationship with the aggrieved person and against whom the aggrieved person has sought any relief under this Act:

Provided that an aggrieved wife or female living in a relationship in the nature of a marriage may also file a complaint against a relative of the husband or the male partner;

(r) "service provider" means an entity registered under sub-section (1) of section 10;

(s) "shared household" means a household where the person aggrieved lives or at any stage has lived in a domestic relationship either singly or along with the respondent and includes such a household whether owned or tenanted either jointly by the aggrieved person and the respondent, or owned or tenanted by either of them in respect of which either the aggrieved person or the respondent or both jointly or singly have any right, title, interest or equity and includes such a household which may belong to the joint family of which the respondent is a member, irrespective of whether the respondent or the aggrieved person has any right, title or interest in the shared household;

(t) "shelter home" means any shelter home as may be notified by the State Government to be a shelter home for the purposes of this Act.

CHAPTER II

DOMESTIC VIOLENCE

3. Definition of domestic violence.

For the purposes of this Act, any act, omission or commission or conduct of the respondent shall constitute domestic violence in case it

(a) harms or injures or endangers the health, safety, life, limb or well-being, whether mental or physical, of the aggrieved person or tends to do so and includes causing physical abuse, sexual abuse, verbal and emotional abuse and economic abuse; or

(b) harasses, harms, injures or endangers the aggrieved person with a view to coerce her or any other person related to her to meet any unlawful demand for any dowry or other property or valuable security; or

(c) has the effect of threatening the aggrieved person or any person related to her by any conduct mentioned in clause (a) or clause (b); or

(d) otherwise injures or causes harm, whether physical or mental, to the aggrieved person.

Explanation I : For the purposes of this section,-

(i) "physical abuse" means any act or conduct which is of such a nature as to cause bodily pain, harm, or danger to life, limb, or health or impair the health or development of the aggrieved person and includes assault, criminal intimidation and criminal force;

(ii) "sexual abuse" includes any conduct of a sexual nature that abuses, humiliates, degrades or otherwise violates the dignity of woman;

(iii) "verbal and emotional abuse" includes :

(a) insults, ridicule, humiliation, name calling and insults or ridicule specially with regard to not having a child or a male child; and

(b) repeated threats to cause physical pain to any person in whom the aggrieved person is interested.

(iv) "economic abuse" includes-

(a) deprivation of all or any economic or financial resources to which the aggrieved person is entitled under any law or custom whether payable under an order of a court or otherwise or which the aggrieved person requires out of necessity including, but not limited to, household necessities for the aggrieved person and her children, if any, stridhan, property, jointly or separately owned by the aggrieved person, payment of rental related to the shared household and maintenance;

(b) disposal of household effects, any alienation of assets whether movable or immovable, valuables, shares, securities, bonds and the like or other property in which the aggrieved person has an interest or is entitled to use by virtue of the domestic relationship or which may be reasonably required by the aggrieved person or her children or her stridhan or any other property jointly or separately held by the aggrieved person; and

(c) prohibition or restriction to continued access to resources or facilities which the aggrieved person is entitled to use or enjoy by virtue of the domestic relationship including access to the shared household.

Explanation II. For the purpose of determining whether any act, omission, commission or conduct of the respondent constitutes "domestic violence" under this section, the overall facts and circumstances of the case shall be taken into consideration.

CHAPTER III

POWERS AND DUTIES OF PROTECTION OFFICERS, SERVICE PROVIDERS

4. Information to Protection Officer and exclusion of liability of informant.

(1) Any person who has reason to believe that an act of domestic violence has been, or is being, or is likely to be committed, may give information about it to the concerned Protection Officer.

(2) No liability, civil or criminal, shall be incurred by any person for giving in good faith of information for the purpose of sub-section (1).

5. Duties of police officers, service providers and Magistrate.

A police officer, Protection Officer, service provider or Magistrate who has received a complaint of domestic violence or is otherwise present at the place of an incident of domestic violence or when the incident of domestic violence is reported to him, shall inform the aggrieved person

(a) of her right to make an application for obtaining a relief by way of a protection order, an order for monetary relief, a custody order, a residence order, a compensation order or more than one such order under this Act;

(b) of the availability of services of service providers;

(c) of the availability of services of the Protection Officers;

(d) of her right to free legal services under the Legal Services Authorities Act, 1987 (39 of 1987);

(e) of her right to file a complaint under section 498A of the Indian Penal Code (45 of 1860), wherever relevant:

Provided that nothing in this Act shall be construed in any manner as to relieve a police officer from his duty to proceed in accordance with law upon receipt of information as to the commission of a cognizable offence.

6. Duties of shelter homes.

If an aggrieved person or on her behalf a Protection Officer or a service provider requests the person in charge of a shelter home to provide shelter to her, such person in charge of the shelter home shall provide shelter to the aggrieved person in the shelter home.

7. Duties of medical facilities.

If an aggrieved person or, on her behalf a Protection Officer or a service provider requests the person in charge of a medical facility to provide any medical aid to her, such person in charge of the medical facility shall provide medical aid to the aggrieved person in the medical facility.

8. Appointment of Protection Officers.

(1) The State Government shall, by notification, appoint such number of Protection Officers in each district as it may

consider necessary and shall also notify the area or areas within which a Protection Officer shall exercise the powers and perform the duties conferred on him by or under this Act.

(2) The Protection Officers shall as far as possible be women and shall possess such qualifications and experience as may be prescribed.

(3) The terms and conditions of service of the Protection Officer and the other officers subordinate to him shall be such as may be prescribed.

9. Duties and functions of Protection Officers.

(1) It shall be the duty of the Protection Officer:

(a) to assist the Magistrate in the discharge of his functions under this Act;

(b) to make a domestic incident report to the Magistrate, in such form and in such manner as may be prescribed, upon receipt of a complaint of domestic violence and forward copies thereof to the police officer in charge of the police station within the local limits of whose jurisdiction domestic violence is alleged to have been committed and to the service providers in that area;

(c) to make an application in such form and in such manner as may be prescribed to the Magistrate, if the aggrieved person so desires, claiming relief for issuance of a protection order;

(d) to ensure that the aggrieved person is provided legal aid under the Legal Services Authorities Act, 1987 (39 of 1987) and make available free of cost the prescribed form in which a complaint is to be made;

(e) to maintain a list of all service providers providing legal aid or counselling, shelter homes and medical facilities in a local area within the jurisdiction of the Magistrate;

(f) to make available a safe shelter home, if the aggrieved person so requires and forward a copy of his report of having lodged the aggrieved person in a shelter home to the police station and the Magistrate having jurisdiction in the area where the shelter home is situated;

(g) to get the aggrieved person medically examined, if she has sustained bodily injuries and forward a copy of the medical report to the police station and the Magistrate having jurisdiction in the area where the domestic violence is alleged to have taken place;

(h) to ensure that the order for monetary relief under section 20 is complied with and executed, in accordance with the procedure prescribed under the Code of Criminal Procedure, 1973 (2 of 1974);

(i) to perform such other duties as may be prescribed.

(2) The Protection Officer shall be under the control and supervision of the Magistrate, and shall perform the duties imposed on him by the Magistrate and the Government by, or under, this Act.

10. Service providers.

(1) Subject to such rules as may be made in this behalf, any voluntary association registered under the Societies Registration Act, 1860 (21 of 1860) or a company registered under the Companies Act, 1956 (1 of 1956) or any other law for the time being in force with the objective of protecting the rights and interests of women by any lawful means including providing of legal aid, medical, financial or other assistance, shall register itself with the State Government as a service provider for the purposes of this Act.

(2) A service provider registered under sub-section (1) shall have the power to:

(a) record the domestic incident report in the prescribed form if the aggrieved person so desires and forward a copy thereof to the Magistrate and the Protection Officer having jurisdiction in the area where the domestic violence took place;

(b) get the aggrieved person medically examined and forward a copy of the medical report to the Protection Officer and the police station within the local limits of which the domestic violence took place;

(c) ensure that the aggrieved person is provided shelter in a shelter home, if she so requires and forward a report of the lodging of the aggrieved person in the shelter home to the police station within the local limits of which the domestic violence took place.

(3) No suit, prosecution or other legal proceeding shall lie against any service provider or any member of the service provider

who is, or who is deemed to be, acting or purporting to act under this Act, for anything which is in good faith done or intended to be done in the exercise of powers or discharge of functions under this Act towards the prevention of the commission of domestic violence.

11. Duties of Government.

The Central Government and every State Government, shall take all measures to ensure that

(a) the provisions of this Act are given wide publicity through public media including the television, radio and the print media at regular intervals;

(b) the Central Government and State Government officers including the police officers and the members of the judicial services are given periodic sensitisation and awareness training on the issues addressed by this Act;

(c) effective co-ordination between the services provided by concerned Ministries and Departments dealing with law, home affairs including law and order, health and human resources to address issues of domestic violence is established and periodical review of the same is conducted;

(d) protocols for the various Ministries concerned with the delivery of services to women under this Act including the courts are prepared and put in place.

CHAPTER IV

PROCEDURE FOR OBTAINING ORDERS OF RELIEFS

12. Application to Magistrate.

(1) An aggrieved person or a Protection Officer or any other person on behalf of the aggrieved person may present an application to the Magistrate seeking one or more reliefs under this Act:

Provided that before passing any order on such application, the Magistrate shall take into consideration any domestic incident report received by him from the Protection Officer or the service provider.

(2) The relief sought for under sub-section (1) may include a relief for issuance of an order for payment of compensation or damages without prejudice to the right of such person to institute a suit for compensation or damages for the injuries caused by the acts of domestic violence committed by the respondent:

Provided that where a decree for any amount as compensation or damages has been passed by any court in favour of the aggrieved person, the amount, if any, paid or payable in pursuance of the order made by the Magistrate under this Act shall be set off against the amount payable under such decree and the decree shall, notwithstanding anything contained in the Code of Civil Procedure, 1908 (5 of 1908), or any other law for the time being in force, be executable for the balance amount, if any, left after such set off.

(3) Every application under sub-section (1) shall be in such form and contain such particulars as may be prescribed or as nearly as possible thereto.

(4) The Magistrate shall fix the first date of hearing, which shall not ordinarily be beyond three days from the date of receipt of the application by the court.

(5) The Magistrate shall Endeavour to dispose of every application made under sub-section (1) within a period of sixty days from the date of its first hearing.

13. Service of notice.

(1) A notice of the date of hearing fixed under section 12 shall be given by the Magistrate to the Protection Officer, who shall get it served by such means as may be prescribed on the respondent, and on any other person, as directed by the Magistrate within a maximum period of two days or such further reasonable time as may be allowed by the Magistrate from the date of its receipt.

(2) A declaration of service of notice made by the Protection Officer in such form as may be prescribed shall be the proof that such notice was served upon the respondent and on any other person as directed by the Magistrate unless the contrary is proved.

14. Counselling.

(1) The Magistrate may, at any stage of the proceedings under this Act, direct the respondent or the aggrieved person, either singly or jointly, to undergo counselling with any member of a service provider who possess such qualifications and experience in counselling as may be prescribed.

(2) Where the Magistrate has issued any direction under sub-section (1), he shall fix the next date of hearing of the case within a period not exceeding two months.

15. Assistance of welfare expert.

In any proceeding under this Act, the Magistrate may secure the services of such person, preferably a woman, whether related to the aggrieved person or not, including a person engaged in promoting family welfare as he thinks fit, for the purpose of assisting him in discharging his functions.

16. Proceedings to be held in camera.

If the Magistrate considers that the circumstances of the case so warrant, and if either party to the proceedings so desires, he may conduct the proceedings under this Act in camera.

17. Right to reside in a shared household.

(1) Notwithstanding anything contained in any other law for the time being in force, every woman in a domestic relationship shall have the right to reside in the shared household, whether or not she has any right, title or beneficial interest in the same.

(2) The aggrieved person shall not be evicted or excluded from the shared household or any part of it by the respondent save in accordance with the procedure established by law.

18. Protection orders.

The Magistrate may, after giving the aggrieved person and the respondent an opportunity of being heard and on being prima facie satisfied that domestic violence has taken place or is likely to take place, pass a protection order in favor of the aggrieved person and prohibit the respondent from:

(a) committing any act of domestic violence;

(b) aiding or abetting in the commission of acts of domestic violence;

(c) entering the place of employment of the aggrieved person or, if the person aggrieved is a child, its school or any other place frequented by the aggrieved person;

(d) attempting to communicate in any form, whatsoever, with the aggrieved person, including personal, oral or written or electronic or telephonic contact;

(e) alienating any assets, operating bank lockers or bank accounts used or held or enjoyed by both the parties, jointly by the aggrieved person and the respondent or singly by the respondent, including her stridhan or any other property held either jointly by the parties or separately by them without the leave of the Magistrate;

(f) causing violence to the dependants, other relatives or any person who give the aggrieved person assistance from domestic violence;

(g) committing any other act as specified in the protection order.

19. Residence orders.

(1) While disposing of an application under sub-section (1) of section 12, the Magistrate may, on being satisfied that domestic violence has taken place, pass a residence order:

(a) restraining the respondent from dispossessing or in any other manner disturbing the possession of the aggrieved person from the shared household, whether or not the respondent has a legal or equitable interest in the shared household;

(b) directing the respondent to remove himself from the shared household;

(c) restraining the respondent or any of his relatives from entering any portion of the shared household in which the aggrieved person resides;

(d) restraining the respondent from alienating or disposing off the shared household or encumbering the same;

(e) restraining the respondent from renouncing his rights in the shared household except with the leave of the Magistrate; or

(f) directing the respondent to secure same level of alternate accommodation for the aggrieved person as enjoyed by her in the shared household or to pay rent for the same, if the circumstances so require:

Provided that no order under clause (b) shall be passed against any person who is a woman.

(2) The Magistrate may impose any additional conditions or pass any other direction which he may deem reasonably necessary to protect or to provide for the safety of the aggrieved person or any child of such aggrieved person.

(3) The Magistrate may require from the respondent to execute a bond, with or without sureties, for preventing the commission of domestic violence.

(4) An order under sub-section (3) shall be deemed to be an order under Chapter VIII of the Code of Criminal Procedure, 1973 (2 of 1974) and shall be dealt with accordingly.

(5) While passing an order under sub-section (1), sub-section (2) or sub-section (3), the court may also pass an order directing the officer in charge of the nearest police station to give protection to the aggrieved person or to assist her or the person making an application on her behalf in the implementation of the order.

(6) While making an order under sub-section (1), the Magistrate may impose on the respondent obligations relating to the discharge of rent and other payments, having regard to the financial needs and resources of the parties.

(7) The Magistrate may direct the officer in-charge of the police station in whose jurisdiction the Magistrate has been approached to assist in the implementation of the protection order.

(8) The Magistrate may direct the respondent to return to the possession of the aggrieved person her stridhan or any other property or valuable security to which she is entitled to.

20. Monetary Reliefs.

(1) While disposing of an application under sub-section (1) of section 12, the Magistrate may direct the respondent to pay monetary relief to meet the expenses incurred and losses suffered by the aggrieved person and any child of the aggrieved person as a result of the domestic violence and such relief may include, but not limited to,

(a) the loss of earnings;

(b) the medical expenses;

(c) the loss caused due to the destruction, damage or removal of any property from the control of the aggrieved person; and

(d) the maintenance for the aggrieved person as well as her children, if any, including an order under or in addition to an order of maintenance under section 125 of the Code of Criminal Procedure, 1973 (2 of 1974) or any other law for the time being in force.

(2) The monetary relief granted under this section shall be adequate, fair and reasonable and consistent with the standard of living to which the aggrieved person is accustomed.

(3) The Magistrate shall have the power to order an appropriate lump sum payment or monthly payments of maintenance, as the nature and circumstances of the case may require.

(4) The Magistrate shall send a copy of the order for monetary relief made under sub-section (1) to the parties to the application and to the in charge of the police station within the local limits of whose jurisdiction the respondent resides.

(5) The respondent shall pay the monetary relief granted to the aggrieved person within the period specified in the order under sub-section (1).

(6) Upon the failure on the part of the respondent to make payment in terms of the order under sub-section (1), the Magistrate may direct the employer or a debtor of the respondent, to directly pay to the aggrieved person or to deposit with the court a portion of the wages or salaries or debt due to or accrued to the credit of the respondent, which amount may be adjusted towards the monetary relief payable by the respondent.

21. Custody orders.

Notwithstanding anything contained in any other law for the time being in force, the Magistrate may, at any stage of hearing of the application for protection order or for any other relief under this Act grant temporary custody of any child or children to the aggrieved person or the person making an application on her behalf and specify, if necessary, the arrangements for visit of such child or children by the respondent:

Provided that if the Magistrate is of the opinion that any visit of the respondent may be harmful to the interests of the child or children, the Magistrate shall refuse to allow such visit.

22. Compensation orders.

In addition to other reliefs as may be granted under this Act, the Magistrate may on an application being made by the aggrieved person, pass an order directing the respondent to pay compensation and damages for the injuries, including mental torture and emotional distress, caused by the acts of domestic violence committed by that respondent.

23. Power to grant interim and ex parte orders.

(1) In any proceeding before him under this Act, the Magistrate may pass such interim order as he deems just and proper.

(2) If the Magistrate is satisfied that an application prima facie discloses that the respondent is committing, or has committed an act of domestic violence or that there is a likelihood that

the respondent may commit an act of domestic violence, he may grant an ex parte order on the basis of the affidavit in such form, as may be prescribed, of the aggrieved person under section 18, section 19, section 20, section 21 or, as the case may be, section 22 against the respondent.

24. Court to give copies of order free of cost.

The Magistrate shall, in all cases where he has passed any order under this Act, order that a copy of such order, shall be given free of cost, to the parties to the application, the police officer in-charge of the police station in the jurisdiction of which the Magistrate has been approached, and any service provider located within the local limits of the jurisdiction of the court and if any service provider has registered a domestic incident report, to that service provider.

25. Duration and alteration of orders.

(1) A protection order made under section 18 shall be in force till the aggrieved person applies for discharge.

(2) If the Magistrate, on receipt of an application from the aggrieved person or the respondent, is satisfied that there is a change in the circumstances requiring alteration, modification or revocation of any order made under this Act, he may, for reasons to be recorded in writing pass such order, as he may deem appropriate.

26. Relief in other suits and legal proceedings.

(1) Any relief available under sections 18, 19, 20, 21 and 22 may also be sought in any legal proceeding, before a civil court, family court or a criminal court, affecting the aggrieved person and the respondent whether such proceeding was initiated before or after the commencement of this Act.

(2) Any relief referred to in sub-section (1) may be sought for in addition to and along with any other relief that the aggrieved person may seek in such suit or legal proceeding before a civil or criminal court.

(3) In case any relief has been obtained by the aggrieved person in any proceedings other than a proceeding under this Act, she shall be bound to inform the Magistrate of the grant of such relief.

27. Jurisdiction.

(1) The court of Judicial Magistrate of the first class or the

Metropolitan Magistrate, as the case may be, within the local limits of which:

(a) the person aggrieved permanently or temporarily resides or carries on business or is employed; or

(b) the respondent resides or carries on business or is employed; or

(c) the cause of action has arisen, shall be the competent court to grant a protection order and other orders under this Act and to try offences under this Act.

(2) Any order made under this Act shall be enforceable throughout India.

28. Procedure.

(1) Save as otherwise provided in this Act, all proceedings under sections 12, 18, 19, 20, 21, 22 and 23 and offences under section 31 shall be governed by the provisions of the Code of Criminal Procedure, 1973 (2 of 1974).

(2) Nothing in sub-section (1) shall prevent the court from laying down its own procedure for disposal of an application under section 12 or under sub-section (2) of section 23.

29. Appeal.

There shall lie an appeal to the Court of Session within thirty days from the date on which the order made by the Magistrate is served on the aggrieved person or the respondent, as the case may be, whichever is later.

CHAPTER V
MISCELLANEOUS

30. Protection Officers and members of service providers to be public servants.

The Protection Officers and members of service providers, while acting or purporting to act in pursuance of any of the provisions of this Act or any rules or orders made thereunder shall be deemed to be public servants within the meaning of section 21 of the Indian Penal Code (45 of 1860).

31. Penalty for breach of protection order by respondent.

(1) A breach of protection order, or of an interim protection order, by the respondent shall be an offence under this Act and shall be punishable with imprisonment of either description for a term which may extend to one year, or

with fine which may extend to twenty thousand rupees, or with both.

(2) The offence under sub-section (1) shall as far as practicable be tried by the Magistrate who had passed the order, the breach of which has been alleged to have been caused by the accused.

(3) While framing charges under sub-section (1), the Magistrate may also frame charges under section 498A of the Indian Penal Code (45 of 1860) or any other provision of that Code or the Dowry Prohibition Act, 1961 (28 of 1961), as the case may be, if the facts disclose the commission of an offence under those provisions.

32. Cognizance and proof.

(1) Notwithstanding anything contained in the Code of Criminal Procedure, 1973 (2 of 1974), the offence under sub-section (1) of section 31 shall be cognizable and non-bailable.

(2) Upon the sole testimony of the aggrieved person, the court may conclude that an offence under sub-section (1) of section 31 has been committed by the accused.

33. Penalty for not discharging duty by Protection Officer.

If any Protection Officer fails or refuses to discharge his duties as directed by the Magistrate in the protection order without any sufficient cause, he shall be punished with imprisonment of either description for a term which may extend to one year, or with fine which may extend to twenty thousand rupees, or with both.

34. Cognizance of offence committed by Protection Officer.

No prosecution or other legal proceeding shall lie against the Protection Officer unless a complaint is filed with the previous sanction of the State Government or an officer authorised by it in this behalf.

35. Protection of action taken in good faith.

No suit, prosecution or other legal proceeding shall lie against the Protection Officer for any damage caused or likely to be caused by anything which is in good faith done or intended to be done under this Act or any rule or order made thereunder.

36. Act not in derogation of any other law.

The provisions of this Act shall be in addition to, and not in derogation of the provisions of any other law, for the time being in force.

37. Power of Central Government to make rules.

(1) The Central Government may, by notification, make rules for carrying out the provisions of this Act.

(2) In particular, and without prejudice to the generality of the foregoing power, such rules may provide for all or any of the following matters, namely:-

(a) the qualifications and experience which a Protection Officer shall possess under subsection (2) of section 8;

(b) the terms and conditions of service of the Protection Officers and the other officcrs subordinate to him, under sub-section (3) of section 8;

(c) the form and manner in which a domestic incident report may be made under clause (b) of sub-section (1) of section 9;

(d) the form and the manner in which an application for protection order may be made to the Magistrate under clause (c) of sub-section (1) of section 9;

(e) the form in which a complaint is to be filed under clause (d) of sub-section (1) of section 9;

(f) the other duties to be performed by the Protection Officer under clause (i) of sub-section (1) of section 9;

(g) the rules regulating registration of service providers under sub-section (1) of section 10;

(h) the form in which an application under sub-section (1) of section 12 seeking reliefs under this Act may be made and the particulars which such application shall contain under subsection (3) of that section;

(i) the means of serving notices under sub-section (1) of section 13;

(j) the form of declaration of service of notice to be made by the Protection Officer under subsection (2) of section 13;

(k) the qualifications and experience in counselling which a member of the service provider shall possess under sub-section (1) of section 14;

(l) the form in which an affidavit may be filed by the aggrieved person under sub-section (2) of section 23;

(m) any other matter which has to be, or may be, prescribed.

(3) Every rule made under this Act shall be laid, as soon as may be after it is made, before each House of Parliament, while it is in session, for a total period of thirty days which may be comprised in one session or in two or more successive sessions, and if, before the expiry of the session immediately following the session or the successive sessions aforesaid, both Houses agree in making any modification in the rule or both Houses agree that the rule should not be made, the rule shall thereafter have effect only in such modified form or be of no effect, as the case may be; so, however, that any such modification or annulment shall be without prejudice to the validity of anything previously done under that rule.

References

1. *The Tribune*, Chandigarh, India - Punjab
2. Save Family Foundation
3. ibnlive.com
4. timesofindia.indiatimes.com

11

Indecent Representation of Women

The Indecent Representation of Women (Prohibition) Act, 1986

Modern Indian society, while undergoing many socio-economic changes, largely remains a conservative society, placing a high value on the morals of restraint, chastity and the limits on sexuality. In this regard, a legislation curbing the dissemination of obscene material would be more than welcome. Scholars have held that in many societies, many people are made anxious by the existence of obscene publications as they may induct feelings of guilt or uncertainty on discussion or perusal, and as a result, feel it is necessary and apt to punish the distribution of such objectionable material. Keeping in mind the Indian social-set up, the Act seeks to regulate the depiction of women in various sectors of the mass media in present day India. In dealing with a society as culturally diverse as ours, special heed needs to be paid to the sentiments of the community, and the same need to be protected by the State. Morality, while highly subjective, remains a sensitive issue in India, and reflects a large variety of personally culturally related and historically changing values and attitudes. In light of the aforementioned, the Indecent Representation of Women Act, 1986, enacted in the thirty-seventh year of the Republic of India, is a pioneering legislation in the area of protection of the rights and welfare of women in India. In addition to the above mentioned objectives, the researcher seeks to understand the objectives of the Act, the recent controversies and developments regarding it, and its application in various decisions of the courts.

The right to live with dignity has been enshrined in the Constitution and has been read into Article 21 by the Supreme Court on numerous occasions. The Preamble of the Act, stating its purpose as the prohibition of depiction of women in an indecent manner, be it through advertisements, publications, writings, paintings, figures or in any other manner and for purposes connected with or incidental with any of these. The Act may be treated as a legislation that strengthens the demands of millions of women across India, that is, to live without being objectified and not have their persons treated as promotion and selling instruments in the sphere of business and commerce. The Indecent Representation of Women Act (IRWA) was enacted in 1987, supposedly in response to demands from the women's movement to tackle the derogatory depiction of women in the media.

The Act prohibits publishing, causing to be published, or arranging or participating in the publication or exhibition of, any advertisement which contains indecent representation of women in any manner whatsoever, according to Section 3. In addition to that, the Act also prohibits the publication or sending by post of books, pamphlets, papers, slides, films, writing, drawings, paintings, photographs or any other medium of representation that contain indecent representation of women. In the wider ambit of the term publication is included production, selling, leasing, distribution and circulation. However, exceptions have been made for representations for public good on the grounds of the publication being necessary in the interests of science, literature, art, or learning, art, or learning or other objects of general concern, or used bona fide for religious purposes. The same has been listed under Section 4 of the legislation. Representations sculptured, engraved, painted or otherwise represented on or in any ancient monument within the meaning of the Ancient Monument and Archaeological Sites and Remains Act, 1958.

The Text of THE INDECENT REPRESENTATION OF WOMEN (PROHIBITION) ACT, 1986 (NO. 60 OF 1986)

An Act to prohibit indecent representation of women through advertisements or in publications, writings, paintings, figures or in any other manner and for matters connected therewith or incidental thereto.

Be it enacted by Parliament in the Thirty-seven Year of the Republic of India as follows:-

1. Short title, extent and commencement :

(1) This Act may be called the Indecent Representation of Women (Prohibition) Act, 1986.

(2) It extends to the whole of India, except the State of Jammu and Kashmir.

(3) It shall come into force on such date as the Central Government may, by notification in the Official Gazette, appoint.

2. Definitions

In this Act, unless the context otherwise requires,-

"advertisement" includes any notice, circular, label, wrapper or other document and also includes any visible representation made by means of any light, sound, smoke or gas;

"distribution" includes distribution by way of samples whether free or otherwise;

"indecent representation of women" means the depiction in any manner of the figure of a woman; her form or body or any part thereof in such way as to have the effect of being indecent, or derogatory to, or denigrating women, or is likely to deprave, corrupt or injure the public morality or morals;

"label" means any written, marked, stamped, printed or graphic matter, affixed to, or appearing upon, any package;

"package" includes a box, a carton, tin or other container;

"prescribed" means prescribed by rules made under this Act.

3. Prohibition of advertisements containing indecent representation of Women

No person shall publish, or cause to be published, or arrange or take part in the publication or exhibition of, any advertisement which contains indecent representation of women in any form.

4. Prohibition of publication or sending by post of books, pamphlets, etc; containing indecent representation of women

No person shall produce or cause to be produced, sell, let to hire, distribute, circulate or send by post any book, pamphlet, paper, slide, film, writing, drawing, painting, photograph, representation or figure which contains indecent representation of women in any form:

Provided that nothing in this section shall apply to :

(a) any book, pamphlet, paper, slide, film, writing, drawing, painting, photograph, representation or figure –

(i) the publication of which is proved to be justified as as being for the public good on the ground that such book, pamphlet, paper, slide, film, writing, drawing, painting, photography, representation or figure is in the interest of science, literature, art, or learning or other objects of general concern; or

(ii) which is kept or used bona fide for religious purpose; any representation sculptured, engraved, painted or otherwise represented on or in:

(i) any ancient monument within the meaning of the Ancient Monument and Archaeological Sites and Remains Act, 1958 (24 of 1958); or

(ii) any temple, or on any car used or the conveyance of idols, or kept or used for any religious purpose;

any film in respect of which the provisions of Part II of the Cinematograph Act, 1952 (37 of 1952), will be applicable.

5. Powers to enter and search

(1) Subject to such rules as may be prescribed, any Gazetted Officer authorised by the State Government may, within the local limits of the area for which he is so authorised:

enter and search at all reasonable times, with such assistance, if any, as he considers necessary, any place in which he has reason to believe that an offence under this Act has been or is being committed;

seize any advertisement or any book, pamphlet, paper, slide, film, writing, drawing, painting, photograph, representation or figure which he has reason to believe contravenes any of the provisions of this Act;

examine any record, register, document or any other material object found in any place mentioned in Cl.(a) and seize the same if he has reason to believe that it may furnish evidence of the commission of an offence punishable under this Act.

Provided that no entry under this sub-section shall be made into a private dwelling-house without a warrant:

Provided further that the power of seizure under this sub-section may be exercised in respect of any document, article or thing which contains any such advertisement, including the contents, if any, of such document, article or thing if the advertisement cannot be separated by reason of its being embossed or otherwise from such document, article or thing without affecting the integrity, utility or saleable value thereof.

(2) The provisions of the Code of Criminal Procedure, 1973(2 of 1974), shall, so far as may be, apply to any search or seizure made under the authority of a warrant issued under Sec.94 of the said Code.

(3) where any person seizes anything under Cl.(b) or Cl.(c) of sub section (1), he shall, as soon as may be, inform the nearest Magistrate and take his orders as to the custody thereof.

6. Penalty

Any person who contravenes the provisions of Sec 3 or Sec 4 shall be punishable on first conviction with imprisonment of either description for a term which may extend to two years, and with fine which may extend to two thousand rupees, and in the event of a second or subsequent conviction with imprisonment for term of not less than six months but which may extend to five years and also with a fine not less than ten thousand rupees but which may extend to one lakh rupees.

7. Offences by companies

(1) Where an offence under this Act has been committed by a company, every person, who, at the time the offence was committed was in-charge of, and was responsible to, the company for the conduct of the business of the company, as well as the company, shall be deemed to be guilty of the offence and shall be liable to be proceeded against and punished accordingly:

Provided that nothing contained in this sub-section shall render any such person liable to any punishment, if he proves that the offence was committed without his knowledge or that he had exercised all due diligence to prevent the commission of such offence.

(2) Notwithstanding anything contained in sub-section (1), where any offence under this Act has been committed by a company and it is proved that the offence has been committed with

the consent or connivance of, or is attributable to any neglect on the part of, any director, manager, secretary or other officer of the company, such director, manager, secretary or other officer shall be proceeded against and punished accordingly.

Explanation – For the purpose of this section.-

"company" means any body corporate and includes a firm or other association of individuals; and

"director", in relation to a firm, means a partner in the firm.

8. Offences to be cognizable and bailable

(1) Notwithstanding anything contained in the Code of Criminal Procedure, 1973 (2of 1974), an offence punishable under this Act shall be bailable.

(2) An offence punishable under this Act shall be cognizable.

9. Protection of action taken in good faith

No suit, prosecution or other legal proceeding shall lie against the Central Government or any State Government or any officer of the Central Government or any State Government for anything which is in good faith done or intended to be done under this Act.

10. Power to make rules.

(1) The Central Government may, by notification in the Official Gazette, make rules to carry out the provisions of this Act.

(2) In particular and without prejudice to the generality of the foregoing power, such rules may provide for all or any of the following matters, namely:

(a) the manner in which the seizure of advertisement or other articles shall be made, and the manner in which the seizure list shall be prepared and delivered to the person from whose custody any advertisement or other article has been seised;

any other matter which is required to be, or may be, prescribed.

(3) Every rule made under this Act, shall be laid, as soon as may be after it is made, before each House of Parliament, while it is in session for a total period of thirty days, which may be comprised in one session or in two or more successive sessions, and if, before the expiry of the session immediately following the session or the successive session aforesaid,

both Houses agree in making any modification in the rule or both Houses agree that the rule should not be made, the rule shall thereafter have effect only in such modified form or be of no effect, as the case may be; so, however, that any such modification or annulment shall be without prejudice to the validity of anything previously done under that rule.

Indecent Representation of Women (Prohibition) Rules, 1987

G.S.R.822 (E), dated 25th September, 1987.- In exercise of the powers conferred by Sec.10 of the Indecent representation of Women (Prohibition) Act, 1986 (60 of 1986), the Central Government hereby makes the following rules, namely :

1. Short title and commencement

(1) These rules may be called the Indecent Representation of Women (Prohibition) Rules, 1987.

(2) They shall come into force on the 2nd October, 1987.

2. Definitions

(1) In these rules, unless the context otherwise requires,-

'Act' means the Indecent Representation of women (Prohibition) Act, 1986 (60 of 1986) ;

(b) 'article' means any book, pamphlet, paper, slide, film, writing, drawing, painting, photograph, representation of figure;

(c) 'authorised officer' means any Gazetted Officer authorised by the State Government for the purpose of section 5 of the Act.

(d) 'section' means a section of the Act.

(2) Words and expressions used in these rules and not defined, shall have the meanings respectively, assigned to them in the Act.

3. Manner of seizure of articles

(1) Every seizure made in pursuance of the provisions of sub-section (1) of section 5 shall be made in the manner hereinafter provided in these rules.

(2) The authorised officer seizing any advertisements or articles under sub-section (1) of section 5 shall prepare a list of such advertisements or articles containing such details relating to the description, quality, quantity, mark, number and other particulars thereof as he may consider relevant to the identity

of such advertisements or articles in any proceeding under the Act, in the Form annexed to these rules.

(3) The authorised officer shall pack and seal such advertisements or articles in the manner provided in rule 4 and shall deliver a copy of the list so prepared to the person from whom such advertisements or articles are seised.

(4) The advertisements or articles so seised shall be marked with a distinguishing number and shall also be signed by the authorised officer, the person from whom such advertisements or articles have been seised and two respectable inhabitants of the locality. If it is not possible to mark any such advertisement or article, the marking may be done on the packaging or in any other manner which the authorised officer thinks proper.

4. Manner of packing and dealing with advertisements or articles seized

(1) The advertisements or articles seized shall be packed in adequately strong paper, cloth or in any other packing material in such a way that the advertisements or articles may not be tampered with and the ends of the paper, cloth or other packing material shall be neatly folded and affixed by means of gum or other adhesive or stitched in or tied.

(2) The package shall be further secured by means of strong twine or thread and the twine or thread shall be fastened on the package by means of sealing wax on which there shall be at least four distinct and clear impressions of the seal of the authorised officer of which one shall be on the top of the package, one at the bottom and the other two at the body of the package and knots of the twine or thread shall be covered by means of sealing wax bearing the impression of the seal of the authorised officer.

(3) Where necessary, the authorised officer shall put the advertisements or articles in a box, a container of a suitable material and size and seal it in the manner provided in sub-rule (2).

5. Manner of seizing and sealing advertisements or articles in certain cases

Notwithstanding anything contained in rules 3 and 4, where the authorised officer is of the opinion that it is not possible to seize and seal any advertisement or article in the manner prescribed in rules 3 and 4 due to the size or the nature of such advertisement or article, he may take such steps as he thinks fit for the seizure and sealing of such advertisement or article without affecting the integrity, utility or saleable value thereof.

THE INDECENT REPRESENTATION OF WOMEN (PROHIBITION) RULES, 1987

FORM

(See rule 3(2))

List of Advertisements or Articles Seized

To

(Name and address of the person from whom the advertisement(s) or article(s) are seized)

....

....

The advertisement(s), article(s) detailed below has/have this day been seized by me under sub-section (1) of section 5 of the Indecent Representation of Women (Prohibition) Act, 1986 (60 of 1986), from the premises..........................situated at ....

Details of advertisement(s), article(s) seized:

Place........ ....

(Authorised Officer)

(Seal) Area...........

12

Indian Law for Prohibiting Dowry

Dowry Law in India

Payment of a dowry, gift—often financial, has a long history in many parts of the world. In India, the payment of a dowry was prohibited in 1961 under Indian civil law and subsequently by Sections 304B and 498a of the Indian Penal Code were enacted to make it easier for the wife to seek redress from potential harassment by the husband's family. Dowry laws have come under criticism as they have been misused by women and their families.

In India, there are civil laws, criminal laws and special legislative acts against the tradition of Dowry. Someone accused of taking dowry is therefore subject to a multiplicity of legal processes.

Definitions

Many judicial experts consider the definitions as vague and subject to misuse.

Dowry

As per section 2 of the Dowry Prohibition Act

... "dowry" means any property or valuable security given or agreed to be given either directly or indirectly

(a) By one party to a marriage to the other party to the marriage, or

(b) By the parent of either party to a marriage or by any other person, to either party to the marriage or to any other person,

at or before ... or any time after the marriage ... in connection with the marriage of the said parties ...

Stridhan

Stridhan is, generally speaking, what a woman can claim as her own property within a marital household. It may include her jewelry (gifted either by her family or by her in-laws), gifts presented to her during the wedding or later, and the dowry articles given by her family.

> Gifts given by the parents of the bride are considered "stridhan", i.e. property of the woman, traditionally representing her share of her parent's wealth.

The Dowry Prohibition (DP) Act

Introduced and taken up by then Indian law minister Ashoke Kumar Sen, this Act prohibits the request, payment or acceptance of a dowry, "as consideration for the marriage". where "dowry" is defined as a gift demanded or given as a precondition for a marriage. Gifts given without a precondition are not considered dowry, and are legal. Asking or giving of dowry can be punished by an imprisonment of up to six months, or a fine of up to Rs. 15000 or the amount of dowry whichever is higher and imprisonment up to 5 years. It replaced several pieces of anti-dowry legislation that had been enacted by various Indian states.

Section 4 of the said Act states:

4. Penalty for demanding dowry. If any person demands, directly or indirectly, from the parents or other relatives or guardian of a bride or bridegroom, as the case may be, any dowry, he shall be punishable with imprisonment for a term which shall not be less than six months, but which may extend to two years and with fine which may extend to ten thousand rupees.

   Provided that the Court may, for a adequate and special reasons to be mentioned in the judgment, impose a sentence of imprisonment for a term of less than six months.

However, as per section 3 of the Act, both the giver and the receiver are sought to be punished.

3. Penalty for giving or taking dowry.- [(Note: Section 3 re-numbered as sub-section (1) thereof by Act No. 63 of 1984, sec. 3) (1)] If any person, after the commencement of this Act, gives or takes or abets the giving or taking of dowry, he shall be punishable with imprisonment for a term which shall not be less than [(Note: Subs. by Act 43 of 1986, Sec.3)

five years, and with fine which shall not be less than fifteen thousand rupees or the amount of the value of such dowry, whichever is more:]

Provided that the Court may, for a adequate and special reasons to be recorded in the judgment, impose a sentence of imprisonment of a term of less than [(Note: Subs. by Act 43 of 1986, Sec. 3) five years.]

(2) [(Note: Ins. by Act 63 of 1984, sec. 3) Nothing in sub section (1) shall apply to, or in relation to, -

(a) Presents which are given at the time of a marriage to the bride (without any demand having been made in that behalf).

(b) Presents which are given at the time of a marriage to the bridegroom (without any demand having been made in that behalf).

Provided that such presents are entered in a list maintained in accordance with the rules made under this Act.

Provided further that where such presents are made by or on behalf of the bride or any person related to the bride, such presents are of a customary nature and the value thereof is not excessive having regard to the financial status of the person by whom, or on whose behalf, such presents are given.

IPC Section 406

This section, for offences related to Criminal Breach of Trust, is usually applied in investigation of Stridhan recovery from the husband and his family.

Offences under this section are bailable and cognizable.

Section 406.

Punishment for criminal breach of trust

Whoever commits criminal breach of trust shall be punished with imprisonment of either description for a term which may extend to three years, or with fine, or with both.

IPC Section 304B

This Section of the Indian Penal Code was inserted by a 1986 amendment. The wording of the law states:

Section 304B. Dowry death

(1) Where the death of a woman is caused by any burns or bodily injury or occurs otherwise than under normal circumstances within seven years of her marriage and it is shown that soon before her death she was subjected to cruelty or harassment by her husband or any relative of her husband for, or in connection with, any demand for dowry, such death shall be called "dowry death" and such husband or relative shall be deemed to have caused her death.

Explanation: For the purpose of this sub-section, "dowry" shall have the same meaning as in section 2 of the Dowry Prohibition Act, 1961 (28 of 1961).

(2) Whoever commits dowry death shall be punished with imprisonment for a term which shall not be less than seven years but which may extend to imprisonment for life.

IPC Section 498A

Section 498A was inserted into the Indian Penal Code in 1983 via an amendment.

It reads:

498A. Husband or relative of husband of a woman subjecting her to cruelty.

Whoever, being the husband or the relative of the husband of a woman, subjects such woman to cruelty shall be punished with imprisonment for a term which may extend to three years and shall also be liable to fine.

Explanation: For the purpose of this section, "cruelty" means-

(a) Any willful conduct which is of such a nature as is likely to drive the woman to commit suicide or to cause grave injury or danger to life, limb or health (whether mental or physical) of the woman; or

(b) Harassment of the woman where such harassment is with a view to coercing her or any person related to her to meet any unlawful demand for any property or valuable security or is on account of failure by her or any person related to her to meet such demand.

This section is non-bailable, non-compoundable (i.e. it cannot be privately resolved between the parties concerned) and cognizable.

Prosecution for a non-compoundable offense can only be quashed by a High Court of India under its powers under section 482 of Criminal Procedure Code of India. Usually, cases under

498A are quashed by mutual agreement when the husband and wife reconcile with each other, or agree to divorce by mutual consent.

After registration of an FIR for a cognizable, non-bailable offense, the police in India can arrest any and all of the accused named in the complaint.

Status of Second wife under Anti-Dowry Law- I [2008] DMC 279- Bombay High Court- *Justice C.L. Pangarkar —Ranjana Gopalrao Thorat Vs. State of Maharashatra*- Hindu Marriage Act,1955—Section 17—Bigamy—Second wife cannot assume a character as wife--- It is no marriage in eyes of law—[Pg.280 {Para6}]-- Indian Penal Code—Section 498A—cruelty—word "relative"—meaning of- "Person who is related to husband either by blood or marriage—Thus, she does not fall within scope of Section 498A-- Indian Penal Code— Pg. 280 {Para6}]

"Every Suicide After Marriage cannot be presumed to be Suicide due to Dowry Demand"- 2011[1] JCC Page No.668- In The High Court of Delhi- Hon'ble Mr. Justice Shiv Narayan Dhingra- Dated: - 2 December 2010- *Rani Vs. State of NCT of Delhi*- Criminal Appeal No. 93 of 2004- Indian Penal Code, 1860- Section 304B/ 498A Read With Section 34- Conviction- allegation of demanding of Rs.50,000/- and scooter were vague in nature- Whether it was done by husband, mother-in-law or father-in-law- Answers to all these questions are absent—Ingredients of Section 304B IPC were totally absent- Unnatural Death can be called a dowry death only if after making a demand made by accused is not fulfilled by perpetuation of cruelty upon the victim- The list of dowry show that both parties belonged to poor strata of society- No evidence, whatsoever was collected by police about the real facts- Every suicide after marriage cannot be presumed to be a suicide due to dowry demand- The tendency of the court should not be that since a young bride has died after marriage, now somebody must be held culprit and the noose must be made to fit some neck.

Relationship between dowry and Domestic Violence Act (2005/2006)

The above being criminal remedies, a civil remedy was brought into the picture in 2005 (amended in 2006). This was called the "Protection of Women from Domestic Violence Act".

For the purpose of this act, Domestic Violence includes the demand for dowry:

For the purposes of this Act, any act, omission or commission or conduct of the respondent shall constitute domestic violence in case it -

(a) harms or injures or endangers the health, safety, life, limb or well-being, whether mental or physical, of the aggrieved person or tends to do so and includes causing physical abuse, sexual abuse, verbal and emotional abuse and economic abuse; or

(b) harasses, harms, injures or endangers the aggrieved person with a view to coerce her or any other person related to her to meet any unlawful demand for any dowry or other property or valuable security; or

(c) has the effect of threatening the aggrieved person or any person related to her by any conduct mentioned in clause (a) or clause (b); or(d) otherwise injures or causes harm, whether physical or mental, to the aggrieved person.

This Act empowered the lower courts to issue "protection orders" on the complaint of a woman against her male relatives. The protection orders could include restraining orders on the husband and others, monetary compensation, and residence orders.

Though it is a Civil remedy, violation of protection orders result in Criminal penalties (including imprisonment).

Criticism of Anti-Dowry Laws

Criticism by Judiciary

The Supreme Court of India and the various High Courts have noted the gross misuse of IPC 498A in various judgments:

- Supreme court declared 498a as "Legal Terrorism" while giving judgment in matter of *Sushil Kumar Sharma* Vs. *Union of India* (UOI) and Ors - Jul 19 2005 (Citation: JT 2005 (6) SC 266).

Criticism outside India

Several reports of the abuse of Section 498A have involved couples based outside India especially in the US & Canada. The United States Department of State has published the following travel warning:

A number of US men who have come to India to marry Indian nationals have been arrested and charged with crimes related to dowry extraction. Many of the charges stem from the US citizen's inability to provide an immigrant visa for his prospective spouse to travel immediately to the United States.

The courts sometimes order the US citizen to pay large sums of money to his spouse in exchange for the dismissal of charges. The courts normally confiscate the American's passport, and he must remain in India until the case has been settled.

It is stated in Travel Advisory by US, since the police may arrest anyone who is accused of committing a crime (even if the allegation is frivolous in nature), the Indian criminal justice system is often used to escalate personal disagreements into criminal charges. This practice has been increasingly exploited by dissatisfied business partners, contractors, estranged spouses, or other persons with whom the US citizen has a disagreement, occasionally resulting in the jailing of US citizens pending resolution of their disputes. At the very least, such circumstances can delay the US citizen's timely departure from India, and may result in an unintended long-term stay in the country. Corruption in India, especially at local levels, is a concern, as evidenced by Transparency International's Corruption Perception Index of 3.5, ranking India in 72nd place of the world's countries.

In a well publicised case, Dr. Balamurali Ambati, who earned his MD at age 17, and his family were detained in India for over three years in a suit related to alleged dowry demands by the family for his brother's wife Archana, which delayed Dr. Ambati's entry to the ophthalmology program for two years, leaving him to begin his residency in 1998. All charges against him were dismissed in October 1996 and all his family members were acquitted in June 1999.

During the course of the trial the Ambatis produced a tape in which the father of Archana demanded US $500,000 to drop all the charges although the details of this particular case are still debated in India.

Criticism by Social Groups

Criticism by Men's Rights movements

According to the Men's Rights movement in India, the laws suffer from the following shortcomings:

- **Gender Bias:** The laws do not recognise cruelty and domestic violence against men. The police in India almost never register complaints of extortion or violence against men in a domestic relationship, whereas registering a complaint under 498A (where a woman is the aggrieved party) is widespread.

- Vague definitions of Dowry and Stridhan.
- Presumption of guilt. IPC 304B assumes that if the accidental death of a wife happens within 7 years of marriage, it should be assumed to be murder, unless the husband can prove his innocence. Similarly, the Dowry Prohibition Act (section 8-A) states that "Where any person is prosecuted for taking or abetting the taking of any dowry under Sec. 3, or the demanding of dowry under Sec.4, the burden of proving that he had not committed an offence under those sections shall be on him."
- Duplication of existing laws: Laws already exist to deal with offences against intimidation, violence, extortion and murder. A "dowry death" can be considered a murder, and a demand for dowry can be considered extortion under existing laws. The additional laws, instead of reforming the police, mostly serve to shift the burden of proof onto the accused.
- A corrupt police force which often does no investigation before arresting innocent people.
- Human Rights violations: In most cases involving Non-Resident Indians, their passports are impounded and they are restricted from traveling outside the country.
- No penalties, in practice, for false complaints or for perjury.

Police Circulars

The Ministry of Home Affairs, as well as various State governments, have issued notifications and circulars which limit the arbitrary arrests made by police during investigation of dowry-related offences.

Demands for Amending the law

The Malimath committee in 2003 proposed making amendments to this section although such amendments were opposed by Women's groups.

The Centre for Social Research India has released a research report opposing amendments to section 498A. According to this report, in the studied cases there were no convictions based solely on section 498A. The report however states that 6.5 percent of the studied cases were falsified. They also state that many people believe the law has been abused by "educated and independent minded women." A police official asserted that in his district one-third of dowry murder cases were found totally false by the police.

However, on December 17, 2003, the then Minister of State for Home Affairs, I.D. Swami said: "There is no information available with the Government to come to the conclusion that many families in India are suffering due to exaggerated allegations of harassment and dowry cases made by women against their husbands and other family members involving them in criminal misappropriation and cruelty."

On 20 July 2005, Justices Arijit Pasayat and H.K. Seema of the Indian Supreme Court declared Section 498A to be constitutional."The object is to strike at the root of dowry menace. But by misuse of the provision a new legal terrorism can be unleashed. The provision is intended to be used as a shield and not an assassin's weapon. If [the] cry of "wolf" is made too often as a prank, assistance and protection may not be available when the actual wolf appears," the Bench said.

In August 2010, the Supreme Court asked the Government of India to amend the Dowry Laws to prevent their misuse.

In February 2011, the Law Commission of India is considering grounds to recommend amendments to IPC 498A.

Social Repercussions

In urban India, the majority of families have inadequate knowledge regarding section 498A of the Indian Penal Code, 1860.

Even temporary imprisonment followed by acquittal leads to loss of social standing.

As per the judgements given by many courts in India including Supreme Court, once a women files a false 498a case against her husband or her relatives she had caused cruelty to the other party and the husband can claim divorce and it is assured.

A women who files a false 498a case against the husband or husbands relatives finds it difficult to get remarried as the other person feels that he might also be in the same position if he marries her.

Revisiting the Important Sections of the Dowry Prohibition Act

Penalty for giving or taking dowry- 5[(1) If any person, after the commencement of this Act, gives or takes or abets the giving or taking of dowry, he shall be punishable 6[with imprisonment for a term which shall not be less than 7 [five years, and with fine which shall not be less than fifteen thousand rupees or the amount of the value of such dowry, whichever is more].

Provided that the Court may, for adequate and special reasons to be recorded in the judgement, impose a sentence of imprisonment for a term of less than 8[five years].

1[(2) Nothing in sub-section (1) shall apply to, or in relation to,

1. presents which are given at the time of a marriage to the bride (without any demand having been made in that behalf).

   Provided that such presents are entered in a list maintained in accordance with the rules made under this Act;

2. presents which are given at the time of a marriage to the bridegroom (without any demand having been made in the behalf).

   Provided that such presents are entered in a list maintained in accordance with the rules made under this Act.

   Provided further that where such presents are made by or on behalf of the bride or any person related to the bride, such presents are of a customary nature and the value thereof is not excessive having regard to the financial status of the person by whom, or on whose behalf, such presents are given].

8A. Burden of proof in certain cases : Where any person is prosecuted for taking or abetting the taking of any dowry under section 3, or the demanding of dowry under section 4, the burden of proving that he had no committed an offence under those sections shall be on him.

The Dowry Prohibition (Maintenance of Lists of Presents to the Bride and Bridegroom) Rules, 1985

G.S.R.664(E)-In exercise of the powers conferred by section 9 of the Dowry Prohibition Act, 1961 (28 of 1961), the Central Government hereby made the following rules, namely:-

1. Short title and commencement-

   (1) These rules may be called the Dowry Prohibition (Maintenance of lists of Presents to the Bride and Bridegroom) Rules, 1985.

   (2) They shall come into force on the 2nd day of October, 1985 being the date appointed for the coming into force of the Dowry Prohibition (Amendment) Act, 1984 (63 of 1984).

2. Rules in accordance with which lists of presents are to be maintained:

    (1) The list of presents which are given at the time of the marriage to the bride shall be maintained by the bride.

    (2) The list of presents which are given at the time of the marriage to the bridegroom shall be maintained by the bridegroom.

    (3) Every list of presents referred to in sub-rule (1) or sub-rule (2)-

    1. shall be prepared at the time of the marriage or as soon as possible after the marriage;
    2. shall be in writing;
    3. shall contain-
        1. a brief description of each present;
        2. the approximate value of the present;
        3. the name of the person who has given the present; and
        4. where the person giving the present is related to the bride or bridegroom, a description of such relationship;
    4. shall be signed by both the bride and the bridegroom.

        Explanation I- Where the bride is unable to sign, she may affix her thumb-impression in lieu of her signature after having the list read out to her and obtaining the signature, on the list, of the person who has so read out the particulars contained in the list.

        Explanation II- Where the bridegroom is unable to sign he may affix his thumb-impression in lieu of his signature after having the list read out to him and obtaining the signature, on the list, of the person who has so read out the particulars contained in the list.

    (4) The bride or the bridegroom may, if she or he so desires, obtain on either or both of the lists referred to in sub-rule (1) or sub-rule (2) the signature or signatures of any relations of the bride or the bridegroom or of any other person present at the time of the marriage.

Section 498 IPC of Dowry Prohibition Act : A Critique

"I am the woman who holds up the sky
The rainbow runs through my eyes
The sun makes a path to my womb
My thoughts are in the shape of clouds
But my words are yet to come."

The issue of women's rights and family law reform has been increasingly entangled within the polemics of politics and minority rights. It is true that the hardships and sufferings experienced by women of all communities, minority as well as majority, cannot be overlooked with the help of persuasive or effective freedom of religion. The life of an average Hindu woman has always been difficult and pitiable due to existing social customs and practices of time.

Historical Background

The beginning of 19th century plays an important role in degrading Indian women till its depth. The fear of insecurity is not only envisaged in unmarried young women but also married women. In India, "family" has always been of prime importance. Marriage being an important social institution since Vedic period was biased against women. It was regarded as the social alliance between two families instead of two persons. The bride was expected to serve her husband and his family and ensure their happiness and well being. There was no question of her happiness, expectation or content. There were three main objectives of Hindu marriage: dharma or religious duties to be performed by the couple, proja or procreation, and rati or conjugal love.[1]

The exploitation of women began with the child marriage. A girl too young to take life seriously, a girl too young to understand the meaning of 'life' and 'marriage', had to step into the world of thorns. She was subjugated by her mother-in-law and other members of her husband's family, most of the time including even her husband. She was expected to observe 'purdah', not to speak to elders, speak in low voice to younger members of family, not to speak or meet her husband except midnight and bear all harsh words and sufferings for even minor fault and above all never to express her sorrows or utter a word of distress to anyone.

A woman had no freedom, neither personal nor economic. Traditionally, the Hindu woman had distinct economic right called 'stridhan'.[2] In order to partially set off the disability suffered under the notion of joint ownership by male members, the smritikars assigned a special category of property to women termed as 'stridhana'.[3] The first mention of this term is found in Gautama Dharma sutra. He provided not only for the women's separate property but also distinct and separate rules for its succession. But the definition of 'stridhana' changed over from time to time, granting all the rights and power to husbands. Consent of the girl was not considered to be relevant and hence, she was left with no choice, except to accept all pains and marry.

The traditional concept of marriage has greatly changed and Hindu marriage is considered tc be of dual nature i.e. of both religious sacrament and contract, where mutual consent and benefit of both the parties are duly aided by different legal provisions and reforms. Attempts to bring about changes in the status of women either through legislation or judicial activism can achieve little success without a simultaneous movement to transform the social and economic structures and the culture (values, ideologies and attitudes) of society.

One of those attempts to bring changes in status of women and relieve her from her sufferings, pains and gloomy environment is given under chapter XX-A of Indian Penal Code, 1860.

Introduction

Chapter XX-A of Indian Penal Code, 1860, refers to 'cruelty by husband or relatives of husband' and includes section 498-A.

Section 498-A states, that whoever being the husband or relative of the husband of woman, subjects such woman to cruelty shall be punished with the imprisonment for a term which may extend to three years and also be liable to fine.

Explanation- For the purpose of this section, "cruelty" means-

(a) Any wilful conduct which is of such nature as is likely to drive the woman to commit suicide or to cause grave injury or danger to life, limb or health (whether mental or physical) of the woman; or

(b) Harassment of the woman where such harassment is with view to coercing her or any person related to her meet any unlawful demand for any person related to her to meet such demand.

The section was enacted to combat the menace of dowry deaths. It was introduced in the code by the Criminal Law Amendment Act, 1983 (Act 46 of 1983). By the same Act section 113-A has been added to the Indian Evidence Act to raise presumption regarding abetment of suicide by married woman. The main objective of section 498-A of I.P.C is to protect a woman who is being harassed by her husband or relatives of husband.

Section 113-A of Indian Evidence Act, reads as follows:

Sec. 113-A, Presumption as to dowry death- When the question is whether a person has committed the dowry death of a woman and it is shown that soon before her death such woman has been subjected by such person to cruelty or harassment for, or in connection with, any demand for dowry, the Court shall presume that such person had caused the dowry death.

Explanation : For the purpose of this section 'dowry death' shall have the same meaning as in section 304-B of the Indian Penal Code (45 of 1860).

The object for which section 498A IPC was introduced is amply reflected in the Statement of Objects and Reasons while enacting Criminal Law (Second Amendment) Act No. 46 of 1983. As clearly stated therein the increase in number of dowry deaths is a matter of serious concern. The extent of the evil has been commented upon by the Joint Committee of the Houses to examine the work of the Dowry Prohibition Act, 1961. In some of cases, cruelty of the husband and the relatives of the husband which culminate in suicide by or murder of the helpless woman concerned, which constitute only a small fraction involving such cruelty. Therefore, it was proposed to amend IPC, the Code of Criminal Procedure,1973 (in short 'the Cr.P.C') and the Evidence Act suitably to deal effectively not only with cases of dowry deaths but also cases of cruelty to married women by the husband, in- law's and relatives. The avowed object is to combat the menace of dowry death and cruelty.

The act of harassment would amount to cruelty for the purpose of this section. Drinking and late coming habits of the husband coupled with beating and demanding dowry have been taken to amount to cruelty within the meaning of this section, but this section has been held not to include a husband who merely drinks as a matter of routine and comes home late.[6] In a case before Supreme Court it was observed that this section has given a new dimension to the concept of cruelty for the purposes of matrimonial remedies and that the type of conduct described here would be relevant for proving cruelty.

Meaning of Cruelty

It was held in '*Kaliyaperumal vs. State of Tamil Nadu*', that cruelty is a common essential in offences under both the sections

304B and 498A of IPC. The two sections are not mutually inclusive but both are distinct offences and persons acquitted under section 304B for the offence of dowry death can be convicted for an offence under sec.498A of IPC. The meaning of cruelty is given in explanation to section 498A. Section 304B does not contain its meaning but the meaning of cruelty or harassment as given in section 498-A applies in section 304-B as well. Under section 498-A of IPC cruelty by itself amounts to an offence whereas under section 304-B the offence is of dowry death and the death must have occurred during the course of seven years of marriage. But no such period is mentioned in section 498-A.

In the case of '*Inder Raj Malik vs. Sumita Malik*', it was held that the word 'cruelty' is defined in the explanation which inter alia says that harassment of a woman with a view to coerce her or any related persons to meet any unlawful demand for any property or any valuable security is cruelty.

Kinds of cruelty covered under this section includes following:

(a) Cruelty by vexatious litigation

(b) Cruelty by deprivation and wasteful habits

(c) Cruelty by persistent demand

(d) Cruelty by extra-marital relations

(e) Harassment for non-dowry demand

(f) Cruelty by non-acceptance of baby girl

(g) Cruelty by false attacks on chastity

(h) Taking away children

The presumption of cruelty within the meaning of section 113-A, Evidence Act,1872 also arose making the husband guilty of abetment of suicide within the meaning of section 306 where the husband had illicit relationship with another woman and used to beat his wife making it a persistent cruelty within the meaning of Explanation (a) of section 498-A.

Constitution Validity of Section 498-A

In '*Inder Raj Malik and others vs. Mrs. Sumita Malik*', it was contended that this section is ultra vires Article 14 and Article 20 (2) of the Constitution. There is the Dowry Prohibition Act which also deals with similar types of cases; therefore, both statutes together create a situation commonly known as double jeopardy. But Delhi High Court negatives this contention and held that this section does not create a situation for double jeopardy. Section

498-A is distinguishable from section 4 of the Dowry Prohibition Act because in the latter mere demand of dowry is punishable and existence of element of cruelty is not necessary, whereas section 498-A deals with aggravated form of the offence. It punishes such demands of property or valuable security from the wife or her relatives as are coupled with cruelty to her. Hence a person can be prosecuted in respect of both the offences punishable under section 4 of the Dowry Prohibition Act and this section.

This section gives wide discretion to the courts in the matters of interpretation of the words occurring in the laws and also in matters of awarding punishment. This provision is not ultra vires. It does not confer arbitrary powers on courts.

In the leading case of '*Wazir Chand vs. State of Haryana*', involving the death by burning of a newly married woman, the circumstances did not establish either murder or an abetted suicide and thus in-laws escaped the jaws of section 300 and 306, but they were caught in the web of this newly enacted section for prevention of harassment for dowry. Not to speak of the things they are persistently demanding from the girl's side, the fact that a large number of articles were taken by her father after her death from her matrimonial abode, showed that there was pressure being exerted on-in laws and continued to be exerted till death for more money and articles.

The other face of the coin

Though section 498-A aims at protection and safety of woman from her husband's and his relatives cruelty and harassment, this shield is used as a weapon by many females for their own purposes. Many women are using this section against their husbands and his relatives without any attempt or cruelty practiced. Indian law has always laid emphasis on protection of the innocent. It has always been emphasised that ten guilty person's can be acquainted rather punishing a single innocent person. But this section is being misused and innocents are punished.

Abuse of section 498-A has always been a matter of discussion in Rajya Sabha. It was observed there that, Section 498-A has become an instrument of oppression in the hands of certain people who are seeking to get minor children, aged in-laws are being arrested on absolutely whimsical allegations. The issue is not only of compounding it, the question is how you ensure a just investigation of such complaints. Low police officers are investigating it in a manner that is ruining the sanctity of families; minor children and girls are hauled up. This is a scathing indictment of how this law which was intended to subserve a noble purpose has in fact, been prostituted.

It was also stated that, in many cases, there are complaints where the provisions of section 498-A are misused or abused or excessively used. And for that, the investigating agency is the only agency which can remedy this. From time to time, these instructions are issued even from the Government of India, and the State Governments are already cognisant of this fact. But, for the investigating officer, the problem arises when a case is registered and the persons have been mentioned in the FIR; it becomes difficult for him. Till such time, he really satisfies himself. During that period, some harassment is certainly made; it is expected from the investigating officers, it is expected from the police officers. They are sensitised on this matter by the State Government, and also by the Central Government, that they should see to it that they are not harassed.

Observing that anti-dowry laws were being increasingly misused by wives to harass their husbands and in-laws, the Delhi High Court has urged the Government to review their provisions. Judge J.D.Kapoor urged the review while rejecting a plea by a woman petitioner, Savitri Devi, seeking the arrest of her brothers in-law and sister in-law for allegedly harassing her by demanding more dowries. Kapoor said in his order passed: "I feel constrained to comment upon the misuse of the provisions (of law) to such an extent that it is hitting at the foundation of marriage itself and has proved to be not so good for the health of the society at large".The judge observed: "There is a growing tendency to come out with inflated and exaggerated allegations, roping in each and every relation of the husband. If one of them happens to be of higher status or of vulnerable standing, he or she becomes an easy prey for better bargaining and blackmailing."

He added: "The ground realities have persuaded this court to recommend to the authorities and law makers to have a review of the situation and legal provisions." Judge Kapoor, in his order said the provisions of the anti-dowry laws "were made with good intentions but the implementation has left a very bad taste and has been counter-productive."

According to the anti-dowry laws, a non-bailable warrant is issued against the accused if a woman alleges she is being harassed by her husband and/or his relatives for dowry. People found guilty can be sent to jail for up to three years and/or fined. Savitri Devi had filed a case urging her brothers-in-law and sister-in-law be arrested for demanding dowry. City Court rejected the plea, but ordered the framing of charges against Savitri Devi's husband and father-in-law. She then challenged the lower court's order in the High Court.

Judge Kapoor agreed with the lower court's decision and found no evidence of harassment against Savitri Devi's brothers-in-law and sister-in-law. "The only allegation against the respondents is that they did not like the customary gifts the petitioner had brought", said Kapoor. This, according to him, did not amount to cruelty or harassment. "The petition is highly misconceived and is being used as a tool to hold the entire household to ransom and jeopardy," he said. He also pulled up the investigating agencies not doing their work properly.

Misuse of section 498-A has also been called as legal terrorism by the Supreme Court of India. Many instances have come to light where the complaints are not bonafide and have been filed with oblique motive. In such cases acquittal of the accused does not in all cases wipe out the ignomy suffered during and prior to trial. A new legal terrorism can be unleashed by the misuse of the provision. The provision is intended to be used as a shield and not as an assassin's weapon. If cry of "wolf" is made too often as a prank assistance and protection may not be available when the actual "wolf" appears. There is no question of investigating agency and Courts casually dealing with the allegations. They cannot follow any strait jacket formula in the matters relating to dowry tortures, deaths and cruelty. It cannot be lost sight of that ultimate objective of every legal system is to arrive at truth, punish the guilty and protect the innocent. It is to be noted that the role of the investigating agencies and the courts is that of watch dog and not of a bloodhound. It should be their effort to see that an innocent person is not made to suffer on account of unfolded, baseless and malicious allegations.

Supreme Court also contended that 'false case by wife amounts to mental cruelty'. It was also found that the allegations made in the police complaint by the respondent were "void" and that such void allegations without proving the same amounted to cruelty. It was found that given the falsity of the allegations against the appellant he was entitled to a decree of divorce on the ground of cruelty under section 13(1)(i)(a) of the Act.

In a landmark judgment, the Delhi High Court has ruled that lodging false dowry complaints against men amounts to cruelty and can be a ground for dissolution of marriage. The court granted divorce to a man who alleged mental cruelty by his wife.

The act of appellant in filing a false complaint case and getting her husband and other in-laws arrested clearly amounts to cruelty. The statement of the appellant and her brother before CJM points towards falsity of the complaint.

In the present case the situation is still worse. Not only the wife made a false complaint and got the husband and other in-laws arrested, she also took money and then resiled from the agreement.

Delhi High Court also added that Section 498-A and 406 of IPC should be made bailable. The Chief Justice said that, "for the foregoing reasons, the petition is highly misconceived and is being used as a tool to hold the entire household to ransom and jeopardy. Petition is dismissed. I feel constrained to comment upon the misuse of the provisions of Section 498-A/406 IPC to such an extent that it is hitting at the foundation of marriage itself and has proved to be not so good for the health of the society at large."

"There is a growing tendency amongst the women which is further perpetuated by their parents and relatives to rope in each and every relative- including minors and even school going kids nearer or distant relatives and in some case against every person of the family of the husband whether living away or in other town or abroad and married, unmarried sisters, sister-in-laws, unmarried brothers, married uncles and in some cases grand-parents or as many as 10 to 15 or even more relatives of the husband. Once a complaint is lodged under Section 498-A/406 IPC whether they are vague, unspecific or exaggerated allegations or there is no evidence of any physical or mental harm or injury inflicted upon woman that is likely to cause grave injury or danger to life, limb or health, it comes as an easy tool in the hands of police and agencies like Crime against Women Cell to hound them with the threat of arrest making them run here and there and force them to hide at their friends or relatives houses till they get anticipatory bail as the offence has been made cognizable and non-bailable. Thousands of such complaints and cases are pending and are being lodged day in and day out."

"To start with, marital offences under Sections 498-A/406 IPC be made bailable, if no grave physical injury is inflicted and necessarily compoundable. If the parties decide to either settle their disputes amicably to salvage the marriage or decide to put an end to their marriage by mutual divorce, they should be allowed to compound the offences so that criminal proceedings don't chase them if they want to start their marital life afresh or otherwise."

Several other cases have raised a debate on whether the

stringent and well meaning provisions of the laws governing dowry and cruelty against women were actually being increasingly misused to settle scores. "Husbands and their families are harassed by the stringent and outdated Dowry Act as majority of the cases these days are either exaggerated claims or are simply fabricated. This results in endless mental torture to the boy's family who have no way out," says Neena Tiwari, president of an NGO, Nari Jagriti Manch, which has started "crime against men" cell five months ago to provide counselling to the 'suffering husbands'.

Conclusion

Anyone who has been awake the last two decades knows how section 498-A of IPC has been heavily misused, dragging innocent men and women into police stations, lock-ups and courts, thus depriving many young children of a happy childhood, many youth of productive careers and many senior citizens of mental peace in the last leg of their lives.

As if this 498-A fiasco is not enough jingoistic feminists have come up with another Act, along the same lines of 498-A only with larger loopholes waiting to be used against many more Indian citizens. Many women who really need protection from Domestic Violence will probably never know about it and even if they do, never use it. This law will be yet another weapon in the hands of unscrupulous women who will misuse it at the slightest opportunity. In a society where men and women live together what affects one affects the other. When a man is thrown out of his own house under true or false allegations of domestic violence or cruelty everyone who is dependent on him is bound to suffer. That will include dependent parents and siblings who can be male or female. It is unfair enough to penalise an entire family even if an accused man is truly abusive. Unfair is a subtle word to describe a situation in which an innocent man, along with his family, is tortured by misuse of law. Injustice is a subtle word to describe how women, who commit perjury and harass families for years on end go unpunished.

Own Inference

In sum we can conclude that though Section 498-A of IPC was brought in for the protection of women from the cruelty of her husband and his relatives it is being abused by some thoughtless women. These women are turning the law other way round by being cruel to their husband's and his relatives and getting them tried under Section 498 A of IPC which deals with "Cruelty by husband or relatives of husband". Henceforth certain legal actions should be taken as soon as possible to curtail growth of "legal terrorism", by misuse of provisions of law.

Misuse of Sec. 498 A of IPC and Dowry Prohibition Act : An Indepth Analysis

Sec. 498 A of IPC

This is the most controversial Section of the Indian Penal Code and one that receives the highest media attention these days. It reads as follows:

"498A" - Husband or relative of husband of a woman subjecting her to cruelty

Whoever, being the husband or the relative of the husband of a woman, subjects such woman to cruelty shall be punished with imprisonment for a term which may extend to three years and shall also be liable to fine.

Explanation: For the purpose of this section, "cruelty" means-

(a) Any willful conduct which is of such a nature as is likely to drive the woman to commit suicide or to cause grave injury or danger to life, limb or health whether mental or physical of the woman; or

(b) Harassment of the woman where such harassment is with a view to coercing her or any person related to her to meet any unlawful demand for any property or valuable security or is on account of failure by her or any person related to her to meet such demand.

The Dowry Prohibition Act of 1961

The DP Act is a related law which defines giving, abetting and taking of dowry as criminal acts, and it also prescribes many rules as to the exchange of gifts, expenditure at the time of marriage and declaration of the same to the Government.

The purported aim of the DP Act is to curb the practice of dowry and to prevent extravagant marriages.

Anti-dowry laws ineffective

Together, IPC Section 498A and the DP Act are promoted under the label of women-protection laws.

Law enforcement officials, judiciary, general public and even feminists criticise these laws for being ineffective in curbing dowry or dowry harassment.

This factsheet highlights the magnitude and intensity of harm caused by Section 498A and the current implementation of the DP Act. The information presented below sheds light on the reasons why anti-dowry laws are ineffective.

Table 1: Number of cases filed:

Case Type	*2005*	*2006*	*2007*
498A	58319	63128	75930
DP Act	5243	4504	3204

Table 2 : Number of Persons arrested in Section 498A

Gender	*2005*	*2006*	*2007*
Male	98815	105927	120745
Female	28745	31253	35667
Total	127560	137180	156412

Note: The total number of persons arrested under Section 498A is 421,152 in just 3 years!

Low conviction rate

Ad-hoc studies have hinted at a very low rate of conviction – 2% or even less – under section 498A.

There are several instances where convictions by lower courts have been reversed by the Higher Judiciary.

Taking the conviction rate to be 2%, out of the 421,152 people arrested, 8423 people could not prove their innocence while 412,279 people were successful in proving their innocence.

Unfortunately, proving oneself innocenct is an extremely expensive and time consuming affair, costing an individual lakhs of rupees and 4-10 years of one's life.

Voices of reason ignored

Numerous authorities including Her Excellency the President of India Smt. Pratibha Devisingh Patil, the Supreme Court of India, Chief Justice of India Shri K G Balakrishan, various High Courts, eminent lawyers, and several NGOs under the aegis of the Save Indian Family movement have raised concerns over the misuse of Section 498A and the arrest of innocent people under false cases filed by greedy, disgruntled women.

So far, no measures have been taken to curb the arrests of innocent citizens or to prevent misuse of the law.

Constitutional and Human Rights violated

IPC Section 498A and DP Act consider the accused as guilty until proven innocent, and under these laws, the accused are punished even before investigation or trial.

The criminal justice system, which has been thoroughly sensitised by radical feminists, is jeopardising the life and liberty of everyone in the accused husband's family (including minor children, pregnant sisters and senior citizens) just to satisfy the greed and ego of one woman as the wife/daughter-in-law.

These laws violate a citizen's basic right to life and liberty, right to due process, and right to be presumed innocent until proven guilty.

The Paradox

Radical feminists vehemently reject all proposals to amend Section 498A claiming that its enactment was the result of years of tireless campaigning to provide protection to the married woman.

Radical feminists ignore the fact that over 123,000 innocent women (mothers and sisters of men who were implicated in 498A cases) were arrested under Section 498A over a span of just 4 years (2004–2007) without evidence or investigation.

Radical feminists ignore the fact that for every woman who files a false case under Section 498A and DP Act, at least two women in the husband's family suffer unnecessary arrest and legal harassment.

Radical feminists ignore the fact that due to a spate of false cases, timely justice is denied to genuinely abused women.

This is the most deplorable fact about Section 498A as the law claiming to protect women is their worst abuser.

DP Act not implemented, only misused

The DP Act came into effect 48 years ago, and yet women's rights activists claim that the problem of dowry is only getting worse every day.

Basing their claim on the rising number of dowry cases, they constantly urge the Government to introduce more stringent provisions against the husband and his family.

The current DP Act is sufficient to contain the dowry menace if it is implemented in its true spirit i.e. penalising both dowry givers and dowry takers.

To date, not a single woman or her family has been punished for either giving dowry or admitting to giving dowry, whereas scores of husbands and their relatives have been arrested upon mere allegations every day.

Section 498A and DP Act destroy families:

Once a case is filed under IPC Section 498A and DP Act, the marriage invariably ends in divorce.

Section 498A and DP Act have not only converted marriage into a crime, but also serve as weapons that break marriages and destroy families.

Section 498A and DP Act are two examples which illustrate the success of the radical feminist campaign of hatred against men and disdain for the family.

TEXT OF THE DOWRY PROHIBITION ACT, 1961
(Act No. 28 of 1961)

(20th May, 1961)

An Act to prohibit the giving or taking of dowry

Be it enacted by Parliament in the Twelfth Year of the Republic of India as follows:

1. Short title, extent and commencement. (1) This Act may be called the Dowry Prohibition Act, 1961.

It extends to the whole of India except the State of Jammu and Kashmir.

It shall come into force on such date as the Central Government may, by notification in the official Gazette, appoint.

**2. Definition of `dowry'.** In this act, `dowry' means any property or valuable security given or agreed to be given either directly or indirectly:

(a) by one party to a marriage to the other party to the marriage; or;

(b) by the parents of either party to a marriage or by any other person, to either party to the marriage or to any other person;

at or before or any time after the marriage in connection with the marriage of said parties but does not include dower or *mehr* in the case of persons to whom the Muslim Personal Law (Shariat) applies.

Explanation II. The expression `valuable security' has the same meaning as in Sec. 30 of the Indian Penal Code (45 of 1860).

3. Penalty for giving or taking dowry. (1) If any person, after the commencement of this Act, gives or takes or abets the giving or taking of dowry, he shall be punishable with imprisonment for a term which shall not be less than five years, and with the fine which shall not be less than fifteen thousand rupees or the amount of the value of such dowry, whichever is more:

Provided that the Court may, for adequate and special reasons to be recorded in the judgment, impose a sentence of imprisonment for a term of less than five years.

Explanation I omitted by Sec.2 w.e.f 2nd October, 1985

(2) Nothing in sub-section (1) shall apply to or, in relation to,-

presents which are given at the time of a marriage to the bride (without any demand having been made in that behalf):

Provided that such presents are entered in list maintained in accordance with rule made under this Act;

presents which are given at the time of marriage to the bridegroom (without any demand having been made in that behalf):

Provided that such presents are entered in a list maintained in accordance with rules made under this Act;

Provided further that where such presents are made by or on behalf of the bride or any person related to the bride, such presents are of a customary nature and the value thereof is not excessive having regard to the financial status of the person by whom, or on whose behalf, such presents are given.

4. Penalty for demanding dowry. If any person demands directly or indirectly, from the parents or other relatives or guardian of a bride or bridegroom as the case may be, any dowry, he shall be punishable with imprisonment for a term which shall not be less than six months but which may extend to two years and with fine which may extend to ten thousand rupees:

Provided that the Court may, for adequate and special reasons to be mentioned in the judgment, impose a sentence of imprisonment for a term of less than six months.

4-A. Ban on advertisement. If any person:

(a) offers, through any advertisement in any newspaper, periodical, journal or through any other media any share in his property or of any money or both as a share in any business or other interest as consideration for the marriage of his son or daughter or any other relative,

(b) prints or publishes or circulates any advertisement referred to Cl. (a), he shall be punishable with imprisonment for a term which shall not be less than six months, but which may extend to five years, or with fine which may extend to fifteen thousand rupees:

Provided that the Court may, for adequate and special reasons to be recorded in the judgment, impose a sentence of imprisonment for a term of less than six months.

5. Agreement for giving or taking dowry to be void. Any agreement for the giving or taking of dowry shall be void.

6. Dowry to be for the benefit of the wife or heirs.-

(1) Where any dowry is received by any person other than the woman in connection with whose marriage it is given, that person shall transfer it to the woman:

(a) if the dowry was received before marriage, within three months after the date of marriage; or

(b) if the dowry was received at the time of or after the marriage within three months after the date of its receipt; or

(c) if the dowry was received when the woman was a minor, within three months after she has attained the age of eighteen years, and pending such transfer, shall hold it in trust for the benefit of the woman.

(2) If any person fails to transfer any property as required by sub-section (1) within the time limit specified there of or as required by sub-section(3), he shall be punishable with imprisonment for a term which shall not be less than six months, but which may extend to two years or with fine which shall not be less than five thousand rupees, but which may extend to ten thousand rupees or with both.

(3) Where the woman entitled to any property under sub-section (1) dies before receiving it, the heirs of the woman shall be entitled to claim it from the person holding it for the time being:

Provided that where such woman dies within seven years of her marriage, otherwise than due to natural causes, such property shall if she has no children, be transferred to her parents, or

if she has children, be transferred to such children and pending such transfer, be held in trust for such children.

(3-A) Where a person convicted under sub-section (2) for failure to transfer any property as required by sub-section (1) or sub-section (3) has not, before his conviction under that sub-section, transferred such property to the women entitled thereto or, as the case may be, her heirs, parents or children, the Court shall, in addition to awarding punishment under that sub-section, direct, by order in writing, that such person shall transfer the property to such woman, or as the case may be, her heirs, parents or children within such period as may be specified in the order, and if such person fails to comply with the direction within the period so specified, an amount equal to the value of the property may be recovered from him as if it were a fine imposed by such Court and paid to such woman, as the case may be, her heirs, parents or children.

(4) Nothing contained in this section shall affect provisions of Sec. 3 or Sec. 4.

7. Cognisance of offences.

(1) Notwithstanding anything contained in the Code of Criminal Procedure, 1973 (2of 1974),-

no Court inferior to that of a Metropolitan magistrate or a Judicial Magistrate of the first class shall try any offence under this Act;

no Court shall take cognizance of an offence under this Act except upon:

(i) its own knowledge or a police report of the facts which constitute such offence, or

(ii) a complaint by the person aggrieved by offence or a parent or other relative of such person, or by any recognised welfare institution or organisation:

it shall be lawful for a Metropolitan Magistrate or a Judicial Magistrate of the first class to pass any sentence authorised by this Act on any person convicted of any offence under this Act.

Explanation. For the purposes of this sub-section, "recognised welfare institution or organisation" means a social welfare institution or organisation recognised in this behalf by the Central or State Government.

(2) Nothing in Chapter XXXVI of the Code of Criminal Procedure, 1973 (2of 1974), shall apply to any offence punishable under this Act.

Notwithstanding anything contained in any law for the time being in force, a statement made by the person aggrieved by the offence shall not subject such person to a prosecution under this Act.

8. Offences to be congnizable for certain purposes and to be bailable and non-compoundable.

(1) The Code of Criminal Procedure, 1973 (2 of 1974) shall apply to offences under this Act as if they were cognizable offences-

(a) for the purpose of investigation of such offences; and

(b) for the purpose of matters other than:

(i) matters referred to in Sec. 42 of that Code, and

(ii) the arrest of person without a warrant or without an order of a Magistrate.

(2) Every offence under this Act shall be non-bailable and non-compoundable.

8-A. Burden of proof in certain cases. Where any person is prosecuted for taking or abetting the taking of any dowry under Sec. 3, or the demanding of dowry under Sec.4, the burden of proving that he had not committed an offence under those sections shall be on him.

8-B. Dowry Prohibition Officers.

(1) The State Government may appoint as many Dowry Prohibition Officers as it thinks fit and specify the areas in respect of which they shall exercise their jurisdiction and powers under this Act.

(2) Every Dowry Prohibition Officer shall exercise and perform the following powers and functions, namely, -

(a) to see that the provisions of this Act are complied with;

(b) to prevent, as far as possible, the taking or abetting the taking of, of the demanding of, dowry;

(c) to collect such evidence as may be necessary for the prosecution of persons committing offences under the Act; and

(d) to perform such additional functions as may be assigned to him by the State Government, or as may be specified in the rules made under this Act.

(3) The State Government may, by notification in the official Gazette, confer such powers of a police officer as may be specified in the notification, the Dowry Prohibition Officer who shall exercise such powers subject to such limitations and conditions as may be specified by rules made under this Act.

(4) The State Government may, for the purpose of advising and assisting the Dowry Prohibition Officers in the efficient performance of their functions under this Act, appoint an advisory board consisting of not more than five social welfare workers (out of whom at least two shall be women) from the area in respect of which such Dowry Prohibition Officer exercises jurisdiction under sub-section (1).

9. Power to make rules.

(1) The Central Government may, by notification in the official Gazettee, make rules for carrying out the purposes of this Act.

(2) In particular, and without prejudice to the generality of the foregoing power, such rules may provide for-

(a) the form and manner in which, and the persons by whom, any list of presents referred to in sub-section (2) of Sec. 3 shall be maintained and all other matters connected therewith; and

(b) the better co-ordination of policy and action with respect to the administration of this Act.

(3) Every rule made under this section shall be laid as soon as may be after it is made before each House of Parliament while it is in session for a total period of thirty days which may be comprised in one session or in two or more successive sessions, and if, before the expiry of the session immediately following the session or the successive sessions aforesaid both Houses agree in making any modification in the rule or both Houses agree that the rule should not be made, the rule shall thereafter have effect only in such modified form or be; of no effect, as the case may be, so, however, that any such modification or annulment shall be without prejudice to the validity of anything previously done under that rule.

10. Power of the State Government to make rules.

(1) The State Government may, by notification in the official Gazette, make rules for carrying out the purposes of this Act.

(2) In particular, and without prejudice to the generality of the foregoing power, such rules may provide for all or any of the following matters, namely:

(a) the additional functions to be performed by the Dowry Prohibition Officers under sub-section(2) of Sec. 8-B;

(b) limitations and conditions subject to which a Dowry Prohibition Officer may exercise his functions under sub-section (3) of Sec. 8-B.

(3) Every rule made by the State Government under this section shall be laid as soon as may be after it is made before the State Legislature.

THE DOWRY PROHIBITION (MAINTENANCE OF LISTS OF PRESENTS TO THE BRIDE AND BRIDEGROOM) RULES, 1985

G.S.R. 664 (E), dated 19th August, 1985.- In exercise of the powers conferred by Sec.9 of the Dowry Prohibition Act, 1961 (28 of 1961), the Central Government hereby makes the following rules, namely:

1. Short title and commencement.

(1) These rules may be called the Dowry Prohibition (Maintenance of Lists of Presents to the Bride and Bridegroom) Rules, 1985.

2) They shall come into force on the 2nd day of October, 1985, being the date appointed for the coming into force of the Dowry Prohibition (Amendment) Act, 1984 (63 of 1984).

2. Rules in accordance with which lists of presents are to be maintained.

(1) The list of presents which are given at the time of the marriage to the bride shall be maintained by the bride.

(2) The list of presents which are given at the time of the marriage to the bridegroom shall be maintained by the bridegroom.

Every list of presents referred to in sub-rule (1) or sub-rule (2),-

(a) shall be prepared at the time of the marriage or as soon as possible after the marriage:

(b) shall be in writing;

(c) shall contain,-

(i) a brief description of each present;

(ii) the approximate value of the present;

(iii) the name of the person who has given the present; and

(iv) where the person giving the present is related to the bride or bridegroom, a description of such relationship;

(d) shall be signed by both the bride and the bridegroom.

Explanation. 1. Where the bride is unable to sign, she may affix her thumb impression in lieu of her signature after having the list read out to her and obtaining the signature on the list, of the person who has so read out the particulars contained in the list.

Explanation 2. Where the bridegroom is unable to sign he may affix his thumb-impression in lieu of his signature after having the list read out to him and obtaining the signature on the list of the person who has so read out the particulars contained in the list.

The bride or the bridegroom may, if she or he so desires, obtain on either or both of the lists referred to in sub-rule (1) or sub-rule (2) the signature or signatures of any relations of the bride or the bridegroom or of any other person or persons present at the time of the marriage.

TEXT OF THE DOWRY PROHIBITION (MAINTENANCE OF LISTS OF PRESENTS TO THE BRIDE AND BRIDEGROOM) RULES, 1985

G.S.R. 664 (E), dated 19th August, 1985. In exercise of the powers conferred by Sec.9 of the Dowry Prohibition Act, 1961 (28 of 1961), the Central Government hereby makes the following rules, namely:

1. Short title and commencement.

(1) These rules may be called the Dowry Prohibition (Maintenance of Lists of Presents to the Bride and Bridegroom) Rules, 1985.

(2) They shall come into force on the 2nd day of October, 1985, being the date appointed for the coming into force of the Dowry Prohibition (Amendment) Act, 1984 (63 of 1984).

2. Rules in accordance with which lists of presents are to be maintained.

(1) The list of presents which are given at the time of the marriage to the bride shall be maintained by the bride.

(2) The list of presents which are given at the time of the marriage to the bridegroom shall be maintained by the bridegroom.

Every list of presents referred to in sub-rule (1) or sub-rule (2),-

(a) shall be prepared at the time of the marriage or as soon as possible after the marriage:

(b) shall be in writing;

(c) shall contain:

(i) a brief description of each present;

(ii) the approximate value of the present;

(iii) the name of the person who has given the present; and

(iv) where the person giving the present is related to the bride or bridegroom, a description of such relationship;

(d) shall be signed by both the bride and the bridegroom.

Explanation. 1. Where the bride is unable to sign, she may affix her thumb impression in lieu of her signature after having the list read out to her and obtaining the signature on the list, of the person who has so read out the particulars contained in the list.

Explanation 2. Where the bridegroom is unable to sign he may affix his thumb-impression in lieu of his signature after having the list read out to him and obtaining the signature on the list of the person who has so read out the particulars contained in the list.

The bride or the bridegroom may, if she or he so desires, obtain on either or both of the lists referred to in sub-rule (1) or sub-rule (2) the signature or signatures of any relations of the bride or the bridegroom or of any other person or persons present at the time of the marriage.

Indecent Representation of Women (Prohibition) Rules, 1987

G.S.R.822 (E), dated 25th September, 1987- In exercise of the powers conferred by Sec.10 of the Indecent representation of Women (Prohibition) Act, 1986 (60 of 1986), the Central Government hereby makes the following rules, namely :

1. Short title and commencement.

(1) These rules may be called the Indecent Representation of Women (Prohibition) Rules, 1987.

(2) They shall come into force on the 2nd October, 1987.

2. Definitions.

(1) In these rules, unless the context otherwise requires,-

(a) 'Act' means the Indecent Representation of Women (Prohibition) Act, 1986 (60 of 1986) ;

(b) 'article' means any book, pamphlet, paper, slide, film, writing, drawing, painting, photograph, representation of figure;

(c) 'authorised officer' means any Gazetted Officer authorised by the State Government for the purpose of section 5 of the Act.

(d) 'section' means a section of the Act.

(2) Words and expressions used in these rules and not defined, shall have the meanings respectively, assigned to them in the Act.

3. Manner of seizure of articles.

(1) Every seizure made in pursuance of the provisions of sub-section (1) of section 5 shall be made in the manner hereinafter provided in these rules.

(2) The authorised officer seizing any advertisements or articles under sub-section (1) of section 5 shall prepare a list of such advertisements or articles containing such details relating to the description, quality, quantity, mark, number and other particulars thereof as he may consider relevant to the identity of such advertisements or articles in any proceeding under the Act, in the Form annexed to these rules.

(3) The authorised officer shall pack and seal such advertisements or articles in the manner provided in rule 4 and shall deliver a copy of the list so prepared to the person from whom such advertisements or articles are seized.

(4) The advertisements or articles so seized shall be marked with a distinguishing number and shall also be signed by the authorised officer, the person from whom such advertisements or articles have been seized and two respectable inhabitants of the locality. If it is not possible to mark any such advertisement or article, the marking may be done on the packaging or in any other manner which the authorised officer thinks proper.

4. Manner of packing and dealing with advertisements or articles seized.

(1) The advertisements or articles seized shall be packed in adequately strong paper, cloth or in any other packing material in such a way that the advertisements or articles may not be tampered with and the ends of the paper, cloth or other packing material shall be neatly folded and affixed by means of gum or other adhesive or stitched in or tied.

(2) The package shall be further secured by means of strong twine or thread and the twine or thread shall be fastened on the package by means of sealing wax on which there shall be at least four distinct and clear impressions of the seal of the authorised officer of which one shall be on the top of the package, one at the bottom and the other two at the body of the package and knots of the twine or thread shall be covered by means of sealing wax bearing the impression of the seal of the authorised officer.

(3) Where necessary, the authorised officer shall put the advertisements or articles in a box, a container of a suitable material and size and seal it in the manner provided in sub-rule (2).

5. Manner of seizing and sealing advertisements or articles in certain cases. Notwithstanding anything contained in rules 3 and 4, where the authorised officer is of the opinion that it is not possible to seize and seal any advertisement or article in the manner prescribed in rules 3 and 4 due to the size or the nature of such advertisement or article, he may take such steps as he thinks fit for the seizure and sealing of such advertisement or article without affecting the integrity, utility or saleable value thereof.

THE INDECENT REPRESENTATION OF WOMEN (PROHIBITION) RULES, 1987

FORM

(See rule 3(2))

List of Advertisements or Articles Seized

To

(Name and address of the person from whom the advertisement(s) or article(s) are seized)

....

....

The advertisement(s), article(s) detailed below has/have this day been seized by me under sub-section (1) of section 5 of the Indecent Representation of women (Prohibition) Act, 1986 (60 of 1986), from the premises...........................situated at ....

Details of advertisement(s), article(s) seized:

Place......... ....

(Authorised Officer)

(Seal) Area...........

COMMISSION OF SATI (PREVENTION) RULES, 1988

G.S.R. 360(E), dated 21st March, 1988.- In exercise of the powers conferred by Sec. 21 of the Commission of Sati (Prevention) Act, 1987 (3 of 1988), the Central Government hereby makes the following rules, namely:

1. Short title and commencement.

(1) These rules may be called the Commission of Sati (Prevention) Rules, 1988.

(2) They shall come into force on the date of their publication in the Official Gazette.

2. Definitions.

(1) In these rules, unless the context otherwise requires,-

"Act" means the Commission of Sati (Prevention) Act, 1987 (3 of 1988);

"prohibitory order" means an order issued under Sec. 6;

"section" means section of the Act.

(2) Words and expressions used but not defined in these rules and defined in the Act shall have the same meanings as are respectively assigned to them in the Act.

3. Delegation of power to prohibit certain acts.

(1) The State Government may, by order and subject to such conditions as it may deem fit to impose, direct that the powers of the Collector or the District Magistrate under Sec. 6 may also be exercised by such other officers not below the rank of the village officers.

4. Prohibitory orders under Sec. 6 : how made

(1) Every prohibitory order under Sec. 6 shall be made by beat of drum or other customary mode, in the concerned village, or in case of town or city, in the locality in which the act prohibited is likely to occur or has taken place.

(2) The prohibitory order shall be displayed at some conspicuous place in the area or areas to which such acts relate and a copy thereof shall also be displayed in the office of the officer issuing the prohibitory order and such display shall be taken as a sufficient notice to all persons concerned in the area of areas to which such order relates.

5. Manner of making order for removal of temples or structures under sub-section (1) of Sec. 7

(1) Before making any order under sub-section (1) of Sec. 7 for removal of any temple or structure, the State Government or any other officer authorised by the State Government in this behalf, shall give at least ninety days' notice to the person or persons involved in the acts complained of, and also to the owners and occupiers of the temple or structure proposed to be removed.

(2) The notice under sub-rule (1) shall specify:

(1) the temple/structure proposed to be removed, its location and other particulars,

(2) the owners/occupiers of the temple/structure, and

(3) the specific instance or instances of worship or ceremony contravening the provisions of Sec.7.

(3) The Government or the officer authorised by the State Government in this behalf shall, after giving reasonable

opportunity of being heard to the persons specified in the notice, order the removal of the temple or structure through a police not below the rank of the Sub-Inspector.

6. **Manner of making order for removal of temples or structures under sub-section (2) of Sec. 7.**

(1) After issue of a prohibitory order under Sec. 6, the Collector or the District Magistrate, or such other officer as directed by the State Government by order under rule 3 shall, before making any order for removal of any temple or structure under sub-section (2) of Sec. 7 give at least ninety days' notice to the owners and occupiers of the temple or structure proposed to be removed.

(2) The Collector of the District Magistrate, or such other officer as directed by the State Government by order under rule 3, shall follow the provisions of sub-rules (2) and (3) of rule 4 in the case of orders made under this rule.

7. **Inventory and forfeiture of the property of temple or structure.** As soon as the order of removal of the temple or structure is executed, the State Government or the Collector or the District Magistrate, or as the case may be, the officer as directed by the State Government by order under rule 3, shall prepare an inventory of all the material and other property obtained after removal of such temple or structure specifying in it the place where it is lodged or kept, and shall forward the intimation thereof to the Special court for declaration of forfeiture of the said material or property to the State under Sec. 13, if the Special Court considers it necessary to do so, and shall also give a copy of the inventory to the owners/occupiers of the temple/structure removed.

References

1. http://www.indiatogether.com/manushi/issue148/dowry.htm
2. http://wcd.nic.in/dowryprohibitionact.htm
3. Hindu Woman's Right to Property (Past and Present), Review author[s]: Ludwik Sternbach, *Journal of the American Oriental Society*, 1962, p.94 American Oriental Society
4. http://indiacode.nic.in/rsPaging.asp?tfnm=196128&Page=1
5. http://www.vakilno1.com/bareacts/dowryprohibitionact/s4.html
6. http://www.vakilno1.com/bareacts/dowryprohibitionact/s3.html
7. http://www.vakilno1.com/bareacts/indianpenalcode/s406.htm
8. http://www.vakilno1.com/bareacts/indianpenalcode/S304B.htm

9. http://www.vakilno1.com/bareacts/indianpenalcode/s498a.htm
10. http://pwdvhyd.ap.nic.in/bareacts.html#s1
11. "India". The Bureau of Consular Affairs website. US Department of State. July 9, 2009. http://travel.state.gov/travel/cis_pa_tw/cis/cis_1139.html#criminal_penalties. Retrieved 2010-01-21.
12. http://www.umiacs.umd.edu/users/sawweb/sawnet/news/news408.txt
13. http://www.vakilno1.com/bareacts/indianpenalcode/S304B.htm
14. http://wcd.nic.in/dowryprohibitionact.htm
15. http://www.saveindianfamily.org/knowledge/circulars.html
16. "Amend dowry law to stop its misuse, SC tells govt". *The Times of India*. 17 August 2010. http://timesofindia.indiatimes.com/india/Amend-dowry-law-to-stop-its-misuse-SC-tells-govt/articleshow/6321987.cms.
17. http://www.hindustantimes.com/Misuse-forces-a-review-of-dowry-law/Article1-667632.aspx

13

Rights on Muslim Women Divorce

The Muslim Women (Protection of Rights on Divorce) Act 1986

The Muslim Women (Protection of Rights on Divorce) Act was a landmark legislation passed by the Parliament of India in 1986 to protect the rights of Muslim women who have been divorced by, or have obtained divorce from, their husbands and to provide for matters connected therewith or incidental thereto. .The Act was passed by the Rajiv Gandhi government to nullify the decision in Shah Bano case.

The law applies to the whole of India except Jammu and Kashmir. It is administered by any magistrate of the first class exercising jurisdiction under the Code of Criminal Procedure 1973.

Shah Bano Case

The Shah Bano case was a controversial divorce lawsuit in India, in which Shah Bano, a 62 year old Muslim woman and mother of five from Indore, Madhya Pradesh, was divorced by her husband in 1978 and was subsequently denied alimony. The case created considerable debate and controversy about the extent of having different civil codes for different religions, especially for Muslims in India. This case caused the Rajiv Gandhi government, with its absolute majority, to pass the Muslim Women (Protection of Rights on Divorce) Act, 1986 which diluted the secular judgment of the Supreme Court and, in reality, denied even utterly destitute Muslim divorcees the right to alimony from their former husbands.

Overview

Shah Bano, a 62 year old Muslim woman and mother of five from Indore, Madhya Pradesh, was divorced by her husband in 1978. The Muslim family law (marriage, gifts, inheritance, adoption and a few other civil laws are under the purview of personal laws in India - they are different for Christians, Muslims and Hindus) allows the husband to do this and not the wife: the husband just needs to say the word Talaq (meaning divorce) three times before two witnesses for a valid divorce.

Shah Bano, because she had no means to support herself and her children, approached the courts for securing maintenance from her husband. When the case reached the Supreme Court of India, seven years had elapsed. The Supreme Court invoked Section 125 of Code of Criminal Procedure, which applies to everyone regardless of caste, creed, or religion. It ruled that Shah Bano be given maintenance money, similar to alimony.

Some Muslims felt threatened by what they perceived as an encroachment of the Muslim Personal Law, and protested loudly at the judgment. Their spokesmen were Obaidullah Khan Azmi and Syed Shahabuddin. They had formed an organisation in 1973 known as the All India Muslim Personal Law Board devoted to upholding what they saw as Muslim Personal Law.

The Indian Government's Reaction

In 1986, the Congress (I) party, which had an absolute majority in Parliament at the time, passed an act The Muslim Women (Protection of Rights on Divorce) Act 1986 that nullified the Supreme Court's judgment in the Shah Bano case. This act upheld the Muslim Personal Law and writ as excerpted below:

"Every application by a divorced woman under section 125... of the Code of Criminal Procedure, 1973, pending before a magistrate on the commencement of this Act shall, notwithstanding anything contained in that code... be disposed of by such magistrate in accordance with the provisions of this Act."

The Statement of Objects and Reasons of this Act (the objective of the Act) needs a mention. According to the stated objects of the Act, when a Muslim divorced woman is unable to support herself after the period that she must observe after the death of her spouse or after a divorce, during which she may not marry another man, the magistrate is empowered to make an order for the payment of maintenance by her relatives who would be entitled to inherit her property on her death according to Muslim Law. But when a divorced woman has no such relatives, and does not have enough means to pay the maintenance, the magistrate would order the State Waqf Board to pay the maintenance. The 'liability' of husband to pay the maintenance was thus restricted to the period of the *iddat* only.

Consequences

The Shah Bano case generated tremendous debate in India. Critics argued that Muslim minorities can exert pressure on government and judicial decisions. The mainstream media disapproved of the decision. The opposition reacted strongly against the Congress party's policies.

The case has led to Muslim women receiving a large, one-time payment from their husbands during the period of iddat, instead of a maximum monthly payment of 500 - an upper limit which has since been removed. Cases of women getting lump sum payments for lifetime maintenance are becoming common.

Critics of the Shah Bano case point out that while divorce is within the purview of personal laws, maintenance is not, and thus it is discriminatory to exclude Muslim women from a civil law. Exclusion of non-Muslim men from a law that appears inherently beneficial to men is also pointed out by them.

The Shah Bano case once again spurred the debate on the Uniform Civil Code in India. Ironically, the Hindu Right led by parties like the Jan Sangh which had strongly opposed reform of Hindu law in the 50's, in its metamorphosis as the Bharatiya Janata Party became an advocate for secular laws across the board. However, their opposition to the reforms was based on the argument that no similar provisions would be applied for the Muslims on the claim that they weren't sufficiently advanced. The pressure exerted by orthodox Muslims caused women's organisations and secularists to cave in.

The Passing of Muslim Women Protection Act allegedly sent a message of Muslim appeasement practised by the Congress party. To counter this charge Rajiv Gandhi began his election campaign in 1989 from Ram Janma Bhumi (birth place of Lord Rama) in Ayodhya.

Personal Laws

Personal Laws have been part of the Civil Law since the British Raj. They have been criticised by feminists for their orthodox approach and for disadvantaging women.

High Courts have interpreted "just and fair provision" that a woman is entitled to during her iddat period very broadly to include amounts worth lakhs (hundreds of thousands) of rupees. More recently the Supreme Court in *Danial Latifi* v. *Union of India* read the Act with Art 14 and 15 of the constitution which prevent discrimination on the basis of sex and held that the intention of the framers could not have been to deprive Muslim women of their rights. Further the Supreme Court construed the statutory provision in such a manner that it does not fall foul of Articles 14 and 15. The provision in question is Section 3(1)(a) of the Muslim Women (Protection of Rights on Divorce) Act, 1986 which states that "a reasonable and fair provision and maintenance to be made and paid to her within the iddat period by her former husband". The Court held this provision means that reasonable and fair provision and maintenance is not limited for the iddat period (as evidenced by the use of word "within" and not "for"). It extends for the entire life of the divorced wife until she remarries.

Text of the THE MUSLIM WOMEN (PROTECTION OF RIGHTS ON DIVORCE) ACT, 1986
ACT NO. 25 OF 1986

Preamble

[19th May, 1986.]

An Act to protect the rights of Muslim women who have been divorced by, or have obtained divorce from, their husbands and to provide for matters connected therewith or incidental thereto.

Be it enacted by Parliament in the Thirty-seventh year of the Republic of India as follows:

1. **Short title and extent.**

   (1) Short title and extent.

   (1) This Act may be called the Muslim Women (Protection of Rights on Divorce) Act, 1986.

   (2) It extends to the whole of India except the State of Jammu and Kashmir.

2. **Definitions.** In this Act, unless the context otherwise requires,

   (a) "divorced woman" means a Muslim woman who was married according to Muslim law, and has been divorced by, or has obtained divorce from, her husband in accordance with Muslim law;

(b) "iddat period" means, in the case of a divorced woman,-

(i) three menstrual courses after the date of divorce, if she is subject to menstruation; and

(ii) three lunar months after her divorce, if she is not subject to menstruation; and

(iii) if she is enceinte at the time of her divorce, the period between the divorce and the delivery of her child or the termination of her pregnancy, whichever is earlier;

(c) "Magistrate" means a Magistrate of the First class exercising jurisdiction under the Code of Criminal Procedure, 1973 (2 of 1974) in the area where the divorced woman resides;

(d) "prescribed" means prescribed by rules made under this Act.

3. Mehr or other properties of Muslim woman to be given to her at the time of divorce

(1) Notwithstanding anything contained in any other law for the time being in force, a divorced woman shall be entitled to :

(a) a reasonable and fair provision and maintenance to be made and paid to her within the *iddat* period by her former husband;

(b) where she herself maintains the children born to her before or after her divorce, a reasonable and fair provision and maintenance to be made and paid by her former husband for a period of two years from the respective dates of birth of such children;

(c) an amount equal to the sum of mehr or dower agreed to be paid to her at the time of her marriage or at any time thereafter according to Muslim law; and

(d) all the properties given to her before or at the time of or after her marriage by her relatives or friends or the husband or any relatives of the husband or his friends. marriage.

(2) Where a reasonable and fair provision and maintenance or the amount of mehr or dower due has not been made or paid or the properties referred to in clause (d) of sub-section (1) have not been delivered to a divorced woman on her divorce, she or any one duly authorised by her may, on her behalf, make an application to a

Magistrate for an order for payment of such provision and maintenance, mehr or dower or the delivery of properties; as the case may be.

(3) Where an application has been made under sub-section (2) by a divorced woman, the Magistrate may, if he is satisfied that

(a) her husband having sufficient means, has failed or neglected to make or pay her within the iddat period a reasonable and fair provision and maintenance for her and the children; or

(b) the amount equal to the sum of mehr or dower has not been paid or that the properties referred to in clause (d) of sub-section (1) have not been delivered to her, make an order, within one month of the date of the filing of the application, directing her former husband to pay such reasonable and fair provision and maintenance to the divorced woman as he may determine it as and having proper regard to the needs of the divorced woman, the standard of life enjoyed by her during her marriage and the means of her former husband or, as the case may be, for the payment of such mehr or dower or the delivery of such properties referred to in clause (d) of sub-section (1) of the divorced woman:

Provided that if the Magistrate finds it impracticable to dispose of the application within the said period, he may, for reasons to be recorded by him, dispose of the application after the said period.

(4) If any person against whom an order has been made under sub-section (3) fails without sufficient cause to comply with the order, the Magistrate may issue a warrant for levying the amount of maintenance or mehr or dower due in the manner provided for levying fines under the Code of Criminal Procedure, 1973 (2 of 1974), and may sentence such person, for the whole or part of any amount remaining unpaid after the execution of the warrant, to imprisonment for a term which may extend to one year or until payment if sooner made, subject to such person being heard in defence and the said sentence being imposed according to the provisions of the said Code.

4. Order for payment of maintenance.

(1) Notwithstanding anything contained in the foregoing provisions of this Act or in any other law for the time being in force, where a Magistrate is satisfied that a divorced woman has not re-married and is not able to maintain herself after the *iddat* period, he may make an order directing such of her relatives as would be entitled to inherit her property on her death according to Muslim law to pay such reasonable and fair maintenance to her as he may determine fit and proper, having regard to the needs of the divorced woman, the standard of life enjoyed by her during her marriage and the means of such relatives and such maintenance shall be payable by such relatives in the proportions in which they would inherit the property and at such periods as he may specify in his order:

Provided that where such divorced woman has children, the Magistrate shall order only such children to pay maintenance to her, and in the event of any such children being unable to pay such maintenance, the Magistrate shall order the parents of such divorced woman to pay maintenance to her:

Provided further that if any of the parents is unable to pay his or her share of the maintenance ordered by the Magistrate on the ground of his or her not having the means to pay the same, the Magistrate may, on proof of such inability being furnished to him, order that the share of such relatives in the maintenance ordered by him be paid by such of the other relatives as may appear to the Magistrate to have the means of paying the same in such proportions as the Magistrate may think fit to order.

(2) Where a divorced woman is unable to maintain herself and she has no relatives as mentioned in sub-section (1) or such relatives or any one of them have not enough means to pay the maintenance ordered by the Magistrate or the other relatives have not the means to pay the shares of those relatives whose shares have been ordered by the Magistrate to be paid by such other relatives under the second proviso to sub-section (1), the Magistrate may, by order, direct the State Wakf Board established under section 9 of the Wakf Act, 1954 (29 of

1954), or under any other law for the time being in force in a State, functioning in the area in which the woman resides, to pay such maintenance as determined by him under sub-section (1) or, as the case may be, to pay the shares of such of the relatives who are unable to pay, at such periods as he may specify in his order.

5. **Option to be governed by the provisions of sections 125 to 128 of Act2 of 1974:** If on the date of the first hearing of the application under sub-section (2) of section 3, a divorced woman and her former husband declare, by affidavit or any other declaration in writing in such form as may be prescribed, either jointly or separately, that they would prefer to be governed by the provisions of sections 125 to 128 of the Code of Criminal Procedure, 1973 (2 of 1974), and file such affidavit or declaration in the court hearing the application, the Magistrate shall dispose of such application accordingly.

   Explanation. For the purposes of this section, "date of the first hearing of the application" means the date fixed in the summons for the attendance of the respondent to the application.

6. **Power to make rules**

   (1) The Central Government may, by notification in the Official Gazette, make rules for carrying out the purposes of this Act.

   (2) In particular and without prejudice to the foregoing power, such rules may provide for-

   (a) the form of the affidavit or other declaration in writing to be filed under section 5;

   (b) the procedure to be followed by the Magistrate in disposing of applications under this Act, including the serving of notices to the parties to such applications, dates of hearing of such applications and other matters;

   (c) any other matter which is required to be or may be prescribed.

   (3) Every rule made under this Act shall be laid, as soon as may be after it is made, before each House of Parliament, while it is in session, for a total period of thirty days which may be comprised in one session or in two or more successive sessions, and if, before the

expiry of the session immediately following the session or the successive sessions aforesaid, both Houses agree in making any modification in the rule or both Houses agree that the rule should not form or be of no effect, as the case may be; so, however, that any such modification or annulment shall be without prejudice to the validity of anything previously done under that rule. be made, the rule shall thereafter have effect only in such modified.

7. **Transitional provisions :** Every application by a divorced woman under section 125 or under section 127 of the Code of Criminal Procedure, 1973 (2 of 1974) pending before a Magistrate on the commencement of this Act, shall, notwithstanding anything contained in that Code and subject to the provisions of section 5 of this Act, be disposed of by such Magistrate in accordance with the provisions of this Act.

14

Indian Law and Rule for Prevention of *Sati*

The Practice of *Sati*

Sati was a religious funeral practice among some Indian communities in which a recently widowed woman either voluntarily or by use of force and coercion would have immolated herself on her husband's funeral pyre. The practice is rare and has been outlawed in India since 1829.

The term is derived from the original name of the goddess Sati, also known as Dakshayani, who self-immolated because she was unable to bear her father Daksha's humiliation of her (living) husband Shiva. The term may also be used to refer to the widow herself. The term *sati* is now sometimes interpreted as "chaste woman."

History

Origin

Few reliable records exist of the practice before the time of the Gupta empire, approximately 400 AD. After about this time, instances of *sati* began to be marked by inscribed memorial stones. The earliest of these are found in Sagar, Madhya Pradesh, though the largest collections date from several centuries later, and are found in Rajasthan. These stones, called *devli*, or sati-stones, became shrines to the dead woman, who was treated as an object of reverence and worship. They are most common in western India.

By about the 10th century sati, as understood today, was known across much of the subcontinent. It continued to occur, usually at a low frequency and with regional variations, until the early 19th century.

Widows did this because it was supposed to cast away any sins the husband had committed, making him able to have a happy afterlife. This was voluntary for the widow, but they were put under much pressure to do it and were looked upon as a bad person if they didn't go through with it.

Some instances of voluntary self-immolation by both women and men that may be regarded as at least partly historical accounts are included in the *Mahabharata* and other works. However, large portions of these works are relatively late interpolations into an original story, rendering difficult their use for reliable dating. Also, neither immolation, nor the desire for self-immolation are regarded as a custom in the Mahabharata. Use of the term 'sati' to describe the custom of self-immolation never occurs in the Mahabarata, unlike other customs such as the Rajasuya Yagna. Rather, the self-immolations are viewed as an expression of extreme grief at the loss of a beloved one.

The ritual has prehistoric roots, and many parallels from other cultures are known. Compare for example the ship burial of the Rus' described by Ibn Fadlan, where a female slave is burned with her master.

Aristobulus of Cassandreia, a Greek historian who traveled to India with the expedition of Alexander the Great, recorded the practice of *sati* at the city of Taxila. A later instance of voluntary co-cremation appears in an account of an Indian soldier in the army of Eumenes of Cardia, whose two wives vied to die on his funeral pyre, in 316 BC. The Greeks believed that the practice had been instituted to discourage wives from poisoning their old husbands.

Voluntary death at funerals have been described in northern India before the Gupta empire. The original practices were called *anumarana*, and were uncommon. Anumarana was not comparable to later understandings of sati, since the practices were not restricted to widows — rather, anyone, male or female, with personal loyalty to the deceased could commit suicide at a loved one's funeral. These included the deceased's relatives, servants, followers, or friends. Sometimes these deaths stemmed from vows of loyalty, and bear a slight resemblance to the later tradition of *seppuku* in Japan.

It is theorised that sati, enforced widowhood, and girl marriage were customs that were primarily intended to solve the problem of surplus women and surplus men in a caste and to maintain its endogamy.

Mughal Period

During the Mughal rule, *sati* became more widely practised, especially in the north.

Humayun issued a royal fiat against sati, which he later withdrew.

Akbar required that permission be granted by his officials, and these officials were instructed to delay the woman's decision for as long as possible. The reasoning was that she was less likely to choose to die once the emotions of the moment had passed. In the reign of Shah Jahan, widows with children were not allowed to burn under any circumstances. In other cases, governors did not readily give permission, but could be bribed to do so. Later on in the Mughal period, pensions, gifts and rehabilitative help were offered to the potential *sati* to wean her away from committing the act. Children were strictly forbidden from following the practice. The later Moghul rulers continued to put obstacles in the way but the practice still persisted in areas outside their capitals.

Guru Nanak, the first Guru of the Sikhs spoke out against the practice of sati.

The strongest attempts under the Mughals to control it were made by Aurangzeb. In 1663, he "issued an order that in all lands under Mughal control, never again should the officials allow a woman to be burnt". Despite such attempts however, the practice continued, especially during periods of war and upheaval.

British and other European Territories

By the end of the 18th century, the practice had been banned in territories held by some European powers. The Portuguese banned the practice in Goa by about 1515, though it is not believed to have been especially prevalent there. The Dutch and the French also banned it in Chinsurah and Pondicherry. The British who by then ruled much of the subcontinent, and the Danes, who held the small territories of Tranquebar and Serampore, permitted it until the 19th century.

Attempts to limit or ban the practice had been made by individual British officers in the 18th century, but without the backing of the British East India Company. The first formal British ban was imposed in 1798, in the city of Calcutta only. The practice continued in surrounding regions. Toward the end of the 18th century, the evangelical church in Britain, and its members in India, started campaigns against sati. Leaders of these campaigns included William Carey and William Wilberforce, and both appeared to be motivated by their love for the Indian people and their desire to introduce Indians to Christianity. These movements put pressure on the company to ban the act, and the Bengal Presidency started collecting figures on the practice in 1813.

The leader of the burgeoning Swaminarayan sect, Sahajanand Swami, was influential in the eventual eradication of sati. He argued that the practice had no Vedic standing and only God could take a life he had given. He also argued that widows could lead a life that would eventually lead to salvation. Governor Malcolm supported Sahajanand in this endeavor, whose domino effect led to other social reforms.

From about 1812, the Bengali reformer Raja Rammohan Roy started his own campaign against the practice. He was motivated by the experience of seeing his own sister-in-law being forced to commit sati. Among his actions, he visited Calcutta cremation grounds to persuade widows not to die so, formed watch groups to do the same, and wrote and disseminated articles to show that it was not required by scripture.

On 4 December 1829, the practice was formally banned in the Bengal Presidency lands, by the then governor, Lord William Bentinck. The ban was challenged in the courts, and the matter went to the Privy Council in London, but was upheld in 1832. Other company territories also banned it shortly after. Although the original ban in Bengal was fairly uncompromising, later in the century British laws included provisions that provided mitigation for murder when "the person whose death is caused, being above the age of 18 years, suffers death or takes the risk of death with his own consent".

Sati remained legal in some princely states for a time after it had been abolished in lands under British control. Jaipur, banned the practice in 1846. Nepal continued to practice *Sati* well into the 20th century.

On the Indonesian island of Bali, *sati* (known as *masatya*) was practised by the aristocracy as late as 1905, until Dutch colonial rule pushed for its termination.

THE COMMISSION OF SATI (PREVENTION) ACT, 1987 (No. 3 of 1988)

An Act to provide for the more effective prevention of the commission of sati and its glorification and for matters connected therewith or incidental thereto.

Whereas *sati* or the burning or burying alive of widows or women is revolting to the feelings of human nature and nowhere enjoined by any of the religions of India as an imperative duty;

And whereas it is necessary to take more effective measure to prevent the commission of *sati* and its glorification;

Be it enacted by Parliament in the Thirty-eighth Year of Republic of India as follows:

PART I

Preliminary

1. Short title, extent and commencement.

(1) This Act may be called the Commission of *Sati* (Prevention) Act, 1987.It extends to the whole of India except the State of Jammu and Kashmir.(3) It shall come into force in a State on such date as the Central Government may, by notification in the Official Gazette, appoint, and different dates may be appointed for different States.

2. Definitions.

(1) In this Act, unless the context otherwise requires.-

(a) "Code" means the Code of Criminal Procedure, 1973 (2 of 1974);

(b) "glorification" in relation to *sati,* whether such *sati*, was committed before or after the commencement of this Act, includes, among other things:

(i) the observance of any ceremony or the taking out of a procession in connection with the commission of *sati*; or

(ii) the supporting, justifying or propagating the practice of *sati* in any manner; or

(iii) the arranging of any function to eulogise the person who has committed *sati*; or

(iv) the creation of a trust, or the collection of funds, or the construction of temple or other structure or the carrying on of any form of worship or the performance of any ceremony there of, with a view to perpetuate the honour of, or to preserve the memory of, a person who has committed sati;

(c) "*sati*" means the burning or burying alive of –

(i) any widow along with the body of her deceased husband or any other relative or with any article, object or thing associated with the husband or such relative; or

(ii) any woman along with the body of any of her relatives, irrespective of whether such burning or burying is claimed to be voluntary on the part of the widow or the women or otherwise;"Special Court" means a Special Court constituted under Sec.9;(e) "temple" includes any building or other structure, whether roofed or not, constructed or made to preserve the memory or a person in respect of whom *sati* has been committed or used or intended to be used for the carrying on of any form of worship or for the observance of any ceremony in connection with such commission.

(2) Words and expressions used but not defined in this Act and defined in the Indian Penal Code (45 of 1860) or in the Code shall have the same meanings as are respectively assigned to them in the Indian Panel Code or the Code.

PART II

Punishment for offences relating to *Sati*

3. Attempt to commit *sati*. Notwithstanding anything contained in the Indian Penal Code (45 of 1860), whoever attempts to commit *sati* and does any act towards such commission shall be punishable with imprisonment for a term which may extend to one year or with fine or with both:Provided that the Special Court trying an offence under this section shall, before convicting any person, take into consideration the circumstances leading to the commission of the offence, the act committed, the state of mind of the person charged of the offence at the time of the commission of the act and all other relevant factors.

4. Abetment of sati

(1) Notwithstanding anything contained in the Indian Penal Code (45 of 1860), if any person commits *sati*, whoever

abets the commission of such sati, either directly or indirectly, shall be punishable with death or imprisonment for life and shall also be liable to fine.

(2) If any person attempts to commit *sati*, whoever abets such attempt, either directly or indirectly, shall be punishable with imprisonment for life and shall also be liable to fine.Explanation.- For the purposes of this section, any of the following acts or the like shall also be deemed to be an abetment, namely:

(a) any inducement to a widow or woman to get her burnt or buried alive along with the body of her deceased husband or with any other relative or with any article, object or thing associated with the husband or such relative, irrespective of whether she is in a fit state of mind or is labouring under a state of intoxication or stupefaction or other cause impeding the exercise of her free will;

(b) making a widow or woman believe that the commission of *sati* would result in some spiritual benefit to her or her deceased husband or relative or the general well being of the family;

(c) encouraging a widow or woman to remain fixed in her resolve to commit *sati* and thus instigating her to commit *sati*;

(d) participating in any procession in connection with the commission of *sati* or aiding the widow or woman in her decision to commit *sati* by taking her along with the body of her deceased husband or relative to the cremation or burial ground;

(e) being present at the place where *sati* is committed as an active participant to such commission or to any ceremony connected with it;

(f) preventing or obstructing the widow or woman from saving herself from being burnt or buried alive;

(g) obstructing, or interfering with, the police in the discharge of its duties of taking any steps to prevent the commission of *sati*.

5. Punishment for glorification of sati. Whoever does any act for the glorification of *sati* shall be punishable with imprisonment for a term which shall not be less than one year but which may extend to seven years and with fine which shall not be less than five thousand rupees but which may extend to thirty thousand rupees.

PART III

Powers of Collector or District Magistrate to prevent offences relating to Sati

6. Power to prohibit certain acts.

(1) where the Collector or the District Magistrate is of the opinion that *sati* or any abetment thereof is being, or is about to be committed, he may, by order, prohibit the doing of any act towards the commission of *sati* by any person in any area or areas specified in the order.

(2) The Collector or the District Magistrate may also, by order, prohibit the glorification in any manner of *sati* by any person in any area or areas specified in the order.

(3) Whoever contravenes any order made under sub-section (1) or sub-section (2) shall, if such contravention is not punishable under any other provision of this Act, be punishable with imprisonment for a term which shall not be less than one year but which may extend to seven years and with fine which shall not be less than five thousand rupees but which may extend to thirty thousand rupees.

7. Power to remove certain temples or other structures.

(1) The State Government may, if it is satisfied in that any temple or other structure which has been in existence for not less than twenty years, any form of worship or the performance of any ceremony is carried on with a view to perpetuate the honour of or to preserve the memory of, any person in respect of whom *sati* has been committed, by order, direct the removal of such temple or other structure.

(2) The Collector or the District magistrate may, if he is satisfied that in any temple or other structure, other than that referred to in sub-section (1), any form of worship or the performance of any ceremony is carried on with a view to perpetuate the honour of, or to preserve the memory of, any person in respect of whom *sati* has been committed, by order, direct the removal of such temple or other structure.

(3) Where any order under sub-section (1) or sub-section (2) is not complied with, the State Government or the Collector or the District Magistrate, as the case may

be, shall cause the temple or other structure to be removed through a police officer not below the rank of a Sub-Inspector at the cost of the defaulter.

8. Power to seize certain properties.

(1) Where the Collector or the District Magistrate has reason to believe that any funds or property have been collected or acquired for the purpose of glorification of the commission of any *sati* or which may be found under circumstances which create suspicion of the commission of any offence under this Act, he may seize such funds or property.

(2) Every Collector or District Magistrate acting under sub-section (1) shall report the seizure to the Special Court, if any, constituted to try any offence in relation to which such funds or property were collected or acquired and shall await the orders of such Special Court as to the disposal of the same.

PART IV

Special Courts

9. Trial of offences under this Act.

(1) Notwithstanding anything contained in the Code, all offences under this Act shall be triable only by a Special Court constituted under this section.

(2) The State Government shall, by notification in the official Gazette, constitute one or more Special Courts for the trial of offences under this Act and every Special Court shall exercise jurisdiction in respect of the whole or such part of the State as may be specified in the notification.

(3) A Special Court shall be presided over by a judge to be appointed by the State Government with the concurrence of the Chief Justice of the High Court.

(4) A person shall not be qualified for appointment as a judge of a Special Court unless he is, immediately before such appointment, a Sessions Judge or an Additional Sessions Judge in any State.

10. Special Public Prosecutions.

(1) For every Special Court, the State Government shall appoint a person to be a Special Public Prosecutor.

(2) A person shall be eligible to be appointed as a Special

Public Prosecutor under this section only if he had been in practice as an advocate for not less than seven years or has held any post for a period of not less than seven years under the State requiring special knowledge of law.

(3) Every person appointed as a Special Public Prosecutor under this section shall be deemed to be a Public Prosecutor within the meaning of Cl. (u) of Sec. 2 of the Code and the Provisions of the Code shall have effect accordingly.

11. Procedure and powers of Special Courts.

(1) A Special Court may take cognizance of any offence, without the accused being committed to it for trial, upon receiving a complaint of facts which constitute such offence, or upon a police report of such facts.

(2) Subject to the other provisions of this Act, a Special Court shall for the purpose of the trial of any offence, have all the powers of a Court of Session and shall try such offence as if it were a Court of Session, so far as may be, in accordance with the procedure prescribed in the Code for trial before a Court of Session.

12. Power of Special Court with respect to other offences.

(1) When trying any offence under this Act, a Special Court may also try any other offence with which the accused may, under the Code, be charged at the same trial if the offence is connected with such other offence.

(2) If, in the course of any trial of any offence under this Act it is found that the accused person has committed any other offence under this Act or any other law, a Special Court may convict such person also of such other offence and pass any sentence authorised by this Act or such other law for the punishment thereof.

(3) In every inquiry or trial, the proceedings shall be held as expeditiously as possible and, in particular, where the examination of witnesses has begun, the same shall be continued from day to day until all the witnesses in attendance have been examined, and if any Special Court finds the adjournment of the same beyond the following date to be necessary, it shall record its reasons for doing so.

13. Forfeiture of funds or property. Where a person has been convicted of an offence under this Act, the Special Court trying such offence may, if it is considered necessary to do so, declare that any funds or property seized under Sec. 8 shall stand forfeited to the State.

14. Appeal. Notwithstanding anything contained in the Code, an appeal shall lie as a matter of right from any judgement, sentence or order, not being an interlocutory order, of a Special Court to the High Court both of facts and on law.(2) Every appeal under this section shall be preferred within a period of thirty days from the date of judgment, sentence or order appealed from:Provided that the High Court may entertain an appeal after the expiry of the said period of thirty days if it is satisfied that the appellant had sufficient cause for not preferring the appeal within the period of thirty days.

PART V

Miscellaneous

15. Protection of action taken under this Act. No suit, prosecution or other legal proceeding shall lie against the State Government or any officer or authority of the State Government for anything which is in good faith done or intended to be done in pursuance of this Act or any rules or orders made under this Act.

16. Burden of proof. Where any person is prosecuted of an offence under Sec. 4, the burden of proving that he had not committed the offence under the said section shall be on him.

17. Obligation of certain persons to report about the commission of offence under this Act.

(1) All officers of Government are hereby required and empowered to assist the police in the execution of the provisions of this Act or any rule or order made there under.

(2) All village officers and such other officers as may be specified by the Collector or the District Magistrate in relation to any area and the inhabitants of such area shall, if they have reason to believe or have the knowledge that *sati* is about to be, or has been, committed in the area shall forthwith report such fact to the nearest police station.

(3) Whoever contravenes the provision of sub-section (1) or sub-section (2) shall be punishable with imprisonment of either description for a term which may extend to two years and shall also be liable to fine.

18. Person convicted of an offence under Sec. 4 to be disqualified form inheriting certain properties. A person convicted of an offence under sub-section (1) of Sec. 4 in relation to the commission of *sati* shall be disqualified from inheriting the property of the person in respect of whom such *sati* has been committed or the property of any other person which he would have been entitled to inherit on the death of person in respect of whom such *sati* has been committed.

Amendment of Act 43 of 1951. In the Representation of the People Act, 1951.

(a) in Sec. 8, in sub-section (2) after the proviso, the following proviso shall be inserted, namely;"Provided further that a person convicted by a Special Court for the contravention of any of the provisions of the Commission of *Sati* (Prevention) Act, 1987 shall be disqualified from the date of such conviction and shall continue to be disqualified for a further period of five years since his release";

(b) in Sec. 123 after Cl.(3-A), the following clause shall be inserted, namely:"(3-B) The propagation of the practice or the commission of *sati* or its glorification by a candidate or his agent or any other person with the consent of the candidate or his election agent for the furtherance of the prospects of the election of that candidate or for prejudicially affecting the election of any candidate.

Explanation. For the purpose of this clause, *"sati"* and "glorification" in relation to *sati* shall have the meanings respectively assigned to them in the Commission of *Sati* (Prevention) Act, 1987."

20. Act to have overriding effect. The provision of this Act or any rule or order made thereunder shall have effect notwithstanding anything inconsistent therewith contained in any enactment other than this Act or in any instrument having effect by virtue of any enactment other than this Act.

21. Power to make rules.

(1) The Central Government may, by notification in the Official Gazette, make rules for carrying out the provisions of this Act.

(2) Every rule made under this section shall be laid, as soon as may be after it is made, before each House of Parliament, while it is in session, for a total period of thirty days which may be comprised in one session or in two or more successive sessions, and if, before the expiry of the session immediately following the session or the successive sessions aforesaid, both Houses agree in making any modification in the rule or both Houses agree that the rule should not be made, the rule shall thereafter have effect only in such modified form or be of no effect, as the case may be; so however, that any such modification or annulment shall be without prejudice to the validity of anything previously done under that rule.

Repeal of existing laws.

(1) All laws in force in any State immediately before the commencement of this Act in that State which provide for the prevention or the glorification of *sati* shall, on such comment, stand repealed.

2) Notwithstanding, such repeal, anything done or any action taken under any law repealed under sub-section (1) shall be deemed to have been done or taken under the corresponding provisions of this Act, and, in particular, any case taken cognizance of by a Special Court under the provisions of any law so repealed and pending before it immediately before the commencement of this Act in that State shall continue to be dealt with by that Special Court after such commencement as if such Special Court had been constituted under Sec. 9 of this Act.

Text of the COMMISSION OF SATI (PREVENTION) RULES, 1988

G.S. 360(E), dated 21st March, 1988. In exercise of the powers conferred by Sec. 21 of the Commission of *Sati* (Prevention) Act, 1987 (3 of 1988), the Central Government hereby makes the following rules, namely:

1. Short title and commencement.

(1) These rules may be called the Commission of *Sati* (Prevention) Rules, 1988.

(2) They shall come into force on the date of their publication in the Official Gazette.

2. Definitions.

(1) In these rules, unless the context otherwise requires,- "Act" means the Commission of *Sati* (Prevention) Act, 1987 (3 of 1988); "prohibitory order" means an order issued under Sec. 6; "section" means section of the Act.

(2) Words and expressions used but not defined in these rules and defined in the Act shall have the same meanings as are respectively assigned to them in the Act.

3. Delegation of power to prohibit certain acts.

(1) The State Government may, by order and subject to such conditions as it may deem fit to impose, direct that the powers of the Collector or the District Magistrate under Sec. 6 may also be exercised by such other officers not below the rank of the village officers.

4. Prohibitory orders under Sec. 6, how made.

(1) Every prohibitory order under Sec. 6 shall be made by beat of drum or other customary mode, in the concerned village, or in case of town or city, in the locality in which the act prohibited is likely to occur or has taken place.

(2) The prohibitory order shall be displayed at some conspicuous place in the area or areas to which such acts relates and a copy thereof shall also be displayed in the office of the officer issuing the prohibitory order and such display shall be taken as a sufficient notice to all persons concerned in the area of areas to which such order relates.

5. Manner of making order for removal of temples or structures under sub-section (1) of Sec. 7

(1) Before making any order under sub-section (1) of Sec. 7 for removal of any temple or structure, the State Government or any other officer authorised by the State Government in this behalf, shall give at least ninety days' notice to the person or persons involved in the

acts complained of, and also to the owners and occupiers of the temple or structure proposed to be removed.

(2) The notice under sub-rule (1) shall specify

(1) the temple/structure proposed to be removed, its location and other particulars,

(2) the owners/occupiers of the temple/structure, and

(3) the specific instance or instances of worship or ceremony contravening the provisions of Sec.7.

(3) The Government or the officer authorised by the State Government in this behalf shall, after giving reasonable opportunity of being heard to the persons specified in the notice, order the removal of the temple or structure through a police not below the rank of the Sub-Inspector.

6. Manner of making order for removal of temples or structures under sub-section (2) of Sec. 7.

(1) After issue of a prohibitory order under Sec. 6, the Collector or the District Magistrate, or such other officer as directed by the State Government by order under rule 3 shall, before making any order for removal of any temple or structure under sub-section (2) of Sec. 7 give at least ninety days' notice to the owners and occupiers of the temple or structure proposed to be removed.

(2) The Collector of the District Magistrate, or such other officer as directed by the State Government by order under rule 3, shall follow the provisions of sub-rules (2) and (3) of rule 4 in the case of orders made under this rule.

7. Inventory and forfeiture of the property of temple or structure. As soon as the order of removal of the temple or structure is executed, the State Government or the Collector or the District Magistrate, or as the case may be, the officer as directed by the State Government by order under rule 3, shall prepare an inventory of all the material and other property obtained after removal of such temple or structure specifying in it the place where it is lodged or kept, and shall forward the intimation thereof to the Special court for declaration of forfeiture of the said material or property to the State under Sec. 13, if the Special Court considers it necessary so to do, and shall also give a copy of the inventory to the owners/occupiers of the temple/structure removed.

Appendix

Indian LAWS RELATED TO VIOLENCE AGAINST WOMEN

Women's Rights Related to Police in India

Rights During Interrogation:

- You cannot be taken to the Police Station or anywhere else for interrogation.
- You can be questioned only at your residence and in presence of your family members.
- You can consult with your lawyer when you are being interrogated whether you are arrested or not.
- You cannot be forced to make confession before the Police or before the Magistrate.

Rights at the Time of Arrest

- You must be told why you are arrested, of your right to bail and of your right to a lawyer of your choice.
- No use of handcuffs at the time of your arrest without a Judge's Permission.
- You can demand that you be produced before the Magistrate within 24 Hours of your arrest.
- A female constable must be present when you are arrested.
- You can take along your relative or friend to the Police Station.
- The Police arresting you must wear clear and visible name tag on uniform.
- Memo of Arrest to be made, with date and time of arrest and signed by a family member/respectable neighbour.
- The Police must inform any person interested in your welfare (or the Legal Aid Committee), if such person lives outside

the Area), your arrest and the location of the place at which you are kept while under arrest.

- An Accurate list of things seized from you must be prepared and you are entitled to a copy immediately.

Rights in the Police Station

- You have the right to demand that you should be placed in a female lockup.
- You have the right to ask the Magistrate for your Medical Examination if you are beaten, abused or tortured by the Police.

Rights of Medical Examination

- Request immediate medical examination on arrest. The medical examiner must record all injuries on a written form. Only sign an accurately filled form.
- Ask for a copy of this form.
- Ask the Magistrate to send you to hospital before the Police Custody is granted.
- A Medical Examination every 48 Hours while in custody.
- If you are under 18 years of age and your age is recorded wrongly, if there is no documentary proof of your age, insist on medical examination to determine your age.
- Make an application for medical treatment in case of unstable health conditions.

Rights At The Time of Search

- Search by a female officer only.
- Two independent witnesses should always be present when you/your premises are searched.
- Call two witnesses (not from your Family) to witness the search.

Production in Court

- You can demand a chair from the Court to sit during trial.
- You have the right to get legible copies of all documents of accusations filed against you in the Court.
- You can demand food and other basic amenities during your custody in the court.
- You have to be produced before a Magistrate within twenty-

four hours of arrest. If you are not produced within 24 hours complain to the Magistrate.

- You cannot be remanded to custody in your absence.

Torture is Illegal

- Torture is illegal. No solitary confinement, punitive cells, hard labor, change in the diet or transfers without permission of Judge.
- If a confession has been taken after torture, inform the Judge immediately and retract it.
- Complain to Court about torture / beating and show any injuries State must pay compensation for illegal arrest / torture.

Children and Juveniles

- In case of persons under 18 years of age, age to be verified by documents or medical examination.
- No remand to jail or police lock up. Must be sent to Juvenile Homes.
- All investigation to be completed within 4 months of complaint/FIR and inquiry before the Juvenile Justice Board disposed of in 6 months. No imprisonment / death sentence to be awarded to the child.
- Children of destitute prisoners, who have no one to take care of them, must be taken care of by the State.

Legal Advice

- If poor, you have a right to demand a competent counsel at State expenses from the Court.
- If your Lawyer is not competent you have the right to change your Lawyer.
- You have a right to interviews, visits, and confidential communications with your lawyer.

Bail

- Keep the following ready for production on grant of Bail: -
  - Proofs of identity like Salary Slips, Rent Receipts, Ration Cards, Bank Passbooks, etc.
  - Sureties with above documents.
- If you are refused bail you have a right to get bail if: -

- The Charge sheet is not filed within 60 days of arrest where your offence is punishable with imprisonment of less than 10 years.
- The Charge sheet is not filed within 90 days of arrest where your offence is punishable with imprisonment of more than 10 years.

- If your bail is set too high, apply for reduction.

First Information Report (FIR)

- You can demand that your FIR be registered.
- You can take along any friend or relative at the time of filing FIR.
- You must read the FIR or have some one else read it to you, before you sign it.
- You have a right to receive a free copy of the FIR.
- You can approach Senior Police Officers or your Area Magistrate, if the Police is not registering your FIR.

Prison Custody

- Persons below the age of 18 must be sent to an observation home only.
- You have the right to write and receive letters.
- You have the right to meet with your family and friends.
- You can receive books, newspapers and other publications.
- You may have a journalist to interview you.
- You have to get reasonable wages for your labor while in prison.
- You have a right to decent food, soap, clothing, bedding etc.
- You cannot be transferred to prisons in far away places.

HIV + or Terminal Illness

- You may be entitled to premature release.

Furlough / Parole

- According to Rules, you may leave from prison for certain periods for specific reasons.

2. Laws Pertaining to Violence Against Women

This chapter deals with the most commonly associated legislations in relation to cases to violence against women. An attempt has been made to explain these laws in a layperson's language. So that it can be easily understood. It is also to inform people and more particularly, women about the protective legislations that are in place to seek redress when subjected to physical and mental torture.

(a) Indian Laws Pertaining to Domestic Violence

There is no specific Law to deal with domestic Violence:

- However the existing criminal law provisions can be used to initiate proceedings against the husband or his relatives in the court of Magistrate where the incident took place.
- A complaint can be filed under Section 498-A for any physical or mental harassment / Torture / Abuse etc.
- If the abuse / harassment / torture/ ill-treatment is not linked with dowry demands, don't mention dowry demands and file the complaint section 498-A only. However, if any monetary / financial demands have been made and you have been subjected to cruelty, then file the complaint under both the provisions i.e., for harassment and also dowry demands.
- File the Complaint as early as possible in the concerned Police Station.
- In the Complaint you must mention all the facts and brief narration of the events-both the past and the immediate cause just before filing of the complaint.
- These events must be of such a nature that it causes grave injury or danger to the life or health of the women or drives a woman to commit suicide.
- Offences under Section 498-A are cognizable and non-bailable i.e., the Police Officer can arrest without a warrant and cannot grant bail themselves. The accused Party has to obtain the Bail Order from the concerned Court.

Civil Remedy (Domestic Violence)

Sometimes, the woman due to personal reasons may not like to go for criminal remedy i.e., registration of FIR or filing the Criminal Complaint. In the said circumstances, there are certain Civil Remedies available in the Case of Domestic Violence:

- You can file suit under Order VII Rule I of the Code of Civil Procedure in the Family Court or where there is no Family Court in a Civil Court against the husband or relatives who are harassing you to seek any of the following orders:

- That the spouse or / and his relatives are restrained from ousting you and your children from the matrimonial house.
- That exclusive possession of the matrimonial house should be granted to you and to your children.
- That the spouse or / and his relatives may be restrained from entering the premises or any part of it, which is in your occupation.
- That your personal property be restored to you.
- That spouse or / and his relatives be restrained from alienating / transferring the matrimonial house by way of sale, gift, rent or inducting any third party into the matrimonial house.
- That the spouse or / and his relatives be restrained from further abusing / molesting you and your children.
- In case of a Hindu woman, she can seek for separate residence under Section 18 of the Hindu Adoption and Maintenance Act.

Rape

- Rape is an offence not against the Individual but like all the crimes in the Indian Penal Code, it is a crime against the State.
- Once the incident occurs, it has to be reported immediately without any delay to the police station of Jurisdiction. As far as possible the complaint must be given in writing containing all relevant facts in order to avoid manipulation. Then the police will investigate the matter and file a chargesheet.
- The information, i.e., the person filing the complaint is entitled to a copy of the First Information Report (FIR).
- The victim must undergo medical examination conducted by a female medical officer.
- The trial is conducted in a Sessions court.
- Like all criminal matters the victim cannot have an independent lawyer, unless she makes an application for appointing a Special Prosecutor. Any advocate with 10 years of practice can be appointed as a Special Public Prosecutor.

Sexual Harassment at Work Place

No specific law regarding sexual harassment, Supreme Court has laid down guidelines in Vishaka's case (AIR 1997 Supreme

Court 3011) Any unwelcome sexually determined behaviour – direct or implicit viz.,

- Physical contact and advances
- Demand or request for sexual favours
- Sexually coloured remarks
- Showing pornography
- Any other unwelcomed physical, verbal or non-verbal conduct of sexual nature.

Such Acts Committed Amounts to Sexual Harassment

- Where the victim has a reasonable apprehension
- That such conduct is humiliating
- Constitutes health and safety problem
- When the victim has a reasonable ground to believe that her objections to such acts would disadvantage, would prejudice her in connection with work, recruitment, promotion, creates a hostile work atmosphere.
- When non-consent /objections to such acts entails adverse consequences.

Duties and Obligations as Per Judgment

(a) Duty to Prevent Commission of Acts of Sexual Harassment

- Identify the acts that constitute sexual harassment
- Prohibit acts of sexual harassment at workplace.
- Penalise commission of acts of sexual harassment.
- Abetment to be defined to include non-action of the official concerned.
- Notify, Publish and circulate – acts prohibited.
- Provide congenial atmosphere – work –leisure and Health-hygiene.
- That no women employee should have grounds to believe that she is disadvantaged in connection with her work.
- Provide optional transfer, if the victim feels necessary.
- Incorporate sexual harassment in conduct rules.
- Incorporate in the Industrial Standing Order.
- Initiate disciplinary proceedings.
- Initiate criminal proceeding under IPC.

- Ensure prevention to victimisation and discrimination of victims and witnesses.
- Facilitate discussions in employee – employer meeting.
- Create awareness among women about sexual harassment.

(b) Duty to Provide Procedure for Resolution Complaint Mechanism headed by women.

(c) Duties of the committee: provide counselling, medical aid, legal aid, maintain confidentiality and time bound inquiry.

THE INDECENT REPRESENTATION OF WOMEN (PROHIBITION) ACT, INDIA, 1986

- The Act prohibits depiction in any manner the figure of woman, body or any part thereof, in such a way that has the effect of being indecent or derogatory to or denigrating women.
- It intends to prevent women being depicted as sex objects in the media for commercial gain or prevent the co-modification of women.
- This Act intends to prohibit indecent representation of women in writing, paintings and figures or in any manner that is likely to corrupt or injure the public morality or morals.
- It penalizes person who publishes or arranges or takes part in the publication or exhibition of any advertisement which contain indecent representation of women in any form.
- It penalizes persons who sell, hire, distribute, circulate or send by posts any books, pamphlets, paper, slide, film, writings, drawings, paintings, photograph, figures or representation which contains indecent representation of women in any form.
- The punishment is imprisonment for a term which may extend to two years with fine up to Rs. 2000/-
- However, certain exceptions are made in favour of religion, art, learning and ancient monuments.
- The Act empowers Gazetted Officers authorised by the State Government to enter and search premises, seize articles and examine records or materials which he has reasons to believe to be in the nature of contraventions of the Act.
- The Indian Penal Code penalizes obscenity.

IMMORAL TRAFFIC (PREVENTION) ACT, 1956

- In India prostitution is tolerated and regulated.
- Prostitution is per se not a crime. Prostitution is not abolished /prohibited/banned.
- The Act intends to criminalise and penalise the Institutions/ Industry (brothel, brothel keepers, procurers, pimps, touts, middlemen, landlords etc.). But actually ends up criminalising and penalising women.
- Trafficking of persons – male/female is prohibited.
- Prevention of sexual exploitation of persons for commercial purposes.
- Soliciting and/or seduction in public places is a crime.
- Offences involving children/minor-stringent punishment.
- Does not address the health concerns of the persons trafficked.
- Provides for Rescue and Rehabilitation of the prostituted women.
- Voluntary rehabilitation
- Removal of prostitutes from any place – on complaint
- Special enforcement mechanism
- This does not focus on persons who are voluntary in this field.
- Provides for mandatory testing for STD.

THE MEDICAL TERMINATION OF PREGNANCY ACT, INDIA, 1971

- Abortion in India has been legalised since the year 1971.
- A pregnancy may be terminated by a Registered Medical Practitioner.
    - (i) where the length of the pregnancy does not exceed twelve weeks, if such medical practitioner is, or
    - (ii) where the length of the pregnancy exceeds twelve weeks but does not exceed twenty weeks, if not less than two registered medical practitioners are consulted.
- If the doctor/s is/are of the opinion that continuance of the pregnancy would involve a risk to the life of the pregnant woman or would cause grave injury to her physical or mental health.

- The continuation of pregnancy would cause substantial risk and if the child were born it would suffer such physical or mental abnormalities as to be seriously handicapped.
- If the pregnancy is caused by rape and the anguish caused by such pregnancy is presumed to constitute a grave injury to the mental health of the pregnant woman.
- If the pregnancy occurs as a result of failure of family planning device, the anguish caused by such unwanted pregnancy may be presumed to constitute a grave injury to the mental health of the pregnant woman.
- No pregnancy shall be terminated without the consent of the pregnant woman.
- Termination of pregnancy shall be made only in the hospital established or maintained by the government or such other places as approved by the government.

THE PRE-NATAL DIAGNOSTIC TECHNIQUES (REGULATION AND PREVENTION OF MISUSE) ACT, INDIA 1994 AS AMENDED: 2003

'The Pre-Natal Diagnostic Techniques (Regulation and Prevention of Misuse) Act' was passed in 1994 and rules were framed in 1996.

The main objective of the Act is to provide for the Regulation of the use of the Pre -Natal Diagnostic Techniques for the purpose of detecting genetic and metabolic disorders or chromosonal abnormalities or certain congenital malformations or sex linked disorders and for the Prevention of the misuse of such techniques leading to female foeticide and for matter connected therewith and incidental thereto. In others words, it can be said that the Act does not prohibited the tests rather it permits the same in certain situations with certain conditions of detecting the genetic disorders of the foetus with a condition not to disclose the Sex of foetus to the woman or her relative or to any person in any form/way.

The Salient Features of the Act are:

- The act is prohibitory as well as regulatory both in nature.
- There is prohibition of the misuse of Pre-Natal Diagnostic Techniques (after amendment the act has become operative before conception also) for determining of the sex of the foetus leading to Female Foeticide.
- Prohibition of advertisement of Pre -Natal Diagnostic Techniques for detection or determination of sex.

- Permission and regulation of the use of Pre-Natal Diagnostic Techniques for the purpose of detecting genetic abnormalities or disorder.
- Permitting the use of such techniques only under certain conditions at registered place by qualified staff.
- Under no circumstances these techniques are to be used to determine the sex of the foetus.
- No person conducting the Pre-Natal Diagnostic Procedure shall communicate to the pregnant woman concerned or her relatives or to any person the sex of the foetus through words, sign or in any other manner.
- The Act is to be implemented by Appropriate Authorities at State Level, District level and sub-district level.
- All offences under the Act are cognizable, non-bailable and non-compoundable.
- An appropriate authority shall take note of violations under the act. Violations may also be brought to the attention of the appropriate authority by a person/ Company/NGO etc. Within 15 days of receiving the complaint the appropriate Authority shall take action.
- The complaint shall lie before the Judicial Magistrate of 1st class.
- The appropriate authority is to file the complaint. If the notice of 15 days has already been given to the appropriate authority by a person/company and no action has been taken on the same, that person can also file the complaint.
- The violations are punishable with imprisonment, which may extend to Rs. fifty thousand.
- On any subsequent conviction imprisonment may extend to five years and fine, which may extend to Rs. one lac
- In case of Registered Medical Practitioner, his name shall be reported by the appropriate authority to the State Medical council concerned for taking necessary action:-
  - Including suspension of the registration if charges are framed by the court and till the case is disposed of, and
  - For the removal of his name from the register of the council on conviction for the period of

    Five years for the first offence;

    Permanently for the subsequent offence.

- Under the Act no role has been assigned to the police. Police can be called only by the appropriate authority at time of search and seizure if he believes that there is any law and order problem.
- There is presumption in the favour of woman unless proved guilty. The PNDT Act, has been amended with a view to banning the use of the sex selection techniques prior to conception as well as the misuse of Pre Natal Diagnostic Techniques for sex selective abortions and to regulate such techniques. Amendments have also been brought about in the Rules to ensure effective implementation of the Act and in view of the observation of the Supreme Court. The amended Act was notified in January 2003 and the amended rules were notified in February 2003. The amended Act and Rules are discussed as below:

Definitions

Sex Selection (before/after conception) prohibited and has been added under definition of Pre-Natal Diagnostic procedure.

The terms Conceptus, Embryo, Foetus, Sex-Selection, Sonologist, Medical Geneticist etc. have been defined in the amended Act.

The term Genetic Clinic and Genetic Laboratory has been re-defined to include a vehicle where ultrasound machine or a portable equipment having potential for detection of sex during pregnancy or selection of sex before conception is used.

Registration

In the PNDT Act 1994 the registration was mandatory for any Genetic Counselling Centre, Genetic Laboratory or Genetic Clinic. There were three things required for the registration i.e. the ultrasound machine, minimum space as mentioned and the qualified staff. Now after amendment in the Act the space has been relaxed as Adequate Space and so far as the staff is concerned the amended Act requires Post Graduation in the technique he is to carry out or MBBS with one years training or six months experience in the technique he is to carry out.

The amended Act further says that the ultrasound machines are only to be sold to the registered bodies. The seller of the machines are required to furnish the quarterly statement of their clients to the Appropriate Authority.

The seller of such machine/equipment to any person/body registered under the act shall take an affidavit from such body or person purchasing or getting authorisation for using such machine/ equipment that the machine/equipment shall not be used for detection of sex of foetus. (Rule 3A (2) and (3).

That vehicle may now be registered as Genetic Clinic if the other requirements are fulfilled and other conditions would apply as to Genetic Clinic.

Provision for Appeal

The amended Act says that the appeal may be made to the Appropriate Authority at the District level if the order is passed by the Appropriate Authority at sub-district level.

"The appeal may be made to the Appropriate Authority at the State/UT level if the order is passed by the Appropriate Authority at District level.

Each appeal shall be disposed of by the District Appropriate Authority or the State/UT as the case may be, within 60 days of its receipt.

Thus, a hierarchy of appellate bodies has been provided and further the time limit for the disposing of the appeals has been laid down. (New Rule 19)"

Prohibitions

In addition to the prohibition in the PNDT Act 1994 the following prohibition has been added to the amended act:

No person including a relative or husband of the pregnant woman shall seek or encourage the conduct of any Pre -Natal Diagnostic Techniques on her except for the purpose specified in clause (2) ('including' added after amendment).

No person including a relative or husband of a woman shall seek or encourage the conduct of any sex selection techniques on her or him or both (section 4) (sub-clause 5) (as amended)

No person, including a specialist or a team of specialists in the field of infertility, shall conduct or cause to be conducted or aid in conducting by himself or by any other person, sex selection on a woman or a man or on both or on any tissue, embryo, conceptus, fluid or gametes derived from either or both of them. (Section 3A).

Advertisements regarding sex selection before/after conception prohibited including advertisement through Internet or any other media in electronic or print form.

Protection to Women

Section 23(4) has been added for protection of pregnant women compelled to undergo the PNDT. In other words it can be said that the presumption is in favour of woman unless proved guilty. But if the contrary is proved, the woman can also be likewise punished.

Who can make a Complaint

Any Appropriate Authority on Suo-motto or on receiving a complaint.

Any person/body who has given a notice of 15 days to the Appropriate Authority (previously it was 30 days).

Instrumentalities for Implementing the Act

Before amendment, generally the Director Health Services, was the State Appropriate Authority. Under the amendments, a Multi-member body has been provided as the State Appropriate Authority consisting of an officer of or above the rank of Joint Director of Health and Family Welfare-Chairperson, women organisation representative and officer of law department of state/ UT concerned.

Such authorities are to be constituted within three months of coming into force of the amended Act and any vacancy occurrence therein is required to be filled within three months.

There shall be appropriate authority at District level as sub-district level i.e. CMO and Civil Surgeon respectively.

Functions of State Appropriate Authority

According to the PNDT Act, 1994 the Appropriate Authority shall have the following functions namely:

- To grant, suspend or cancel registration of a Genetic Counselling Centre, Genetic Laboratory and Genetic Clinic.
- To enforce standards prescribed for the Genetic Counselling Centre, Genetic Laboratory and Genetic Clinic.
- To investigate complaints of breach of the provisions of this Act or the rules made thereunder and take immediate action; and

- To seek and consider the advice of the Advisory Committee constituted under sub-section (5), on application for registration and on complaints for suspension or cancellation of registration.

In addition to the above said functions the Appropriate Authority has been assigned the following functions (as per amended Act).

Summoning of any person who is in possession of any information relating to violation of Act. Production of any document or material object related to clause (a) Issuing search warrant for any place suspected to be indulged in sex determination. Any other matter, which may be prescribed.

Advisory Committee

The Act also provides for the appointment of an Advisory Committee by the Central or the State Government, as the case may be, to aid and advise the Appropriate Authority in the discharge of its functions. The Advisory Committee is to consist of:

- Three medical experts from amongst gynecologists, obstetricians, pediatricians and medical geneticists;
- One legal expert;
- One officer to represent the information and publicity department of the respective government;
- Three eminent social workers with at least one being a representative of a women's organisation.
- A person who in the opinion of the respective government has been associated with the use of promotion of pre-natal diagnostic techniques for determination of sex shall be disqualified from appointment as a member of the Advisory Committee.
- The intervening period between any two meetings of the Advisory Committee shall not exceed 60 days whether any application for registration or cancellation of the same is pending or not.
- At every meeting of the Advisory Committee, four members shall form a quorum. Thus, at least four members should be present for the meeting of the Advisory Committee to be held.

INDIAN LAWS PERTAINING TO RAGGING

- There is no central enactment to deal with ragging

- Some states have enacted special laws to deal with the menace of ragging, which is crime. However, they have not been effective in curbing the menace of ragging.
- Therefore the Supreme Court has laid down certain guidelines in *Vishwa Jagriti Mission Vs. Central Government* (2001, Supreme Court cases page 577) wherein the educational institution in which the student is studying is empowered to be the disciplinary authority and that the police action should not be resorted unless it is unavoidable.

Ragging is Defined as

Any disorderly conduct by words spoken or written or by an act

- That has the effect of treating or handling with rudeness any other student including in roudy or indisciplinary activities.
- Which cause or is likely to cause annoyance, hardship, or psychological harm or to raise fear or apprehension in a fresher or a junior student;

Asking the students to do any act or perform something which such student will not do in the ordinary course.

Duties of the Educational Institutions as per the Supreme Court Judgment

- The prospectus issued at the time of admission must mention clearly that ragging is banned in the institution and that any one who indulges in ragging is likely to be punished.
- The punishment may be expulsion from such institution, suspension from the institution or class for a limited period or fine or public apology, withholding of scholarship, debarring from representation in events withholding results, suspension or expulsion from hostel mess, etc.
- The application form shall have printed undertaking to be filled up and signed by the student and the parents/guardians.
- Students who are already studying in the institution and their parents/guardians shall also give such an undertaking before the commencement of the next education year/session.
- The Management, the Principal, the Teaching Staff should interact with freshers and take them in confidence by

appraising them of their rights as well as obligations to fight against ragging and to generate confidence in their mind that they should report any incident of ragging.

- The student must be made aware of the dehumanising effects of ragging.
- Migration Certificate issued by the institutions should have an entry whether the student had participated in ragging and the punishment
- If individual committing or abetting ragging is not identified, then collective punishment could be resorted to act as deterrent punishment and to ensure collective pressure on the potential raggers.
- The failure to prevent ragging shall be construed as an act of negligence in maintaining discipline in the institutions on the part of the management, the principal and the hostel wardens/superintendents.
- If the institutions fail to curb ragging, UGC / Funding Agency may consider stoppage of financial assistance to such an institution.

THE COMMISSION OF SATI PREVENTION ACT, INDIA 1987

- This Act intends to prevent commission of Sati by any one.
- Any person who commits Sati or does any act towards such commission in punishable with imprisonment that may extend to one year or fine or with both.
- Person who abets the commission of such Sati, either directly or indirectly, shall be punishable with life imprisonment and fine.
- Abetment includes:
  - Encouraging a woman to commit sati;
  - Making the woman believe that the commission of Sati would result in some spiritual benefit to her or to the deceased husband's family;
  - Encouraging a woman to remain fixed in her resolve to commit sati and thus instigating her to commit sati;
  - Participating in any procession in connection with the commission of Sati;

  - Being present at the place where Sati is committed;
  - Preventing or obstructing a woman from saving herself from being burnt or buried alive;
  - Obstructing or interfering with the police in discharge of their duties of taking steps to prevent the commission of Sati;
  - Glorification of Sati is punishable with imprisonment for not less than one year which may extend upto 7 years and fine of Rs. 5,000/- to Rs. 30,000.
- The government has power to remove the temple or any other structure which has been in existence for not less than 20 years, where any form of worship or the performance of any ceremony is carried on with a view to perpetuate the honour or preserve the memory of the person in respect of who such Sati has been committed.
- The Collector or the District Magistrate has power to seize properties or funds that have been acquired or collected for the purpose of glorification of the commission of Sati.

INDIAN LAW ON MOLESTATION (Section 354 IPC)

An assault or use of criminal force with intent to outrage the modesty of any woman shall be punished with imprisonment upto two years, or fine, or with both.

INDIAN LAW ON EVE TEASING (Section 509 & 214 IPC)

An intention to insult the modesty of a woman either by uttering any word or making any sound or gestures or exhibiting any object, is punished with imprisonment upto one year or with fine or both.

Anyone who annoys others by doing obscene acts in public places, or sing songs or recites or utters obscene songs, ballad or words in or near a public place shall be punished with imprisonment upto three months or with fine or with both.

Major Section in Rape Case in India

Section	*Offence*	*Punishment*
RAPE		
375 & 376	Sexual Intercourse by a man with a woman against her will or without her consent or consent obtained fraudulently.	Minimum imprisonment for 7 years or upto life imprisonment and fine
376 A	Intercourse by a man with his wife during separation	Imprisonment for 2 years and fine
376 B	Intercourse by a Public Servant with woman in his Custody	Imprisonment for 5 years and fine
376 C	Intercourse by Superintendent of Jail, / Remand Home	Imprisonment for 5 years and fine
376 D	Intercourse by a member of management, or staff of a hospital with any woman in the hospital	Imprisonment for 5 Years and fine
377	Unnatural Offence, Voluntary Carnal intercourse against the order of nature with any woman i.e. oral sex, man or animal	Imprisonment for 10 Years and fine

Persons may be Charged with the Following Sections in a Rape Case

Section	*Offence*	*Punishment*
511	Attempt to Commit Rape	Imprisonment for life or Imprisonment not exceeding half of the period.
109	Aiding and Abetting Rape	Imprisonment for life and fine
34	Common Intention (Gang Rape)	Imprisonment for life or fine or both
201	Suppressing evidence/false information	Imprisonment for 7 years and fine
342	Wrongful Confinement	Imprisonment for 1 year / fine / both

Section	*Offence*	*Punishment*
363	Kidnapping	Imprisonment for 7 year & fine
417	Cheating	Imprisonment for 1 year / fine / both
458	House tresspassing or house breaking by night after preparation for causing hurt	Imprisonment upto14 years and fine
354	Assault or Criminal force to women with an intention to outrage her modesty	Imprisonment for 2 years or fine or both
509	Outraging the modesty of Women Physically/ Verbally/ gesture/ exhibits	Simple Imprisonment for 1 year or fine or both
499 / 500	Defamation	Imprisonment for 2 years with fine or both
366	Kidnapping, Abducting: With Intention to compel the woman to marry against her will. In order that she may be forced or seduced to illicit Intercourse. Or knowing that she is likely to be compelled into illicit intercourse or seduction	Imprisonment for 10 years and fine
366 A	Procuring a girl below 18 years with intention and knowledge to force or to seduce to illicit intercourse	Imprisonment for 10 Years and Fine
366 B	Importation of girls below 21 years with intention and knowledge to force or to seduce to illicit intercourse	Imprisonment for 10 Years and Fine
372	Selling a minor person below 18 years for purpose of Prostitution or for illicit intercourse or for any unlawful and immoral purpose or knowledge of such intention	Imprisonment for 10 Years and Fine
373	Buying a person below 18 years for prostitution or illicit intercourse or for any unlawful and immoral purpose	Imprisonment for 10 years and fine

Provisions in Indian Penal Code Regarding Obscenity

Section	*Offence*	*Punishment*
292	Sale of Obscene books etc.	Imprisonment for 2 years with fine
292	Printing etc. of grossly indecent or scurrilous matter or matter intended for blackmail	Imprisonment for 2 years / fine / both
293	Sale of Obscene objects to young persons	Imprisonment for 3 years with fine
294	Obscene Songs	Imprisonment for 3 years with fine

Sections in the Indian Penal Code Relating to Violence

Section	*Offence*	*Punishment*
302	Murder	Death or Imprisonment for life and fine.
323	Voluntarily causing hurt-if a man has beaten or threatened to beat	Imprisonment for 1 year, fine of Rs. 1000 or Both.
324	Voluntarily causing hurt by dangerous weapons or means	Imprisonment for 3 years or fine or Both.
325	Voluntarily causing grievous hurt	Imprisonment for 7 years and Fine.
326	Voluntarily causing grievous hurt with dangerous weapons or means	Imprisonment for life or for 10 years and fine.

Section	*Offence*	*Punishment*
327	Voluntarily causing hurt to extort property or a valuable securing or to constrain to do anything which is illegal or which may facilitate the commission of an offence	Imprisonment upto 10 years and fine.
329	Voluntarily causing grievous hurt to extort property or valuable security or do anything which is illegal or which may facilitate the commission of an offence	Imprisonment upto 10 years and fine.
336	Doing any act, which endangers human life or the personal safety of others	Imprisonment for three months fine / Rs. 250/- both.
337	Causing hurt by an act which endangers human life etc.	Imprisonment for 6 months or fine of Rs. 500/- or both.
338	Causing grievous hurt by an act, which endangers human life etc.	Imprisonment for 2 years or fine of Rs. 1000/- or both.
341	Wrongfully restraining any person	Simple imprisonment for 1 month or fine of Rs. 500/- or both.
342	Wrongfully confining any person	Imprisonment for 1 year or fine of Rs. 1000/- or both.
343	Wrongfully confining for 3 or 4 days	Imprisonment for 2 years or fine or both.
344	Wrongfully confining for 10 or more days	Imprisonment for 3 years and fine

Section	*Offence*	*Punishment*
347	Wrongful confinement for the purpose of extorting property constraining to do an illegal act, etc.	Imprisonment for 3 years and fine.
355	Assault or use of criminal force with an intent to dishonor a person otherwise than on a grave provocation	Imprisonment for 2 years or fine of Rs. 1000/ or both.
357	Assault or use of criminal force for wrongful confinement	Imprisonment for 1 year or fine of Rs. 1000/- or both.

Index

S

T

U

Z